Mark Howard

ONE JUMP AHEAD

THE TOP NH HORSES TO FOLLOW FOR **2014/2015**

THE AUTHOR

Mark Howard is 39 and graduated from Manchester University with a BA Honours Degree in History. For the last 21 years, he has written the National Hunt horses to follow book *One Jump Ahead*. He also writes the Flat racing equivalent, *Ahead On The Flat*. In addition, he appears as a pundit on *Racing UK* (Sky Channel 432) and, prior to that, Attheraces. He has also written for *The Irish Field*, *Sports Advisor* and *Racing & Football Outlook* (*Borderer* & *Trainer File*).

FRONT COVER: **VAUTOUR** (Ruby Walsh) wins the Sky Bet Supreme Novices' Hurdle by six lengths at the Cheltenham Festival.

BACK COVER: **VAUTOUR** (Sky Bet Supreme Novices' Hurdle), **FAUGHEEN** (Neptune Investments NH), **O'FAOLAINS BOY** (RSA Chase) & **VERY WOOD** (Albert Bartlett NH).

Cover photograph supplied by GROSSICK RACING PHOTOGRAPHY. The Steadings, Rockhallhead, Collin, Dumfries. DG1 4JW. Telephone: 01387 750 512.

Published by *Mark Howard Publications Ltd.* 69, Fairgarth Drive, Kirkby Lonsdale, Carnforth, Lancashire. LA6 2FB.
Telephone: 015242 71826
Email: mark.howard@mhpublications.co.uk
Website: www.mhpublications.co.uk

(Please note: If you are currently NOT on the *Mark Howard Publications* mailing list and you would like to be, and therefore receive all information about future publications then please post / email / phone your name and address to the above).

Printed by H&H REEDS PRINTERS. Southend Road, Penrith, Cumbria. CA11 8JH. Telephone: 01768 864214. www.reeds-printers.co.uk

All information correct at the time of going to press. Every care is taken with compilation of *One Jump Ahead*, but no responsibility is accepted by the publishers, for error or omissions or their consequences.

ISBN: 978-0-9564615-8-2

CONTENTS

INTRODUCTION

The 2013/2014 National Hunt season was, once again, a thoroughly enjoyable one with some spectacular moments. In many respects, it was business as usual with Paul Nicholls reclaiming his trainer's title, A.P.McCoy set another record at Towcester on the 7th November when Mountain Tunes provided him with his 4000th winner, Pond House dominated the final day of the Paddy Power meeting at Cheltenham with four winners and Willie Mullins' stranglehold on Irish jump racing got even tighter. The head of Closutton won his seventh consecutive title, and ninth overall and rounded off the season with nine winners at the Punchestown Festival. Just for good measure, McCoy broke his own record for the fastest 100 winners in a jumps season when partnering Arabic History to victory at Newton Abbot on the 21st August – his previous record had been set on the 4th September 2002 – which is a remarkable feat.

One of the most common themes I have noticed whilst compiling this year's edition of *One Jump Ahead* is the fact the very top trainers are getting even stronger. A glance at the spring and summer sales returns confirms the vast sums being spent by the likes of Nicholls, Henderson, O'Neill, McCain, Pipe and Mullins. National Hunt racing needs large investors and, while the amounts being spent are minimal compared to Al Shaqab and Qatar Racing on the Flat, it is terrific to see owners like J.P.McManus, Gigginstown House Stud, Chris Giles, John Hales, Roger Brookhouse, Paul Rooney, Professor Caroline Tisdall and Simon Munir enriching the sport with such high profile purchases.

Two other names who can be added to that list are Rich Ricci and Graham Wylie, who are arguably responsible for some of the hottest properties in National Hunt racing. The American enjoyed 43 successes in Ireland last season, plus a further 5 in the UK, including Faugheen and Vautour's brilliant Cheltenham Festival victories. Graham Wylie had four Grade 1 victories last term, including Boston Bob winning the Melling Chase at Aintree before following up at Punchestown. I am delighted to include an interview with the pair, with them both kindly running through their powerful strings.

A big thank you to regular contributor Anthony Bromley for giving me the heads up regarding Vautour in last year's edition. The former Guillaume Macaire trained gelding really was the star of the show as far as the *Top 40 Prospects* were concerned. Unbeaten in five races, culminating in his six lengths victory in the Sky Bet Supreme Novices' Hurdle, he joins the likes of Big Buck's, Kauto Star and Long Run, who all featured in *One Jump Ahead* before making their UK debuts. Anthony has, once again, penned his regular piece, *Bromley's Best Buys*, which features the pick of his purchases during the 'off season' from France and Ireland. Talking of Ireland, regular contributor Declan Phelan has also written his *Irish Pointers* section, which has also unearthed any number of stars over the years.

There are some new names in the *Talking Trainers* section, including rising star Warren Greatrex. Having learned his trade under the guidance of David Nicholson and Oliver Sherwood amongst others, the head of Uplands has made a big impression in recent seasons. A personal best tally of 43, included 15 bumpers winners, last term and it has led to the patronage of high profile owners such as J.P.McManus, Roger Brookhouse and Dai Walters.

Finally, one equine star who will be sadly missing this season and beyond is one of my all time favourites Tidal Bay, who has been retired. The thirteen year old, who enjoyed a wonderful career winning 15 of his 44 races and earning prize-money of £812,978, bowed out after finishing seventh in the Scottish National in April. A three times Grade 1 winner, he was bought originally for 5,800gns by Alistair Charlton before being purchased by Graham Wylie for 300,000gns at the end of his bumper career in May 2006. His victory in the Lexus Chase at Leopardstown in December 2012, when trained by Paul Nicholls, was a thrilling moment but surely the highlight was the day he won the Arkle Trophy under Denis O'Regan in 2008. Howard Johnson produced him spot on and it would have taken an exceptional horse to beat him that day.

Many thanks for buying a copy of *One Jump Ahead*, which I hope you find enjoyable, profitable and, most of all, value for money.

Mark Howard

FOREWORD By Nick Luck
Broadcaster of the Year 2007, 2008, 2009, 2011 & 2013 Channel 4 Racing

Not every season can leave you feeling fulfilled – either emotionally or financially – and I must confess to finding the final weeks of the most recent jumps season rather an anti-climax on both counts.

Perhaps the two most exciting horses pre-Christmas were Cue Card and Annie Power. The former put up the single best chasing performance of the season on a memorable afternoon at Haydock in late November, only to succumb to the remorseless and brilliantly trained overachiever Silviniaco Conti in the King George. Then injury put paid to the rest of the campaign. Let's hope he is back near his peak this time around, and can assist the popular Daryl Jacob's rebirth as a freelance rider.

As for Annie Power, she entertained us with her rare brilliance over two and two and a half miles, only to be asked to morph into a thorough stayer for the first time at a championship meeting in one of its most stamina sapping races.

Of course you can understand why Willie Mullins and Ruby Walsh wanted to keep their stars away from one another – wouldn't you? – but the tea dance surrounding which race might be her target became pretty wearing in the end, and we were all complicit.

It must be tricky having to observe the sensitivities of big spending owners in a stable full of talent, but the beauty of jump racing is that there is rarely a long term commercial knock-on from making a poor decision: it is not as though a horse's stud value is going to be affected.

Happily, access to the sport's participants is one of the most notable attributes of the National Hunt scene, and – even more happily – Annie Power's owner Rich Ricci provides one of the headline interviews in this 22nd edition of *One Jump Ahead*.

The charismatic Ricci arguably owns the most select band of jumpers ever assembled, and his biggest head scratcher this season will not be where to run Annie, but rather how best to plot two distinct campaigns for the brilliant duo Vautour and Faugheen: a high class problem, admittedly.

It won't be a massive surprise to regular readers that Vautour's name first came to our attention courtesy of Mark Howard, who 12 months ago described him as "another budding star" before he had even won a race.

Mark's greatest asset is his ability to identify young jumping fruit that is most likely to grow into something of substance rather than wither on the vine. He knew, for example, that Albert Bartlett winner Very Wood was "Noel Meade's best young prospect since Pandorama," but also stressed that the horse would not be seen at his best until presented with a fairly searching test. If you read that just before the Festival, you might easily have had a few quid each way at 33s.

As well as the usual *Top 40 Prospects*, there are some terrific new additions to the interview section of this year's book. Warren Greatrex asked me to write the Introduction to his Open day brochure last year – I wrote that "if the old adage is true that moderate jump jockeys make the best trainers, he is set to make the very top." 'Many a true word in jest' is the phrase that now springs to mind!

He's having a great season already and, with *One Jump Ahead* already safely in your hands, the likelihood is that you'll have a pretty good one too.

TYPE OF TRACK

AINTREE	National Course	Left-Handed, Galloping
	Mildmay Course	Left-Handed, Tight
ASCOT		Right-Handed, Galloping
AYR		Left-Handed, Galloping
BANGOR-ON-DEE		Left-Handed, Tight
CARLISLE		Right-Handed, Stiff / Undulating
CARTMEL		Left-Handed, Tight
CATTERICK BRIDGE		Left-Handed, Tight / Undulating
CHELTENHAM		Left-Handed, Stiff / Undulating
CHEPSTOW		Left-Handed, Stiff / Undulating
DONCASTER		Left-Handed, Galloping
EXETER		Right-Handed, Stiff / Undulating
FAKENHAM		Left-Handed, Tight / Undulating
FFOS LAS		Left-Handed, Galloping
FONTWELL PARK	Chase Course	Figure of Eight, Tight
	Hurdle Course	Left-Handed, Tight
HAYDOCK PARK	Chase Course	Left-Handed, Galloping
	Hurdle Course	Left-Handed, Tight
HEXHAM		Left-Handed, Stiff / Undulating
HUNTINGDON		Right-Handed, Galloping
KELSO		Left-Handed, Tight / Undulating
KEMPTON PARK		Right-Handed, Tight
LEICESTER		Right-Handed, Stiff / Undulating
LINGFIELD PARK		Left-Handed, Tight / Undulating
LUDLOW		Right-Handed, Tight
MARKET RASEN		Right-Handed, Tight /Undulating
MUSSELBURGH		Right-Handed, Tight
NEWBURY		Left-Handed, Galloping
NEWCASTLE		Left-Handed, Galloping
NEWTON ABBOT		Left-Handed, Tight
PERTH		Right-Handed, Tight
PLUMPTON		Left-Handed, Tight / Undulating
SANDOWN PARK		Right-Handed, Galloping
SEDGEFIELD		Left-Handed, Tight / Undulating
SOUTHWELL		Left-Handed, Tight
STRATFORD-UPON-AVON		Left-Handed, Tight
TAUNTON		Right-Handed, Tight
TOWCESTER		Right-Handed, Stiff / Undulating
UTTOXETER		Left-Handed, Tight / Undulating
WARWICK		Left-Handed, Tight / Undulating
WETHERBY	Chase Course	Left-Handed, Galloping
	Hurdle Course	Left-Handed, Galloping
WINCANTON		Right-Handed, Galloping
WORCESTER		Left-Handed, Galloping

IRELAND

BALLINROBE	Right-Handed, Tight
BELLEWSTOWN	Left-Handed, Tight / Undulating
CLONMEL	Right-Handed, Tight / Undulating
CORK	Right-Handed, Galloping
DOWNPATRICK	Right-Handed, Tight / Undulating
DOWN ROYAL	Right-Handed, Tight / Undulating
FAIRYHOUSE	Right-Handed, Galloping
GALWAY	Right-Handed, Tight / Undulating
GOWRAN PARK	Right-Handed, Tight / Undulating
KILBEGGAN	Right-Handed, Tight / Undulating
KILLARNEY	Left-Handed, Tight
LEOPARDSTOWN	Left-Handed, Galloping
LIMERICK	Right-Handed, Galloping
LISTOWEL	Left-Handed, Tight
NAAS	Left-Handed, Galloping
NAVAN	Left-Handed, Galloping
PUNCHESTOWN	Right-Handed, Galloping
ROSCOMMON	Right-Handed, Tight
SLIGO	Right-Handed, Tight / Undulating
THURLES	Right-Handed, Tight / Undulating
TIPPERARY	Left-Handed, Tight
TRAMORE	Right-Handed, Tight
WEXFORD	Right-Handed, Tight

ACKNOWLEDGEMENTS

I would like to thank all the following Trainers who have given up their time, during the summer, to answer my inquiries:

Talking Trainers: Harry Fry, Warren Greatrex, Nicky Henderson, Philip Hobbs, Alan King, Charlie Longsdon, Donald McCain, Paul Nicholls, David Pipe, John Quinn, Lucinda Russell. Plus: Rebecca Curtis, Gordon Elliott, Tom George, Emma Lavelle, Dr Richard Newland, Colin Tizzard. Thank you also to the following secretaries for organising the appointments: Rowie (Nicky Henderson), Jane Young (Warren Greatrex), Jo Cody-Boutcher (Philip Hobbs), Sarah (Paul Nicholls), Catherine (Jonjo O'Neill), Lauren (Tom George), Antonia (Nicky Richards).

Thank you also to Anthony Bromley, David Minton & Bernice Emanuel (Highflyer Bloodstock), Nick Luck (Foreword), Declan Phelan (Ireland), Michael Meagher, Graham Calder, Mags O'Toole, Michael Shinners & Gary Wilson (Skybet), Niall Hannity, Jonathan Neesom, Ellen Welton (*Racing UK*) and Jon Hughes (Owners For Owners).

THE TOP 40 PROSPECTS FOR 2014/2015

ALISIER D'IRLANDE (FR)

4 b or br g Kapgarde (FR) – Isati'S (FR) (Chamberlin (FR))
OWNER: R.S.BROOKHOUSE
TRAINER: P.J.HOBBS. Minehead, Somerset.
CAREER FORM FIGURES: 1
CAREER WINS: 2014: Apr TEMPLEMORE Heavy 4YO Mdn PTP 3m

With his big race winners Goulanes (Midlands National) and Western Warhorse (Arkle Trophy) currently sidelined, Roger Brookhouse was, once again, busy during the spring buying new talent. His purchases included Alisier D'Irlande (£300,000), Miss Estela (£60,000) and Solomn Grundy (£30,000).

The first named is a potentially very exciting recruit, having won his only Irish point-to-point for Willie Codd at Templemore in April. A half-brother to Venetia Williams five times winner Renard D'Irlande, the Kapgarde gelding justified strong support in the market beforehand (1/2 favourite) and won easily by seven lengths. Bought as a three year old for €52,000 at the Derby Sale, he was ridden in his point by crack amateur Jamie Codd and he commented at the Cheltenham April Sale: **"I loved the horse from day one and he's a potentially top-class horse. Every time we took him away for a schooling session, he just got better and better."**

Irish Point expert Declan Phelan comments: **"A majestic looking bay gelding: he trounced an average cast of rivals at Templemore in early April (Heavy) on his sole start. The actual form lacks substance. However, given the impression he created, he attracted a quota of admirers and the result was that he made £300,000 when the hammer dropped on Roger Brookhouse's bid at Brightwells Cheltenham Sale in April. It is likely that middle distance chases on soft ground may be his main arena, probably on big galloping tracks like Newbury."**

Philip Hobbs has taken charge of Alisier D'Irlande and the Minehead trainer had a fantastic season in 2013/2014 with 106 winners, including two Cheltenham Festival winners. Another former Irish pointer Champagne West sported the familiar light blue Brookhouse silks with distinction in novice hurdles last winter. Expect Alisier D'Irlande to do likewise during 2014/2015.

POINTS TO NOTE:

Probable Best Distance	-	2m 4f
Preferred Going	-	Soft

Connection's Comments: **"There is always pressure with a nice horse like this as they have to go and do it. His equals don't come around too often. He was bought at the Derby Sale and always showed us plenty at home. Jamie (Codd) said he gave him a fantastic feel and there is plenty of improvement to come." Willie CODD at Templemore (6/4/14)**

GOING:	R	W	P	TRACK:	R	W	P
Heavy	1	1	0	Right	1	1	0

TRIP:	R	W	P	JOCKEY:	R	W	P
3m	1	1	0	J.J.Codd	1	1	0

ALTIOR (IRE)

4 b g High Chaparral (IRE) – Monte Solaro (IRE) (Key of Luck (USA))
OWNER: Mrs PATRICIA PUGH
TRAINER: N.J.HENDERSON. Lambourn, Berkshire.
CAREER FORM FIGURES: 1
CAREER WINS: 2014: May MARKET RASEN Good NHF 2m 1f

High Chaparral was a brilliant racehorse winning 10 of his 13 races between 2001 and 2003. A son of Sadler's Wells, he beat stablemate Hawk Wing in the 2002 Epsom Derby before capturing the Irish version less than a month later. Indeed, Aidan's O'Brien colt won 6 Group 1 races, including the Breeders' Cup Turf twice.

He has also developed into a top-class stallion being responsible for Group 1 winners Descarado, It's A Dundeel, So You Think and Toronado amongst others on the Flat. His jumping stock haven't scaled such lofty heights but both Hadrian's Approach (Bet365 Gold Cup) and Hawk High (Cheltenham Festival glory) ensured last season was a successful one.

The former is, of course, trained by Nicky Henderson and the same stable are hoping another of High Chaparral's offspring, namely Altior, will develop into an exciting novice hurdler this winter. A four year old half-brother to three times winner Key To The West, he was purchased for €60,000 at the Goffs Land Rover Sale last year. Sent off 4/6 favourite for a bumper at Market Rasen in mid May, Altior raced keenly early on but barely gave his supporters an anxious moment as he bounded clear inside the final quarter of a length to register a fourteen lengths win under Nico de Boinville. In terms of form and time (nearly 40 seconds outside standard on good ground), it looked a modest event but the manner of his win was striking and the fact he arrived at the Lincolnshire venue with a lofty reputation is encouraging.

Altior will hopefully learn to settle as he gains in experience. He looked all speed in the spring and could emerge as a high-class two mile novice hurdler.

POINTS TO NOTE:

Probable Best Distance	-	**2 miles**
Preferred Going	-	**Good/Soft**

GOING:	R	W	P	TRACK:	R	W	P
Good	1	1	0	Right	1	1	0
				Tight/Undul.	1	1	0

TRIP:	R	W	P	JOCKEY:	R	W	P
2m 1f	1	1	0	N. De Boinville	1	1	0

ALLEZ COLOMBIERES (FR)

4 b g Sageburg (IRE) – Paricolombieres (FR) (Lute Antique (FR))
OWNER: Mrs S.RICCI
TRAINER: W.P.MULLINS. Bagenalstown, Co.Carlow.
CAREER FORM FIGURES: 1P11
CAREER WINS: 2013 July LES SABLES-D'OLONNE Soft APQS NHF 1m 5f; Oct NANTES
Heavy APQS NHF 1m 4f; Nov SAINT-CLOUD Heavy APQS NHF 1m 4f

Owners Rich and Susannah Ricci were responsible for the two most exciting novice hurdlers on either side of the Irish Sea last winter, namely Faugheen and Vautour. Hopes are high their famous pink and green silks will be carried to further big race success this season by French recruit Allez Colombieres. Previously trained by Alain Couetil, who has also supplied Willie Mullins with the likes of So Young, Upazo and Upsie over the years, the gelded son of Sageburg was bought at the Arqana Autumn Sale in November for €300,000.

"We have had a lot of success from this stable and he really was the star of the show. He has great size and scope and I think he will make a lovely hurdler and chaser in time," commented Harold Kirk at the sale. Allez Colombieres won three of his four APQS Flat races, including the prestigious Prix Jacques De Vienne at Saint-Cloud four days before he went under the hammer. On his previous start, he had beaten As De Mee by four lengths at Nantes in a similar event. The runner-up was subsequently bought by Paul Nicholls for €200,000 and finished fourth in a bumper at Kempton in February. The four year old's only blemish came at Craon in September when pulling up.

Allez Colombieres was given plenty of time to settle into his new surrounding at Closutton and purposely didn't run over hurdles last season. He reportedly worked well in a couple of 'away days' and his new connections are eagerly anticipating his hurdles debut. Already prominent in the ante-post lists for next March's Supreme Novices' Hurdle, he is very much a horse to look forward to and could be the Ricci's latest star.

POINTS TO NOTE:

Probable Best Distance	-	**2 miles**
Preferred Going	-	**Soft**

GOING:	R	W	P	TRIP:	R	W	P
Heavy	2	2	0	1m 4f	3	2	0
Soft	1	1	0	1m 5f	1	1	0
Good/Soft	1	0	0				

AU QUART DE TOUR (FR)

4 b g Robin Des Champs (FR) – Qualite Controlee (FR) (Poliglote)
OWNER: Mrs S.RICCI
TRAINER: W.P.MULLINS. Bagenalstown, Co.Carlow.
CAREER FORM FIGURES: 1
CAREER WINS: 2014: Apr DROMAHANE Good/Yielding 4YO Mdn PTP 3m

The Pat Doyle trained Au Quart De Tour was bought as a yearling in France by his owner Walter Connors and the gelded son of Robin Des Champs couldn't have made a better start to his career when winning by five lengths on his pointing debut at Dromahane in late April. Sent off 4/5 favourite, the four year old took charge after the fourth last under Derek O'Connor before running out an easy five lengths winner from the Tom Keating trained Globalisation (subsequently bought by Rebecca Curtis for €50,000).

Irish point expert Declan Phelan comments: **"A French bred son of the popular Robin Des Champs, he was in the care of Pat Doyle when recording a commanding win at Dromahane (Good) in April. He was always racing within his comfort zone and picked it up approaching the third last and changed gears to confirm his superiority. Seemed to possess speed and could become a promising middle distance recruit for Rich Ricci. Given his smooth action, time may relate that he may be seen to maximum effect on a sound surface. Winning a bumper ought to be a formality this season, but it is hard to predict if he is Cheltenham Festival material. A few more performances may enlighten a little more in that regard."**

Willie Mullins has won the Cheltenham Festival bumper a record breaking eight times, including with four ex-Irish pointers. Don't be surprised if Au Quart De Tour emerges as a live contender for the 2015 renewal.

POINTS TO NOTE:

Probable Best Distance	-	**2m – 2m 4f**
Preferred Going	-	**Good/Soft**

GOING:	R	W	P	TRACK:	R	W	P
Good/Yield	1	1	0	Left Handed	1	1	0

TRIP:	R	W	P	JOCKEY:	R	W	P
3m	1	1	0	D.O'Connor	1	1	0

AURORE D'ESTRUVAL (FR)

4 ch f Nickname (FR) – Option D'Estruval (FR) (Epervier Bleu)
OWNER: CARL HINCHY
TRAINER: J.J.QUINN. Settrington, North Yorkshire.
CAREER FORM FIGURES: 2125
CAREER WINS: 2014: Feb WETHERBY Heavy NH 2m

John Quinn, who tasted Royal Ascot and Group 1 glory during the summer with The Wow Signal in the Coventry Stakes and Prix Morny respectively, has done a tremendous job with Cockney Sparrow since being bought for 35,000gns out of Peter Chapple-Hyam's yard at the Newmarket Horses In Training Sale in October 2012. The daughter of Cockney Rebel has won 5 out of 11 over hurdles with an official rating of 152, plus she won a decent handicap on the Flat at Ayr's Western meeting last year. Successful in the Scottish Champion Hurdle in the spring, she also chased home My Tent Or Yours in the Grade 1 Fighting Fifth Hurdle at Newcastle earlier in the season.

Despite that, John Quinn believes he has a potentially even better mare currently in training. Aurore D'Estruval finished a head second on her only start over hurdles at Pau for Guillaume Macaire before being purchased by Anthony Bromley on owner Carl Hinchy's behalf. A big strapping filly by Nickname, she never came off the bridle to win a modest mares' novice hurdle at Wetherby in February on her UK debut. She looked all set to follow up at Haydock a fortnight later in the Victor Ludorum Juvenile Hurdle. However, she didn't find as much off the bridle as appeared likely and was denied by half a length by Nick Williams' Abracadabra Sivola. The pair pulled seventeen lengths clear of the rest with subsequent Cheltenham Festival winner Hawk High a distant sixth. Granted an official rating of 137, Aurore D'Estruval missed the Cheltenham Festival due to a minor setback but she was back in action at Aintree's Grand National meeting. Facing a huge step up in class, she contested the Grade 1 Injured Jockeys Fund 50th Anniversary 4YO Juvenile Hurdle but emerged with a lot of credit. It was the first time she had encountered good ground but was only beaten nine and three quarters of a length in fifth behind Guitar Pete. There were a host of useful juveniles behind her, including Dispour (won since), Activial, Hawk High and Broughton.

John (Quinn) is relishing the prospect of stepping Aurore D'Estruval up in trip this season. Surprisingly, the handicapper dropped her two pounds following her run at Aintree and she looks favourably treated off 135. A superb jumper, she has size and scope and will make a smashing chaser in time. However, there is still unfinished business over hurdles. It represents a major step up in distance but it wouldn't be a surprise if the valuable fixed brush handicap hurdle at Haydock's *Betfair* Chase meeting (22nd November) comes under consideration. Ultimately though, the David Nicholson Mares' Hurdle at the Festival in March will be her principal goal. She couldn't be in better hands.

POINTS TO NOTE:

Probable Best Distance	-	**2m 4f +**
Preferred Going	-	**Soft**

Connection's Comments: "She has a lovely pedigree and she has a very good attitude."
Sean QUINN at Wetherby (1/2/14)

GOING:	R	W	P	TRACK:	R	W	P
Heavy	2	1	1	Left Handed	3	1	1
Very Soft	1	0	1	Right	1	0	1
Good	1	0	0	Galloping	2	1	1
				Tight	2	0	1

TRIP:	R	W	P	JOCKEY:	R	W	P
2m	3	1	1	B.Hughes	2	1	1
2m 1f	1	0	1	T.Scudamore	1	0	0
				V.Cheminaud	1	0	1

BATTLE BORN

5 b g Kayf Tara – Realms of Gold (USA) (Gulch (USA))
OWNER: ALAN HALSALL
TRAINER: C.LONGSDON. Chipping Norton, Oxon.
CAREER FORM FIGURES: 2 - 3116
CAREER WINS: 2014: Jan WARWICK Soft NHF 2m; Feb BANGOR-ON-DEE Heavy NHF 2m 1f

Charlie Longsdon's training career continues to go from strength to strength with a personal best 78 winners during the 2013/2014 campaign. The Chipping Norton based handler is, understandably, excited about the winter ahead and feels the ex-Irish pointer Battle Born could prove the pick of his youngsters.

Featured in Declan Phelan's *Irish Pointers* in *OJA* last season, the Kayf Tara gelding won two of his four races in bumpers and acquitted himself well in the Grade 2 championship event at Aintree's Grand National meeting. Only beaten eight lengths in sixth, Noel Fehily reportedly thinks he would have been even closer with a more aggressive ride. Runner-up in his only point-to-point at Dromahane in April 2013 when trained by Nick Stokes, Battle Born had the misfortune to bump into subsequent dual bumper winner No More Heroes.

Transferred to the Longsdon operation last summer, he was a running on third behind the useful Desoto County on his Rules debut at Haydock in November. However, a change of tactics resulted in emphatic victories at Warwick and Bangor in similar events. He was particularly impressive at the latter venue, destroying three rivals by upwards of thirty one lengths. Allowed to take his chance at Aintree, the five year old couldn't match the principals for speed late on, suggesting he will come into his own over two and a half miles plus over timber.

Charlie Longsdon has done extremely well with his runners at Carlisle in recent seasons. Indeed, he has trained 6 winners from only 19 runners (32%) at the Cumbrian venue during the last five seasons. Don't be surprised if Battle Born heads up the M6 for a two and half mile novices' hurdle at their first meeting on Friday 10th October.

POINTS TO NOTE:

Probable Best Distance	-	**2m 4f +**
Preferred Going	-	**Soft**

GOING:	R	W	P	TRACK:	R	W	P
Heavy	1	1	0	Left Handed	4	2	1
Soft	2	1	1	Tight	3	1	1
Good/Soft	1	0	0	Tight/Undul.	1	1	0

TRIP:	R	W	P	JOCKEY:	R	W	P
2m	2	1	1	N.Fehily	3	1	1
2m 1f	2	1	0	C.Deutsch	1	1	0

BEAT THAT (IRE)

6 b g Milan – Knotted Midge (IRE) (Presenting)
OWNER: MICHAEL BUCKLEY
TRAINER: N.J.HENDERSON. Lambourn, Berkshire.
CAREER FORM FIGURES: 26 - 1211
CAREER WINS: 2013: Nov ASCOT Good/Soft Mdn Hdle 2m 4f: 2014: Apr AINTREE Good/
Soft Grade 1 NH 3m; PUNCHESTOWN Good/Yielding Grade 1 NH 3m

Nicky Henderson has won the Stayers/World Hurdle twice with Rustle (1989) and Bacchanal (2000) and he may have another serious contender in Beat That. From the family of Foxhunters' Chase winner Drombeag, the Milan gelding developed into a top-class staying novice hurdler in the spring, gaining Grade 1 victories at Aintree and Punchestown.

Beat That failed to win either of his bumper starts the previous season, but made a smooth transition to hurdling when beating subsequent three times winner Champagne West by ten lengths at Ascot in November. **"He's just a frame of a horse and has done very well through the summer,"** remarked the Seven Barrows trainer afterwards. A mistake at the final flight almost certainly cost him victory in the Grade 2 Winter Novices' Hurdle at Sandown next time, handing the prize to Charlie Longsdon's Killala Quay. The six year old didn't return to the fray until Aintree's Grand National meeting and his connections elected to step him up in trip and take his chance in the Grade 1 Sefton Novices' Hurdle. It proved the correct decision with Beat That trouncing his seventeen rivals by upwards of four lengths. The Milan gelding sauntered clear after the penultimate flight and provided his owner Michael Buckley with his second high profile victory in a matter of six days following Toast of New York's win in the UAE Derby at Meydan. Nicky Henderson enthused afterwards: **"This is a lovely horse for the future. I think he'll be chasing next year, but he's only had three hurdle races and two bumpers in his life."** Beat That then followed up in the Grade 1 Irish Daily Mirror Novice Hurdle at Punchestown Festival lowering the colours of two Cheltenham Festival winners in the process, namely Don Poli and Very Wood. Despite his three parts of a length win, his trainer said: **"I thought he was very slick over his hurdles. He just wasn't quite the horse he was at Aintree."**

Rated 154, chasing will ultimately bring out the best in Beat That but the staying hurdle route must be tempting. If heading down that direction, races such as the Long Distance Hurdle at Newbury (29th November), Long Walk Hurdle at Ascot (20th December) and Cleeve Hurdle at Cheltenham in January are likely to figure in his programme. Then, all being well, all roads will lead to the Festival in March for the Ladbrokes World Hurdle with Henderson seeking his third win in the race.

POINTS TO NOTE:
Probable Best Distance   -   2m 4f +
Preferred Going   -   Good/Soft
Connection's Comments: **"He's a lovely horse and will make a lovely chaser, but I wouldn't rule out staying over hurdles next season. He could easily go down that route."** Barry GERAGHTY at Punchestown (30/4/14)

GOING:	R	W	P	TRACK:	R	W	P
Soft	1	0	0	Left Handed	1	1	0
Good/Soft	3	2	1	Right	5	2	2
Good/Yield	1	1	0	Galloping	4	2	1
Good	1	0	1	Tight	2	1	1
TRIP:	R	W	P	JOCKEY:	R	W	P
2m	1	0	1	B.Geraghty	5	3	2
2m 2f	1	0	0	K.Harrington	1	0	0
2m 4f	2	1	1				
3m	2	2	0				

BROTHER DU BERLAIS (FR)

5 b or br g Saint Des Saints (FR) – King's Daughter (FR) (King's Theatre (IRE))
OWNER: JOHN HALES & IAN FOGG
TRAINER: P.F.NICHOLLS. Ditcheat, Somerset.
CAREER FORM FIGURES: 84121
CAREER WINS: 2013: Aug AUTEUIL Soft Hdle 2m 2f: 2014: Apr AYR Good/Soft HH 2m 6f

I was working for *Racing UK* at Ayr's Scottish National meeting in April and on both days Paul Nicholls won a handicap hurdle with budding chasers on their handicap debuts. Vivaldi Collonges, a half-brother to Nenuphar Collonges, relished the step up to three miles on day one, while Brother Du Berlais looked a horse of considerable talent when beating six rivals off a mark of 132 on day two.

Highlighted as a horse to follow by Bloodstock agent Anthony Bromley in the Paddy Power *Update*, he won over hurdles at Auteuil for Robert Collet on his third outing. Bought soon afterwards, he made his British debut at Wincanton in February and finished a creditable second behind Knight of Noir over two and a half miles. Paul Nicholls was preparing him for the EBF Final at Sandown in March but Brother Du Berlais incurred a cut during his preparation and was forced to miss the race. His trainer felt he was well treated off 132 and so it proved on the West coast of Scotland with a dominate display. Sat in behind the leaders, the imposing Saint Des Saints gelding took charge after the second last before galloping three and a quarter lengths clear of Rumble of Thunder (won next time).

Raised seven pounds, Brother Du Berlais still looks favourably treated off 139 and looks capable of winning a good prize over hurdles. Indeed, he will have no trouble staying three miles and could be one for the fixed brush handicap hurdle at Haydock (22nd November). Otherwise, he will make a terrific chaser – he has size, scope, a high cruising speed and is a very slick jumper.

POINTS TO NOTE:

Probable Best Distance	-	**2m 6f – 3m**
Preferred Going	-	**Good/Soft**

Connection's Comments: "A grand big stamp of a horse, he should make a lovely chaser next season." Purchaser Anthony BROMLEY discussing the gelding in the *OJA* Paddy Power *Update* November 2013

GOING:	R	W	P	TRACK:	R	W	P
Heavy	1	0	1	Left Handed	2	2	0
Soft	2	1	0	Right	1	0	1
Good/Soft	2	1	0	Galloping	3	2	1

TRIP:	R	W	P	JOCKEY:	R	W	P
2m 1f	2	0	0	S.Twiston-Davies	1	1	0
2m 2f	1	1	0	H.Derham	1	0	1
2m 4f	1	0	1	L.Philipperon	3	1	0
2m 6f	1	1	0				

CAPOTE (IRE)

6 b g Oscar (IRE) – Kinsella's Rose (IRE) (Roselier (FR))
OWNER: TREVOR HEMMINGS
TRAINER: J.J.O'NEILL. Temple Guiting, Gloucestershire.
CAREER FORM FIGURES: 1114
CAREER WINS: 2013: Dec TATTERSALLS FARM Yield/Soft Mdn PTP 3m: 2014: Feb
CATTERICK Heavy NH 3m 1f; Mar EXETER Heavy NH 3m

Fresh from his best ever season of 134 winners (including three at the Cheltenham Festival), Jonjo O'Neill has been very active in the 'transfer' market during the spring/summer. His new purchases from the public sales include Adam Du Breteau (£280,000), Blackthorn Prince (£200,000), Champagne Present (£210,000), Joffrey (£85,000), Mackerye End (£62,000), Matorico (€115,000), Montdragon (€185,000) and Young Mr Gorsky (£190,000).

Irish point winner Capote was acquired for £75,000 at the Cheltenham December Sale, having won his sole outing for Liz Doyle at Tattersalls Farm five days earlier. **"He came from the Cheltenham Breeze-Ups. We bought him from the Costello's and he does everything really well. He is a lovely big chasing type,"** remarked Doyle afterwards. A length and a half winner from Count Massini, he followed up in his next two starts under Rules for his new connections. The Oscar gelding beat the 130 rated I Need Gold by nearly two lengths at Catterick in February with the pair well clear. He then faced an easy task at Exeter the following month when his main market rival, namely Chinatown Boy, failed to fire. He sauntered home by twenty four lengths. Stepped up in class, Capote took his chance in the Grade 1 Sefton Novices' Hurdle at Aintree's Grand National fixture and, whilst beaten thirty six lengths by Beat All in fourth, he ran a solid race and was still in contention jumping the third last. Jonjo O'Neill's gelding travelled strongly until the home turn and certainly didn't look out of place in such company. I spoke to Trevor Hemmings' racing manager Michael Meagher the following day and he was delighted with the performance.

Rated 135, Capote threatens to make an even better chaser and could develop into a smart staying novice this season. His half-brother Summery Justice is a four times winner over the larger obstacles for Venetia Williams.

POINTS TO NOTE:

Probable Best Distance	-	3 miles
Preferred Going	-	Good/Soft

Connection's Comments: **"A.P. (McCoy) was very pleased with him. He said he was a bit novicey, but he handled the ground well and is a nice prospect. He won a point-to-point and is going to be a chaser."** Mick MEAGHER (Trevor Hemmings' racing manager) at Catterick (10/2/14)

GOING:	R	W	P	TRACK:	R	W	P
Heavy	2	2	0	Left Handed	2	1	0
Yield/Soft	1	1	0	Right	1	1	0
Good/Soft	1	0	0	Stiff/Undul.	1	1	0
				Tight	1	0	0
				Tight/Undul.	1	1	0

TRIP:	R	W	P	JOCKEY:	R	W	P
3m	3	2	0	A.P.McCoy	2	1	0
3m 1f	1	1	0	M.Linehan	1	1	0
				J.J.Codd	1	1	0

CARRAIG MOR (IRE)

6 b g Old Vic – Lynrick Lady (IRE) (Un Desperado (FR))
OWNER: MASTERSON HOLDINGS LIMITED
TRAINER: A.KING. Wroughton, Wiltshire.
CAREER FORM FIGURES: 1 - 1236
CAREER WINS: 2012: Dec BALLINDENISK Heavy Mdn PTP 3m: 2013: Nov UTTOXETER Soft NH 2m 4f

There were few more impressive novice hurdle winners last season than Carraig Mor when destroying eleven rivals by upwards of twenty five lengths at Uttoxeter in early November. It may not have been the strongest race of its type but the imposing Old Vic produced a breathtaking display of galloping and jumping before running his opponents into submission. Admittedly, Carraig Mor failed to replicate it in three subsequent starts but he remains a horse of huge potential, especially now his attentions are switched to fences.

A three lengths winner of his only Irish point when handled by Adrian Maguire, he couldn't have made a better start to his Rules career under Alan King with his Uttoxeter demolition. As a result, he was sent off 1/8 favourite to successfully carry his penalty at Ascot but compromised his chance with a terrible mistake at the third last. While Carraig Mor was back in contention by the time the leaders negotiated the penultimate flight, the error had knocked the stuffing out of him. Beaten a length by Doing Fine, he never looked the same horse thereafter. **"Carraig Mor would not be mentally ready for Cheltenham. He's one for next year, when he'll be the finished article, and I can't wait to send him novice chasing. He was impressive first time out at Uttoxeter and was obviously not himself when subsequently beaten at Ascot. He was very quiet afterwards and we've brought him back slowly,"** remarked his trainer before reappearing in the Sidney Banks Memorial Hurdle at Huntingdon in February. Third behind Mosspark at the Cambridgeshire track, he possibly wasn't suited by hold up tactics because the six year old looked very much at home making the running earlier in the season. He rounded off his novice hurdle career with a respectable sixth behind Le Vent D'Antan at the Punchestown Festival.

Following a good summer break, Carraig Mor is reportedly much more relaxed, which bodes well for his chasing career. Ordinary horses don't win like he did at Uttoxeter in November. Unbeaten first time out, he shouldn't be missed on his fencing bow.

POINTS TO NOTE:
Probable Best Distance - 2m 4f – 3 miles
Preferred Going - Soft
Connection's Comments: "If he'd been beaten I'd have been mortified as I think he could be very good. You don't get horses like him very often, so we'll be looking after him." Alan KING at Uttoxeter (1/11/13)

GOING:	R	W	P	TRACK:	R	W	P
Heavy	1	1	0	Left Handed	1	1	0
Soft	2	1	1	Right	4	1	2
Good/Soft	1	0	1	Galloping	3	0	2
Good/Yielding	1	0	0	Tight/Undul.	1	1	0

TRIP:	R	W	P	JOCKEY:	R	W	P
2m 4f	3	1	1	W.Hutchinson	1	0	0
2m 6f	1	0	1	R.Thornton	3	1	2
3m	1	1	0	D.L.Queally	1	1	0

CHIDSWELL (IRE)

5 b g Gold Well – Manacured (IRE) (Mandalus (IRE))
OWNER: LANGDALE BLOODSTOCK
TRAINER: N.G.RICHARDS. Greystoke, Cumbria.
CAREER FORM FIGURES: 1
CAREER WINS: 2013: Nov NEWCASTLE Good NHF 2m

It is great to see Greystoke Stables once again being responsible for some high quality equine talent. Eduard emerged as a high-class novice chaser last spring winning the Future Champions Chase at Ayr's Scottish National meeting by twenty lengths, Simply Ned chased home Balder Succes in the Grade 1 Maghull Novices' Chase at Aintree on Grand National day and Noble Alan turned back the clock to plunder the Cumberland Plate at his local track Carlisle during the summer.

Nicky Richards seemingly has a strong team of novice hurdlers for the winter ahead. The trainer is a big supporter of Gold Well as a stallion and the full brother to Montjeu has produced the likes of Gold Future (3 wins during the summer), Looking Well and Chidswell to win for the stable during the last twelve months. The last named looks a particularly interesting prospect for this season and beyond. A big strapping gelding, who was acquired as a three year old at Tattersalls Ireland for €33,000, he was a half length winner on his debut in a bumper at Newcastle in November. Having travelled strongly, Chidswell was forced to dig deep to beat subsequent four times winner Degooch (rated 120 over hurdles) with the pair two and a half lengths clear of the third. Strong at the finish, the five year old will come into his own over two and a half miles plus over hurdles.

Nicky Richards has adopted his customary patient approach since with Chidswell and such a policy looks sure to be rewarded in the long-term. It was interesting to note when asked to nominate a horse to follow last season, Brian Harding selected this once raced gelding. Expect him to make his jumping debut at either Carlisle or, more likely, Kelso or Newcastle around late October/early November.

POINTS TO NOTE:
Probable Best Distance	-	2m 4f +
Preferred Going	-	Good/Soft

Connection's Comments: "He's a big, beautiful baby – a proper horse. I could show a video of him jumping and I'd swear I could run him in a novice chase next week, he's that good." Nicky RICHARDS at Newcastle (15/11/13)

GOING:	R	W	P	TRACK:	R	W	P
Good	1	1	0	Left Handed	1	1	0
				Galloping	1	1	0
TRIP:	R	W	P	JOCKEY:	R	W	P
2m	1	1	0	B.Harding	1	1	0

DEPUTY DAN (IRE)

6 b g Westerner – Louisas Dream (IRE) (Supreme Leader)
OWNER: TIM SYDER
TRAINER: O.M.C.SHERWOOD. Upper Lambourn, Berkshire.
CAREER FORM FIGURES: 3 - 11 - 22112
CAREER WINS: 2013: Mar UTTOXETER Heavy NHF 2m; Apr EXETER Soft NHF 2m 1f; Dec CHEPSTOW Heavy NH 2m 4f: 2014: Jan WARWICK Heavy Grade 2 NH 2m 5f

Numerically, Oliver Sherwood had his best season last year with 34 winners since the 1998/99 campaign. The Rhonehurst team managed it without stable star Puffin Billy as well, who was sidelined with colic. Indeed, the six year old only raced once last term finishing fifth in the Gerry Feilden Hurdle at Newbury's Hennessy meeting. Found to be suffering with a twist in his small intestine, the Heron Island gelding was operated on the 20th December and, thankfully, has made a full recovery. Novice chasing will be on his agenda this winter.

Like Puffin Billy, stablemate Deputy Dan is also owned by Tim Syder and he, too, is due to embark on a fencing career. Bought for £65,000 as a three year old, he is a half-brother to the 2011 Tolworth Hurdle winner Minella Class and enjoyed a terrific season over timber last season. Officially rated 145, he was a wide margin winner at Chepstow's Welsh National meeting. However, the Westerner gelding produced an even better performance in the Grade 2 Leamington Novices' Hurdle at Warwick in January. Leading three out, his task was simplified when Irish raider Rathvinden fell at the same obstacle but it would have taken a good effort to beat Oliver Sherwood's charge. He registered a nine lengths win from Masters Hill and subsequent *Betfair* Hurdle winner Splash of Ginge. It was reported afterwards that Deputy Dan returned with a nasty cut to a hind leg. The six year old was ready in time for the Cheltenham Festival though and ran a tremendous race to finish runner-up in the Grade 1 Albert Bartlett Hurdle. He was attempting to become his trainer's first winner at the Festival since Coulton won the Cathcart Chase in 1995. Unfortunately, it wasn't to be but he still emerged with a career best effort behind Very Wood. It was the fastest ground he had encountered, too.

Oliver Sherwood has trained some top-class horses over the years with names such as Large Action, Cruising Altitude, Arctic Call, Berude Not Too and Lord of the River readily springing to mind. However, he hasn't sent out a Grade 1 winner since Cenkos won the Maghull Novices' Chase in 2000. Deputy Dan may be the one to end the drought for the resurgent Lambourn handler. The RSA Chase looks an obvious long-term target.

POINTS TO NOTE:
Probable Best Distance	-	2m 4f +
Preferred Going	-	Good/Soft

Connection's Comments: "He's a top-class horse and Leighton (Aspell) said he gave him the best ride he's ever had and pinged every hurdle." Oliver SHERWOOD at Cheltenham (14/3/14)

GOING:	R	W	P	TRACK:	R	W	P
Heavy	4	3	1	Left Handed	6	3	3
Soft	1	1	0	Right	2	1	1
Good/Soft	2	0	2	Stiff/Undul.	5	2	3
Good	1	0	1	Tight/Undul.	3	2	1

TRIP:	R	W	P	JOCKEY:	R	W	P
2m	2	1	1	L.Aspell	5	2	3
2m 1f	1	1	0	Sam Jones	3	2	1
2m 4f	2	1	1				
2m 5f	2	1	1				
3m	1	0	1				

DIAMOND KING (IRE)

6 b g King's Theatre (IRE) – Georgia On My Mind (FR) (Belmez (USA))
OWNER: Mrs DIANA L WHATELEY
TRAINER: D.McCAIN. Cholmondeley, Cheshire.
CAREER FORM FIGURES: 11 - 131
CAREER WINS: 2013 Feb WETHERBY Soft NHF 2m; Apr BANGOR-ON-DEE Good NHF 2m
1f; Nov WETHERBY Good/Soft NH 2m: 2014: Jan DONCASTER Good/Soft NH 2m

As discussed, the leading trainers have been investing heavily on new stock during the spring/ summer and Donald McCain is no exception. Fresh from sending out another 142 winners last term, the Cheshire based handler has purchased the likes of Ballyboker Breeze (£55,000), Big Bad Dude (£55,000), Billy Buff (£70,000), Cracked Rear View (£130,000), Duke Arcado (£80,000), Konig Dax (€160,000), Mahler And Me (£65,000), Operating (£140,000), Starchitect (110,000gns) and Vital Evidence (70,000gns). It is exciting times at Bankhouse Stables.

The Diana Whateley owned Diamond King, who cost €95,000 as a three year old, has won four of his five career starts. Unfortunately, his novice hurdle career was cut short last winter, having incurred a knock following his victory at Doncaster in January. A dual bumper winner, he quickened up smartly to beat subsequent winner Secrete Stream at Wetherby in November on his jumping bow. A mistake at the last next time at Bangor cost him his unbeaten record as he failed to recover in time and handed victory to Masquerade. Despite that, he looked ill at ease on the track and, once again, confirmed the view that he is crying out for further than two miles. He made all to win over the minimum trip though at Doncaster next time, pulling clear after the second last to win by nearly four lengths.

Forced to miss the end of season Festivals, Diamond King has had a long break only returning to Donald McCain's yard in early September. There is little doubt he is fairly treated over hurdles off 135 but he was bought with chasing in mind and that is likely to be his vocation this season. He is a smashing horse and, granted luck, the King's Theatre could develop into a high-class chaser over two and a half miles plus.

POINTS TO NOTE:
Probable Best Distance   -   2m 4f +
Preferred Going   -   Good/Soft
Connection's Comments: "Diamond King could be a smart one. I was pleased with that as I'd left something to work on and he quickened up well when they came to him at the second last. He's not a two miler, he'll stay further and he's going to be a chaser." Donald McCAIN at Wetherby (27/11/13)

GOING:	R	W	P	TRACK:	R	W	P
Soft	1	1	0	Left Handed	5	4	1
Good/Soft	3	2	1	Galloping	3	3	0
Good	1	1	0	Tight	2	1	1
TRIP:	R	W	P	JOCKEY:	R	W	P
2m	3	3	0	J.Maguire	4	3	1
2m 1f	2	1	1	H.Brooke	1	1	0

DJAKADAM (FR)

5 b g Saint Des Saints (FR) – Rainbow Crest (FR) (Baryshnikov (AUS))
OWNER: Mrs S.RICCI
TRAINER: W.P.MULLINS. Bagenalstown, Co.Carlow.
CAREER FORM FIGURES: 2 – U1124 – 11F
CAREER WINS: 2013: Feb GOWRAN PARK Heavy Mdn Hdle 2m; Mar LIMERICK Heavy
Hdle 2m; Dec LEOPARDSTOWN Yielding/Soft NC 2m 3f: 2014: Jan LEOPARDSTOWN Soft
Grade 2 NC 2m 5f

If asked to nominate an ante-post selection for next March's Cheltenham Gold Cup, I wouldn't hesitate in suggesting clients took the 50/1 (Bet365, BetVictor, Stan James) available about Djakadam. Willie Mullins' lightly raced five year old is only rated 147 over fences but is open to significant improvement when stepped up in trip this season.

With time very much on his side, the former Arnaud Chaille-Chaille trained gelding won two of his three races over fences last winter and was still in contention when crashing out at the fourth last in the Jewson Novices' Chase at the Cheltenham Festival. Rated 132 over hurdles, Djakadam was always going to make a better chaser and his breeding suggested racing beyond two miles was going to bring about further progression. A dual winner at Leopardstown, including in the Grade 2 Killiney Novice Chase in late January (Sir Des Champs won the same race in 2012), the five year old beat Bright New Dawn by four lengths with the subsequent Galway Plate winner Road To Riches finishing a tailed off fourth of four. **"He's a really natural jumper. It's very hard to get a horse who jumps and gallops like he does,"** said his trainer afterwards. His victory there ensured a trip to Gloucestershire in March and he was only three lengths behind Uxizandre when coming to grief in the Grade 1 Jewson Novices' Chase. His lack of experience caught him out but hopefully he will have learned from it. Withdrawn from the Punchestown Festival at the eleventh hour, due to the drying ground, he was set to contest the Grade 1 Growise Champion Novice Chase over three miles one. Interestingly, Ruby Walsh chose Djakadam ahead of the 155 rated Ballycasey, who is already a Grade 1 winner over fences and had finished fourth in the RSA Chase. I think that speaks for itself.

Despite history being against him, agewise, the plan is to aim Djakadam at the Hennessy Gold Cup at Newbury (29th November). Willie Mullins saw Be My Royal cross the line in front in 2002 only to be later disqualified after testing positive for a banned substance. The Saint Des Saints gelding could redress the balance because there is a strong belief at Closutton that Djakadam is a well handicapped young chaser. The three and a quarter mile showpiece has been a stepping stone to Cheltenham Gold Cup glory, too, with the likes of Bregawn (1982), Burrough Hill Lad (1983), Denman (2007) and Bobs Worth (2012) completing the double.

POINTS TO NOTE:

Probable Best Distance	-	3m – 3m 2f
Preferred Going	-	Soft

Connection's Comments: "He is a horse with great scope and, on pedigree, he'd have no trouble stepping up to three miles." Willie MULLINS at Leopardstown (28/12/13)

GOING:	R	W	P	TRACK:	R	W	P
Heavy	5	2	1	Left Handed	3	2	0
Soft	1	1	0	Right	5	2	1
Yield/Soft	1	1	0	Galloping	5	3	1
Yielding	1	0	1	Stiff/Undul.	1	0	0
Good	1	0	0	Tight/Undul.	2	1	0

TRIP:	R	W	P	JOCKEY:	R	W	P
2m	6	2	2	R.Walsh	3	2	0
2m 3f	1	1	0	P.Townend	4	2	1
2m 4f	1	0	0	D.Mullins	1	0	0
2m 5f	1	1	0	V.Cheminaud	1	0	1

FORYOURINFORMATION

5 b g Kayf Tara – Sleepless Eye (Supreme Leader)
OWNER: CARL HINCHY
TRAINER: Miss REBECCA CURTIS. Newport, Pembrokeshire.
CAREER FORM FIGURES: 21
CAREER WINS: 2014: Feb FFOS LAS Heavy NHF 2m

Rebecca Curtis trained her third Cheltenham Festival winner courtesy of O'Faolains Boy in the RSA Chase last spring and she is understandably dreaming of possible Gold Cup glory for the Oscar gelding next March.

The stable have done particularly well in bumpers in recent seasons, with 33 winners at a strike-rate of 22%, since the 2010/2011 campaign. Despite that, a number of the Curtis trained horses were under the weather mid winter last term. Indeed, O'Faolains Boy scoped badly after underperforming at Haydock in early January. With that in mind, there is every chance the promising Foryourinformation is considerably better than he showed in his two starts in bumpers. Held in high regard, I spoke to Rebecca prior to the Aintree Grand National meeting and she described the Kayf Tara gelding as a big, leggy horse, who will benefit enormously from a summer break. Entered in the Cheltenham Festival bumper, he probably faced an impossible task when attempting to concede sixteen pounds to the unbeaten A Vos Gardes (won at Ascot since) in a 'newcomers' bumper at Bangor in November. Absent until early February, Foryourinformation made heavy weather of beating Obistar at Ffos Las, having travelled strongly and gone clear a furlong out. Half a length separated the pair with thirteen lengths back to the third Ashford Wood (rated 120 over hurdles).

Put away soon afterwards, the five year old is a good prospect for novice hurdles and I am anticipating plenty of improvement when encountering better ground.

POINTS TO NOTE:
Probable Best Distance   -   2m 4f
Preferred Going   -   Good/Soft
Connection's Comments: "We think he could be very good – he's a big, 16.2hh chaser in the making." Rebecca CURTIS (5/11/13)

GOING:	R	W	P	TRACK:	R	W	P
Heavy	1	1	0	Left Handed	2	1	1
Soft	1	0	1	Galloping	1	1	0
				Tight	1	0	1

TRIP:	R	W	P	JOCKEY:	R	W	P
2m	1	1	0	P.Corbett	1	1	0
2m 1f	1	0	1	A.P.McCoy	1	0	1

FULL SHIFT (FR)

5 b g Ballingarry (IRE) – Dansia (GER) (Lavirco (GER))
OWNER: J.P.McMANUS
TRAINER: N.J.HENDERSON. Lambourn, Berkshire.
CAREER FORM FIGURES: 1 – 1210
CAREER WINS: 2013: Feb MILBORNE ST ANDREW Good/Soft Mdn PTP 3m; Nov NEWCASTLE Good Mdn Hdle 2m: 2014: Feb KEMPTON Soft HH 2m 5f

The former English pointer Full Shift was the subject of a significant gamble in the Martin Pipe Conditional Jockeys' Handicap Hurdle on the final day of the Cheltenham Festival. Sent off 9/2 favourite and partnered by Nico de Boinville, the money, unfortunately, remained in the bookmakers' satchels with Nicky Henderson's five year old trailing in a disappointing eleventh.

Despite that performance, Full Shift remains a horse to follow, especially now his attentions are switched to fences. He wasn't battle hardened enough for the Cheltenham Festival, at that stage in his career. He dropped back early on and never looked like getting involved. A four lengths winner of his only point at Milborne St Andrew in February 2013 when trained by Tom Lacey, he was acquired by J.P.McManus soon afterwards. The Ballingarry gelding was sent novice hurdling last season and he claimed the notable scalp of Clever Cookie (rated 144 over hurdles and 106 on the Flat) at Newcastle's Fighting Fifth meeting. A half length winner, he was always in command and was value for more than the winnng margin. Beaten eight lengths by Warren Greatrex's high-class novice Cole Harden (subsequently runner-up in the Grade 1 Sefton Novices' Hurdle) at Newbury in mid January, Full Shift was allocated a handicap mark of 124. Nicky Henderson elected to go down that route at Kempton towards the end of February and he duly won decisively by three and a quarter lengths. The step up to two miles five at the Sunbury track seemingly played to his strengths.

As discussed, the five year old then headed to Prestbury Park but failed to shine behind Willie Mullins subsequent Grade 1 runner-up Don Poli off his revised rating of 135. Bought with chasing in mind, I am expecting Full Shift to be a different proposition over fences.

POINTS TO NOTE:
Probable Best Distance   -   2m 4f +
Preferred Going   -   Good/Soft
Connection's Comments: "He will be a nice horse, coming from the pointing world." Nicky HENDERSON at Kempton (22/2/14)

GOING:	R	W	P	TRACK:	R	W	P
Soft	2	1	1	Left Handed	3	1	1
Good/Soft	1	1	0	Right	1	1	0
Good	2	1	0	Galloping	2	1	1
				Stiff/Undul.	1	0	0
				Tight	1	1	0

TRIP:	R	W	P	JOCKEY:	R	W	P
2m	1	1	0	A.P.McCoy	3	2	1
2m 3f	1	0	1	S.Drinkwater	1	1	0
2m 4f	1	0	0	N.De Boinville	1	0	0
2m 5f	1	1	0				
3m	1	1	0				

GAITWAY

4 b g Medicean – Milliegait (Tobougg)
OWNER: Mrs J.K.POWELL
TRAINER: N.J.HENDERSON. Lambourn, Berkshire.
CAREER FORM FIGURES: 1
CAREER WINS: 2014: Mar NEWBURY Good/Soft NHF 2m

Christopher and Jenny Powell tasted Grade 1 glory over jumps when the Nigel Twiston-Davies trained Gaelstrom won the Sun Alliance Hurdle in 1993 before developing into a high-class staying chaser.

The same owners will be hoping the unbeaten Gaitway will emerge as a prime contender for next spring's Cheltenham Festival following his sole victory in a bumper at Newbury in March. Bought as a three year old for 50,000gns at the Doncaster May Sales, he is essentially Flat bred but is related to winning jumpers Bold Gait and General Miller. Gaitway made his debut in the DBS Spring Sales Bumper at Newbury and he ran out a comfortable victor from the more experienced and previous winner Tea For Two. The most striking aspect of the performance was the fact the pair pulled thirty four lengths clear of the remainder. The Nick Williams trained runner-up looks a useful sort in his own right (won again since and previously second in a Listed bumper at the same track) and both the fourth (L'Amiral David) and fifth (Rainy City) are well regarded by their respective handlers. Barry Geraghty didn't have to get too serious aboard the Medicean gelding either.

Put away soon afterwards, the four year old will go straight over hurdles in the Autumn. The fact he is Flat bred is a minor concern but it hasn't prevented stablemate My Tent Or Yours (by Desert Prince) developing into a top-class hurdler.

POINTS TO NOTE:

| Probable Best Distance | - | 2m |
| Preferred Going | - | Good/Soft |

GOING:	R	W	P	TRACK:	R	W	P
Good/Soft	1	1	0	Left Handed	1	1	0
				Galloping	1	1	0

TRIP:	R	W	P	JOCKEY:	R	W	P
2m	1	1	0	B.Geraghty	1	1	0

HARGAM (FR)

3 gr g Sinndar (IRE) – Horasana (FR) (Galileo (IRE)
OWNER: J.P.McMANUS
TRAINER: To Be Confirmed
CAREER FORM FIGURES: 214
CAREER WINS: 2014: May LONGCHAMP Good/Soft Mdn 1m 4f

J.P.McManus claimed his eighth British owners' championship with 121 winners and prize-money of £2,052,076. Star hurdlers Jezki, My Tent Or Yours and More of That all provided the Irishman with Grade 1 victories. It was a similar story across the Irish Sea, too, with McManus landing his eighteenth owners' title. Indeed, he has won it every season in Ireland since 1994/1995 with the exception of the 2009/10 and 2012/13 campaigns. His Grade 1 winners included Carlingford Lough (2), Defy Logic and Jezki (2), while Shutthefrontdoor (Irish National) and Carlingford Lough (Galway Plate) plundered big handicaps.

One race J.P.McManus has yet to win is the Triumph Hurdle at the Cheltenham Festival. In attempt to rectify that, his green and gold silks will be sported by A.P.McCoy aboard exciting French recruit Hargam this season. Previously owned and bred by the Aga Khan, the three year old son of Sinndar only raced three times on the Flat for Alain de Royer-Dupre. Unraced as a juvenile, he was only denied by half a length on his debut in a ten furlongs maiden at Longchamp in mid April. The winner, Teletext, has rapidly established himself a high-class middle distance three year old, winning a conditions event next time and then finishing less than three lengths third in the Group 1 Grand Prix de Paris at Longchamp in July. It is a terrific piece of form. Hargam confirmed the promise when appreciating a step up to twelve furlongs next time at the same track less than a month later. A head winner from subsequent Group 3 scorer Guardini, he stayed on strongly under Christophe Soumillon. Sent off 8/5 favourite for the Listed Prix Matchem at Maisons-Laffitte over nine furlongs, he was almost certainly inconvenienced by the drop in trip. Beaten two and three quarter lengths in fourth, he was bought soon afterwards by Anthony Bromley on behalf of McManus. Gelded since, he spent the summer at Martinstown Stud in Ireland.

Binocular is arguably the best juvenile hurdler J.P.McManus has owned this century. He, too, was a smart horse on the Flat in France before being purchased by Anthony Bromley. There is every chance lightning will strike twice with Hargam. He has all the ingredients to develop into a top-class hurdler (ie. he stays well, handles cut in the ground and possesses a touch of class). His jumping bow is eagerly anticipated.

POINTS TO NOTE:

Probable Best Distance	-	2 miles
Preferred Going	-	Good/Soft

GOING:	R	W	P	TRACK:	R	W	P
Good	1	0	1	Right	3	1	1
Good/Soft	1	1	0	Galloping	3	1	1
Soft	1	0	0				

TRIP:	R	W	P	JOCKEY:	R	W	P
1m 1f	1	0	0	C.Soumillon	3	1	1
1m 2f	1	0	1				
1m 4f	1	1	0				

JOSSES HILL (IRE)

6 b g Winged Love (IRE) – Credora Storm (IRE) (Glacial Storm (USA))
OWNER: A.D.SPENCE
TRAINER: N.J.HENDERSON. Lambourn, Berkshire.
CAREER FORM FIGURES: 211221
CAREER WINS: 2013: Nov ASCOT Good/Soft NHF 2m; Dec NEWBURY Soft Mdn Hdle 2m;
2014: Apr AINTREE Good/Soft Grade 2 NH 2m

Nicky Henderson has won the Arkle Trophy no less than five times (Remittance Man (1991), Travado (1993), Tiutchev (2000), Sprinter Sacre (2012) & Simonsig (2013)) and he appears to have a prime candidate for the 2015 renewal in 150 rated hurdler Josses Hill.

No match for subsequent Festival winner Faugheen in a bumper at Punchestown in May last year when trained by Andrew Oliver, he was purchased by Highflyer Bloodstock for £100,000 at the Cheltenham May Sale a few weeks later and joined Nicky Henderson. An imposing gelding by Winged Love, he comfortably won a similar event at Ascot in November before readily beating Communicator in a maiden hurdle at Newbury the following month. **"He's gorgeous and a big baby, too. He was jumping like a chaser most of the way and we think he would be better on better ground. He's a chaser for next year,"** remarked Henderson afterwards. Outstayed by stablemate Royal Boy in the rescheduled Grade 1 Tolworth Hurdle at Kempton, the pair pulled eleven lengths clear of the remainder in testing conditions. Given a two months break, Josses Hill produced a career best when a running on second in the Supreme Novices' Hurdle at the Cheltenham Festival. No match for Vautour, he stayed on well under Andrew Tinkler and gained ample compensation in the Grade 2 Top Novices' Hurdle at Aintree the following month. In a race which has been kind to Seven Barrows, the six year old followed in the hoofprints of Darlan and My Tent Or Yours, who had also been placed in the Festival opener during their novice season. Barry Geraghty's mount was always travelling smoothly and, having taken charge at the second last, Josses Hill bounded six lengths clear of Sgt Reckless. It was a dominant performance from a horse who is seemingly improving with every race.

Expect Josses Hill to make his chasing bow in November before taking in the Wayward Lad Novices' Chase at Kempton's Christmas fixture (27th December). Nicky Henderson has won the Grade 2 contest eight times (Remittance Man (1990), Dusk Duel (2000), Fondmort (2001), Caracciola (2003), Jack The Giant (2006), Riverside Theatre (2009), Sprinter Sacre (2011) and Simonsig (2012)). His main target though will be the Arkle in March as his trainer attempts to make it a record breaking sixth win.

POINTS TO NOTE:
Probable Best Distance	-	2m – 2m 4f
Preferred Going	-	Good/Soft

Connection's Comments: **"I think he's a chaser. I can't believe he won't be chasing next season. He looks like an Arkle horse to me. He is a lovely big frame of a horse and he gallops as well as he looks." Nicky HENDERSON at Aintree (4/4/14)**

GOING:	R	W	P	TRACK:	R	W	P
Soft	2	1	1	Left Handed	3	2	1
Good/Soft	3	2	1	Right	3	1	2
Yielding	1	0	1	Galloping	3	2	1
				Stiff/Undul.	1	0	1
				Tight	2	1	1

TRIP:	R	W	P	JOCKEY:	R	W	P
2m	6	3	3	B.Geraghty	3	2	1
				A.Tinkler	2	1	1
				R.P.Quinlan	1	0	1

KALKIR (FR)

3 b g Montmartre (FR) – Kakira (FR) (Cadoudal (FR))
OWNER: Mrs S.RICCI.
TRAINER: W.P.MULLINS. Bagenalstown, Co.Carlow.
CAREER FORM FIGURES: 4

Guillaume Macaire has been responsible for some top-class horses over the years. The Les Mathes based handler nurtured budding stars Azertyuiop, Long Run, Master Minded and, most recently, Vautour, during the early part of their careers before being bought for lofty sums and joining high profile British and Irish stables.

Willie Mullins, of course, trains last season's Sky Bet Supreme Novices' Hurdle winner and Ireland's champion trainer returned to the same source during the spring to purchase the once raced Kalkir. A half-brother to triple Listed chase winner and Grade 1 runner-up Katkovana, the Montmartre gelding made his debut in the Prix Grandak at Auteuil, which is an event for unraced horses over jumps, in April and he finished three lengths fourth behind stablemate Le Baron Noir. The runner-up, Marracudja has joined Paul Nicholls, and the third Bonito Du Berlais (Arnaud Chaille-Chaille) has won two Listed hurdles at Auteuil since. I know leading bloodstock agent Anthony Bromley feels it was a decent event and the form looks strong.

Willie Mullins won the Triumph Hurdle in 2002 with Scolardy and, while the head of Closutton is likely to have a strong hand once again in the juvenile department. Kalkir could be the pick of the crop because he couldn't have come from a better source.

POINTS TO NOTE:

Probable Best Distance	-	**2 miles**
Preferred Going	-	**Soft**

GOING:	R	W	P	TRACK:	R	W	P
Very Soft	1	0	0	Left Handed	1	0	0
				Galloping	1	0	0

TRIP:	R	W	P	JOCKEY:	R	W	P
1m 7f	1	0	0	J.Ricou	1	0	0

LE MERCUREY (FR)

4 b g Nickname (FR) – Feroe (FR) (Bulington (FR))
OWNER: CHRIS GILES & COLM DONLON
TRAINER: P.F.NICHOLLS. Ditcheat, Somerset.
CAREER FORM FIGURES: 1F1
CAREER WINS: 2013: Oct AUTEUIL Very Soft Hdle 2m 2f; Nov AUTEUIL Heavy Hdle 2m 1f

Champion trainer Paul Nicholls has enjoyed tremendous success with his French recruits with Big Buck's (10), Kauto Star (16) and Master Minded (8) developing into household names and winning 34 Grade 1 races between them.

Paul has, once again, invested heavily in new recruits from France during the spring/summer and he is believed to be excited about the prospect of running Le Mercurey this season. Previously trained by Augustin Adeline De Boisbrunet, the Nickname gelding won two of his three races over hurdles at Auteuil. A length and a quarter winner of the Prix Emilius – a debutants race – in October, he fell next time in a €50,000 hurdle. Reappearing nineteen days later over the same course and distance, Le Mercurey won the €70,000 Prix Chalet by a length and three quarters. The runner-up, Bebe Star, has filled the same position in two Graded chases at Auteuil during the spring/summer.

The Prix Renaud Du Vivier at Auteuil in November has already been touted as a possible target for Le Mercurey. Paul Nicholls won the Grade 1 event last year with Ptit Zig and the step up to two and a half miles for the first time is likely to prove beneficial. Chasing will ultimately be his game and he is a tremendous prospect for the champion trainer.

POINTS TO NOTE:

Probable Best Distance	-	2m 4f – 3 miles
Preferred Going	-	Soft

GOING:	R	W	P	TRACK:	R	W	P
Heavy	2	1	0	Left Handed	3	2	0
Very Soft	1	1	0	Galloping	3	2	0

TRIP:	R	W	P	JOCKEY:	R	W	P
2m 1f	2	1	0	David Cottin	3	2	0
2m 2f	1	1	0				

MAHLER LAD (IRE)

4 b g Mahler – Sister Merenda (IRE) (Dr Massini (IRE))
OWNER: T.G.LESLIE
TRAINER: D.McCAIN. Cholmondeley, Cheshire.
CAREER FORM FIGURES: 1
CAREER WINS: 2014: Mar MARALIN Soft/Heavy 4YO Mdn PTP 3m

Mahler developed into a high-class staying three year old in 2007, winning the Queen's Vase at Royal Ascot by three and a half lengths before finishing second in the St Leger at Doncaster behind Lucarno and third in the Melbourne Cup. Based as a stallion at Beeches Stud in Ireland, he is responsible for winning pointer Mahler Lad, who joined Donald McCain during the summer.

Previously handled by Colin Bowe, he was a length and a half winner of his sole outing at Maralin in March. Irish point expert Declan Phelan reports: **"Oozed a deal of class when accounting for two Willie Mullins bound rivals in a top northern maiden at Maralin (Heavy). A powerful sort with scope for development on the physical side, he has already proved his stamina and resolution by virtue of his debut win. Winning a bumper "up north", should be a matter of "how far"….if he matures and acclimatises quickly he could do enough over hurdles to justify a crack at the Albert Bartlett next March at Cheltenham. A horse of some substance and a candidate with bright prospects of Graded success over hurdles and fences. Over the past eight months, Donald McCain must have stocked up with the bones of two dozen new Irish pointers and, in due course, this gelding may be the most potent of the lot."** Both the runner-up (Bellshill) and third (Bordini) have been subsequently purchased by Willie Mullins on behalf of Graham Wylie and Rich Ricci respectively.

In all likelihood, Mahler Lad will contest a bumper before embarking a novice hurdle career. He could be a smart recruit to the northern jumping circuit.

POINTS TO NOTE:

Probable Best Distance		-	2m 4f – 3 miles
Preferred Going		-	Soft

GOING:	R	W	P	TRACK:	R	W	P
Soft/Heavy	1	1	0	Left Handed	1	1	0

TRIP:	R	W	P	JOCKEY:	R	W	P
3m	1	1	0	B.O'Neill	1	1	0

MAYFAIR MUSIC (IRE)

5 br m Presenting – Native Bid (IRE) (Be My Native (USA))
OWNER: Mrs E.ROBERTS
TRAINER: N.J.HENDERSON. Lambourn, Berkshire.
CAREER FORM FIGURES: 1 - 511
CAREER WINS: 2013: Apr FAKENHAM Good NHF 2m; Dec WINCANTON Good NH 2m 6f:
2014: Mar DONCASTER Good Lstd NH 3m

Fiddling The Facts is the best horse to carry the black and red silks of Elisabeth 'Bunny' Roberts. A Grade 1 winning novice chaser, she went on to be placed twice in the Hennessy Gold Cup and Welsh National. There is every chance Mayfair Music will develop into a very smart chaser herself, having won both her starts over hurdles last term and earning an official rating of 139.

Featured in last year's *Top 40 Prospects*, the five year old stayed on well to fill fifth position in the Listed mares' bumper at Cheltenham's Paddy Power meeting. Beaten nine lengths by the likes of The Govaness and Legacy Gold, she was always going to benefit from a step up in distance once tackling obstacles. Sent hurdling in early December, Mayfair Music looked ill at ease around the tight turns of Wincanton but still prevailed in a two mile six mares' novices hurdle by seven lengths. Barry Geraghty reported afterwards: **"She's a lovely filly who jumped really well. She stays well and could go up to three miles but could drop back in trip on a stiffer course."** Very much at home on decent ground, Mayfair Music wasn't seen again until early March. Stepping up to three miles in a Listed mares' novices' hurdle at Doncaster, she was the subject of strong support beforehand and, while her task was made easier following the early departure of market rival Layla Joan, she bolted up. Geraghty had barely moved a muscle before sauntering four and a half lengths clear. It was the performance of a high-class mare who could be anything over fences. Forced to miss the rest of the season due to a stress fracture to a hind leg, she is reportedly back to full fitness.

While the mares' chase final at Newbury in the spring – the same owner's Classic Fiddle finished second in the race in 2008 – is likely to come under consideration, there is a distinct possibility Nicky Henderson will be eyeing the RSA Chase at the Festival, around the same time, instead. Granted three miles on good ground, Mayfair Music is a very good mare.

POINTS TO NOTE:
Probable Best Distance   -   2m 4f – 3 miles
Preferred Going   -   Good
Connection's Comments: **"She won well the last day and Nicky (Henderson) felt she'd come on a nice bit for that. Her jumping was a bit sketchy early on, but she was very good over the last four. She went well on the ground. I would think she'd be a player for a fence next year." Barry GERAGHTY at Doncaster (1/3/14)**

GOING:	R	W	P	TRACK:	R	W	P
Good	4	3	0	Left Handed	3	2	0
				Right	1	1	0
				Galloping	2	2	0
				Stiff/Undul.	1	0	0
				Tight/Undul.	1	1	0

TRIP:	R	W	P	JOCKEY:	R	W	P
2m	2	1	0	B.Geraghty	3	2	0
2m 6f	1	1	0	J.McGrath	1	1	0
3m	1	1	0				

MILES TO MEMPHIS (IRE)

5 b g Old Vic – Phillis Hill (Karinga Bay)
OWNER: Mrs LESLEY FIELD & JULES SIGLER
TRAINER: A.KING. Wroughton, Wiltshire.
CAREER FORM FIGURES: 11
CAREER WINS: 2014: Mar KEMPTON Good/Soft NHF 2m; Apr AYR Good/Soft NHF 2m

I have expounded the virtues of the bumper at Ayr's Scottish National meeting in previous editions of *One Jump Ahead*. The likes of Skippers Brig, Joes Edge, Knockara Beau, Silver By Nature, Aces Four, Sprinter Sacre and River Maigue have all contested it in recent seasons and there is every possibility the winner of the 2014 version is well above average.

Miles To Memphis was due to go hurdling earlier in the season but his trainer Alan King explained in his *Racing Post* Stable Tour in late October: **"I was absolutely thrilled with the way he was going until we had to have his wind done. He's been hobdayed. He's a gorgeous horse."** The Old Vic gelding, who cost £42,000gns at the Newbury Hennessy Sale in December 2012, made his debut in a bumper at Kempton in Mid March and ran out an emphatic eight lengths winner. Miles To Memphis displayed a sharp turn of foot to quickly settle the issue. The runner-up, Run On Sterling, won his next two starts, including over hurdles at Towcester. Reappearing a month later at Ayr, the five year old defied a penalty to beat Gordon Elliott's The Unsub by a length. The fifteen strong field contained eight previous winners, including point-to-pointers.

Once a horse has undergone a wind operation, there is always a doubt at the back of one's mind. However, Denman was hobdayed as a young horse and it didn't prevent him from winning a Gold Cup and two Hennessy's, and Sprinter Sacre also had breathing issues during the early part of his career. Miles To Memphis has the ability and potential to have a big future, too.

POINTS TO NOTE:
Probable Best Distance	-	2m – 2m 4f
Preferred Going	-	Good/Soft

Connection's Comments: "He's always been a lovely horse, he's exciting and he'll go straight over hurdles in the Autumn." Alan KING at Ayr (12/4/14)

GOING:	R	W	P	TRACK:	R	W	P
Good/Soft	2	2	0	Left Handed	1	1	0
				Right	1	1	0
				Galloping	1	1	0
				Tight	1	1	0

TRIP:	R	W	P	JOCKEY:	R	W	P
2m	2	2	0	R.Thornton	2	2	0

MONBEG GOLD (IRE)

4 b g Gold Well – Little Hand (IRE) (Carroll House)
OWNER: MARTIN BROUGHTON RACING PARTNERS 2
TRAINER: J.J.O'NEILL. Temple Guiting, Gloucestershire.
CAREER FORM FIGURES: 1
CAREER WINS: 2014: Feb TALLOW Soft 4YO Mdn PTP 3m

Gold Well never saw a racecourse, whilst in training with John Hammond in France, but the full-brother to the brilliant Montjeu quickly developed into a high profile National Hunt stallion until sadly dying at the age of twelve last November, following a bout of colic. Jonjo O'Neill has enjoyed a lot of recent success with his stock, including Cheltenham Festival winner Holywell and Paddy Power Gold Cup winner Johns Spirit. The son of Sadler's Wells also sired promising youngsters Legacy Gold and Sausalito Sunrise.

It was therefore no surprise the head of Jackdaws Castle was keen to acquire winning Irish pointer Monbeg Gold following his emphatic ten lengths victory at Tallow in February when trained by Sean Doyle. Pointing expert Declan Phelan takes up the story: **"Signalled his class when trouncing five rivals with a dominant display of jumping and galloping at Tallow (Soft): in hindsight, the vanquished did not amount to a whole lot but, in fairness, Monbeg Gold could do no more than put them in their place and reek of power and quality. Jonjo O'Neill was quick to snap him up privately and, given his good fortune with progeny of the deceased sire Gold Well, the appetite to add another from that stallion was evident. No doubt you will be seeing this horse strut his stuff around Cheltenham in due course, and he is talented enough to make an honest attempt at bagging some lucrative bounty. Whilst scoring on soft ground, I reckon good ground ought to pose him no trouble looking at the way he carried himself over the turf."** Monbeg Gold looks set to develop into a household name for his new connections.

POINTS TO NOTE:

Probable Best Distance	-			2m 4f +			
Preferred Going	-			Soft			

GOING:	R	W	P	TRACK:	R	W	P
Soft	1	1	0	Left Handed	1	1	0

TRIP:	R	W	P	JOCKEY:	R	W	P
3m	1	1	0	B.O'Neill	1	1	0

MOSSPARK (IRE)

6 b g Flemensfirth (USA) – Patio Rose (Petoski)
OWNER: N.MUSTOE & TIM SYDER
TRAINER: Miss EMMA LAVELLE. Hatherden, Hampshire.
CAREER FORM FIGURES: 2 – 111P
CAREER WINS: 2013: Nov EXETER Soft NH 2m 6f; Dec LEICESTER Soft NH 2m 4f: 2014:
Feb HUNTINGDON Soft Lstd NH 2m 4f

It was great to see Emma Lavelle back amongst the winners on a regular basis last season following a wretched 2012/2013 campaign. Shotgun Paddy won the Grade 3 Betfred Classic Chase at Warwick in January before failing by a neck to win the National Hunt Chase at the Cheltenham Festival. Bouggler won a Listed chase at Market Rasen and Le Bec developed into a high-class staying novice chaser. In total, the stable sent out 41 winners, only one short of a personal best set during the 2011/2012 season.

Arguably the most interesting prospect currently residing at Cottage Stables is Listed novice hurdle winner Mosspark. Rated 136 over timber, expectations are high that the gelded son of Flemensfirth will reach an even higher mark over fences. Formerly trained by Colin McKeever on behalf of Wilson Dennison, he finished two and a half lengths second behind subsequent Grade 1 winning chaser Annacotty in his only point-to-point at Kirkistown in November 2012. Mosspark joined Emma Lavelle last year and quickly developed into a very good novice hurdler. **"I've had four runners in this race in the past ten years and they've all won. I think he is a very nice horse for the future and he'll be jumping fences at this time next year,"** commented his trainer following a two lengths winning Rules debut at Exeter in November. An eleven lengths winner next time at Leicester over Christmas, Noel Fehily was on board and he said: **"He will be a nice horse in a year's time and is still learning."** However, the six year old produced his best performance to date in the Listed Sidney Banks Memorial Novices' Hurdle at Huntingdon in February when comfortably beating Spirit of Shankly and the aforementioned Carraig Mor by upwards of five lengths.

Pulled up on quick ground in the Albert Bartlett Novices' Hurdle at the Festival, it is hoped that gruelling contest hasn't left its mark. Indeed, the same connections' Court In Motion finished third in the race in 2011 but has never been the same horse since. Mosspark has all the ingredients to make a very good staying novice chaser and he may be the one to provide his popular trainer with her first ever Grade 1 victory.

NB. The race Emma was referring to at Exeter (won 4 times (from 4 runners) in the last 10 years) is due to be run on Wednesday 12th November (2m 5f) this year. She also won it with Highland Valley (2010) and Highland Lodge (2011).

POINTS TO NOTE:
Probable Best Distance   -   2m 4f – 3 miles
Preferred Going   -   Soft
Connection's Comments: **"In the long-term, we see him as an RSA Chase type."** Nick MUSTOE, part owner at Huntingdon (20/2/14)

GOING:	R	W	P	TRACK:	R	W	P
Soft	4	3	1	Left Handed	1	0	0
Good	1	0	0	Right	4	3	1
				Galloping	1	1	0
				Stiff/Undul.	3	2	0

TRIP:	R	W	P	JOCKEY:	R	W	P
2m 4f	2	2	0	A.Coleman	2	1	0
2m 6f	1	1	0	N.Fehily	1	1	0
3m	2	0	1	L.Aspell	1	1	0
				D.O'Connor	1	0	1

PONT ALEXANDRE (GER)

6 b g Dai Jin – Panzella (FR) (Kahyasi)
OWNER: Mrs S.RICCI.
TRAINER: W.P.MULLINS. Bagenalstown, Co.Carlow.
CAREER FORM FIGURES: 1 – 113/
CAREER WINS: 2012: May CHOLET Good/Soft Hdle 2m 1f; Dec NAVAN Heavy Grade 1 NH 2m 4f: 2013: Jan LEOPARDSTOWN Soft/Heavy Grade 2 NH 2m 4f

Both Miinnehoma (1992) and Hanakham (1997) proved it is possible to win the RSA Chase at the Cheltenham Festival, despite missing the previous season due to injury. The ex-French trained Pont Alexandre is hoping to do likewise next March.

Previously handled by Laurent Viel in France, he is by Dai Jin, who was sold to stand at stud in Turkey 2011 and sired his first Group 1 winner on the Flat in September 2012 with Girolamo. A five lengths scorer of his only race over hurdles in France, Pont Alexandre joined Willie Mullins during the summer of 2012 and made a spectacular start to his career in Ireland. Making all, he won the Grade 1 Navan Hurdle in December by thirteen lengths and immediately announced himself as his trainer's latest star novice hurdler. A four pounds penalty wasn't enough to prevent him following up in a Grade 2 novice hurdle at Leopardstown in January 2013. Once again, he made all and never saw another rival as he bounded clear off the home turn. **"I thought it was a huge performance for him to make all in that weather and that ground, facing into that wind twice coming up the straight. He looks to be one of the best novice hurdlers we've had apart, maybe, from Hurricane Fly,"** enthused Mullins afterwards.

Not surprisingly, Pont Alexandre was sent off a short price favourite for the Neptune Investments Novices' Hurdle at the Cheltenham Festival. However, he could only finish third behind The New One and Rule The World with his trainer commenting: **"I wouldn't like to make the drying ground an excuse and I'm more inclined to think that the whole occasion might have got to him. I think he will go on good ground and he remains a horse with a bright future."**

Unfortunately, the Dai Jin gelding missed the whole of last season, due to injury, but he is back in work and a novice chase campaign is firmly on his agenda. Remember what Willie Mullins said at Leopardstown in January 2013: **"I am particularly looking forward to novice chasing with him. He is a gorgeous horse with a great temperament."**

POINTS TO NOTE:
Probable Best Distance	-	2m 4f – 3 miles
Preferred Going	-	Soft

Connection's Comments: "I've loved this horse since I first saw him and wanted him bought at any cost really. He is a chaser too." Willie MULLINS

GOING:	R	W	P	TRACK:	R	W	P
Heavy	1	1	0	Left Handed	3	2	1
Soft/Heavy	1	1	0	Galloping	2	2	0
Good/Soft	2	1	1	Stiff/Undul.	1	0	1

TRIP:	R	W	P	JOCKEY:	R	W	P
2m 1f	1	1	0	R.Walsh	3	2	1
2m 4f	2	2	0	E.Chayrigues	1	1	0
2m 5f	1	0	1				

POTTERS POINT (IRE)

4 b g Robin Des Champs (FR) – Tango Lady (IRE) (King's Theatre (IRE))
OWNER: GIGGINSTOWN HOUSE STUD
TRAINER: W.P.MULLINS. Bagenalstown, Co.Carlow.
CAREER FORM FIGURES: 2

Gigginstown House Stud finished second in the Irish National Hunt owners list last season. Their 109 domestic winners earned prize-money of €2,311,545, which left Michael O'Leary's operation only €25,592 behind J.P.McManus. Responsible for six Grade 1 winners during the 2013/2014 campaign, the famous maroon and white silks were carried to victory on no less than four occasions on the final day of the Cheltenham Festival in March with Tiger Roll (Triumph Hurdle), Very Wood (Albert Bartlett), Don Poli (Martin Pipe) and Savello (Grand Annual) all winning.

The O'Leary's have been restocking during the spring/summer, including the once raced Potters Point, who finished second on his only start in a point-to-point when trained by Colin Bowe. Beaten half a length at Monksgrange in March, the gelded son of Robin Des Champs was subsequently bought at the Cheltenham April Sales. Expert Declan Phelan reports: "A strapping son of Robin Des Champs, the Closutton handler dug deep and paid £260,000 to acquire him at Brightwells Cheltenham Sale in April following his debut second at Monksgrange (Heavy). At that Wexford venue, he moved with real class, in a galloping style not unlike that of Florida Pearl, and was looking a winner all the way, until just outbattled by a more steely rival (Jeweloftheocean) in the final strides. This is a four year old who looks certain to gain Graded class success, and he will get top style marks in terms of impression when he wins easily. As his point-to-point defeat illustrated, how he reacts under pressure or out of his comfort zone, will define if he can make it to be very top. He still has time to mature his powerful frame. He could end up favourite for the Cheltenham bumper and, if lining up for that race, it may be the one time this season when we find out his attitude with the gun put to his head."

POINTS TO NOTE:
Probable Best Distance   -   2m – 2m 4f
Preferred Going   -   Soft
Connection's Comments: "He's a big, strong, scopey horse by our favourite sire and out of a mare by a good broodmare sire (King's Theatre). He looks a chaser and hopefully a Grade 1 horse – he's a horse for next season." Harold KIRK at the Brightwells Cheltenham April Sale (25/4/14)

GOING:	R	W	P	TRACK:	R	W	P
Heavy	1	0	1	Left Handed	1	0	1

TRIP:	R	W	P	JOCKEY:	R	W	P
3m	1	0	1	B.O'Neill	1	0	1

RED SHERLOCK

5 ch g Shirocco (GER) – Lady Cricket (FR) (Cricket Ball (USA))
OWNER: The JOHNSON FAMILY
TRAINER: D.E.PIPE. Nicholashayne, Somerset.
CAREER FORM FIGURES: 11 - 11119
CAREER WINS: 2013: Jan TOWCESTER Heavy NHF 2m; Feb ASCOT Soft NHF 2m; Nov CHELTENHAM Good Lstd NHF 2m; Dec SOUTHWELL Good Mdn Hdle 2m 4f: 2014: Jan WETHERBY Soft NH 2m 4f, CHELTENHAM Heavy Grade 2 NH 2m 4f

Sunday 17th November 2013 proved to be yet another red letter day in the training career of David Pipe. The head of Pond House sent out 4 winners on the final day of Cheltenham's Paddy Power Festival. Home Run (40/1), The Liquidator (6/4), Dell' Arca (12/1) and Red Sherlock (7/2) all prevailed – it was like the old days when his father Martin regularly cleaned up at Prestbury Park in November.

The final leg of the four timer was provided by the well bred Red Sherlock in the Listed bumper, which rounded off the fixture. A gelding by Shirocco out of the late David Johnson's high-class mare Lady Cricket (won seven times, including the Thomas Pink Gold Cup), he has won six of his seven career starts with his sole defeat coming at the Cheltenham Festival in March. A well beaten ninth behind Faugheen in the Neptune Investments Novices' Hurdle, it is fair to say the five year old was out of sorts having come off the bridle someway from home (possible he was still feeling the effects of a gruelling race on his previous start). Prior to that, he had won three times over hurdles, including the Grade 2 Classic Novices' Hurdle at Cheltenham's 'Trials' meeting in late January. Despite flashing his tail, Red Sherlock showed a terrific attitude to repel the challenge of Irish raider Rathvinden to win by two and a half lengths. The pair pulled twenty nine lengths clear of the 140 rated Aubusson, which speaks for itself.

David Pipe is considering giving Red Sherlock another run over hurdles before embarking on a chasing career. Rated 145, it will be interesting to see if the five year old is tried over three miles this season. His dam failed to win in six attempts over the trip but she did finish fourth in the Hennessy Gold Cup in 2000 and runner-up in the Martell Gold Cup at Aintree three years later. Red Sherlock promises to make an even better chaser.

POINTS TO NOTE:

Probable Best Distance	-	2m 4f +	
Preferred Going	-	Good/Soft	

Connection's Comments: "He'll be an even better horse next year." Timmy MURPHY at Wetherby (11/1/14)

GOING:	R	W	P	TRACK:	R	W	P
Heavy	2	2	0	Left Handed	5	4	0
Soft	2	2	0	Right	2	2	0
Good	3	2	0	Galloping	2	2	0
				Stiff/Undul.	4	3	0
				Tight	1	1	0

TRIP:	R	W	P	JOCKEY:	R	W	P
2m	3	3	0	T.Scudamore	3	2	0
2m 4f	3	3	0	T.J.Murphy	4	4	0
2m 5f	1	0	0				

ROCK THE KASBAH (IRE)

4 ch g Shirocco (GER) – Impudent (IRE) (In The Wings)
OWNER: Mrs DIANA L WHATELEY
TRAINER: P.J.HOBBS. Minehead, Somerset.
CAREER FORM FIGURES: 2

Philip Hobbs looks particularly strong in the novice chase department this season with Champagne West and Sausalito Sunrise set to embark on fencing careers this winter. The Minehead trainer has a couple of promising novice hurdlers, too, with the aforementioned Alisier D'Irlande and the once raced Rock The Kasbah.

From the family of dual Grade 2 winning hurdler Royal Shakespeare, the Shirocco gelding was purchased for €140,000 as a three year old at the Tattersalls Derby Sale in Ireland. He didn't make his racecourse debut until early April this year, but finished a most encouraging second in a bumper at Chepstow. Beaten four and a half lengths by the Charlie Brooks trained Simon Squirrel, the winner has been bought by Paul Nicholls since on behalf of Graham Wylie. The third, Sidbury Hill, had previously chased home Josses Hill in a bumper at Ascot. Despite being sent off 13/8 favourite, Philip Hobbs is adamant Rock The Kasbah wasn't tuned up for his debut and significant improvement ought to be forthcoming.

In all likelihood, the four year old will contest another bumper in the Autumn before going novice hurdling. Once again, Diana and Grahame Whateley have a lot to look forward to and not least from the potentially useful Rock The Kasbah.

POINTS TO NOTE:

Probable Best Distance	-		2m 4f	
Preferred Going	-		Good/Soft	

GOING:	R	W	P	TRACK:	R	W	P
Soft	1	0	1	Left Handed	1	0	1
				Stiff/Undul.	1	1	1

TRIP:	R	W	P	JOCKEY:	R	W	P
2m	1	0	1	M.Nolan	1	0	1

SEMPRE MEDICI (FR)

4 b g Medicean – Sambala (IRE) (Danehill Dancer (IRE))
OWNER: Mrs S.RICCI.
TRAINER: W.P.MULLINS. Bagenalstown, Co.Carlow.
CAREER FLAT FORM FIGURES: 14 - 326336
CAREER WIN: 2012: Oct LONGCHAMP Heavy Mdn 1m 1f

Willie Mullins has won the Grade 1 Royal Bond Novice Hurdle at Fairyhouse (30th November) on four occasions, thanks to Alexander Banquet (1998), Hurricane Fly (2008), Zaidpour (2010) and Sous Les Cieux (2011). The former French Flat racer Sempre Medici has yet to jump a flight of hurdles in public but he is a potentially classy recruit to the National Hunt game and could develop into a candidate for the two mile event.

Trained on the Flat by Myriam Bollack-Badel, he was an impressive four and a half lengths winner on his racecourse debut as a juvenile at Longchamp in October 2012. He then finished a respectable fourth in the Group 1 Criterium De Saint-Cloud. Sempre Medici failed to win any of his six races as a three year old but he was placed four times, including in a ten furlongs Listed event at Compiegne in July. Beaten around three lengths behind the Godolphin owned subsequent Group 2 winner Vancouverite (rated 112), he stayed a mile and a half thoroughly and should be ideally suited by two miles over timber.

Bought by Rich Ricci in the Autumn last year, he was gelded soon afterwards and given plenty of time to mature by Willie Mullins. Indeed, it has become increasingly common for Mullins to buy ex-Flat horses towards the end of their three year old career and then leave them off until the following Autumn before going jumping. He did exactly that with Zaidpour, having bought him for €80,000 at the Arqana October Sale in 2009. Fourteen months later, the former Alain de Royer-Dupre inmate won the Royal Bond Novice Hurdle by a dozen lengths.

POINTS TO NOTE:

| Probable Best Distance | - | 2 miles |
| Preferred Going | - | Soft |

GOING:	R	W	P	TRIP:	R	W	P
Heavy	3	1	1	1m 1f	1	1	0
Soft	1	0	1	1m 2f	3	0	1
Good/Soft	4	0	2	1m 4f	4	0	3

SIR VINSKI (IRE)

5 ch g Vinnie Roe (IRE) – Mill Emerald (Old Vic)
OWNER: LANGDALE BLOODSTOCK
TRAINER: N.G.RICHARDS. Greystoke, Cumbria.
CAREER FORM FIGURES: 1
CAREER WINS: 2014: Mar KELSO Good NHF 2m

When it comes to bumper horses, Nicky Richards invariably runs his best ones at either Kelso (4 winners from only 8 runners during the last five seasons and showing a level £1 stake profit of £16.50) or Newcastle (3 from 7 during the same period and a profit of £19.00). Two seasons ago, stablemates Eduard and Duke of Navan dominated the finish in such an event at the Borders' track, Simply Ned was narrowly beaten on his racecourse bow at the same venue twelve months earlier and Noble Alan was a ten lengths winner on his first ever start in a bumper at Gosforth Park in 2007. It isn't a coincidence.

The 2014 version of the bumper at Kelso in March, which was won by Eduard two years earlier, once again went the way of the Greystoke trainer, courtesy of debutant Sir Vinski. Bought cheaply for €7,000 in Ireland as a three year old, the Vinnie Roe gelding powered clear of his rivals inside the final couple of furlongs to record an impressive ten lengths victory. Having showed signs of greenness throughout the race, the penny dropped late on and he was emphatically on top of his thirteen rivals at the line. Runner-up Major Ivan was beaten a short head by another Richards trained bumper winner, Looking Well, at Perth next time and the third, Shades of Midnight, scored by eight lengths in his only subsequent start for Donald Whillans.

Sir Vinski can only improve with experience and looks a smashing long-term prospect. It wouldn't be a surprise if Nicky Richards starts him off over the minimum trip over timber but his style of racing at Kelso suggested he will excel over further. It will be disappointing if he can't make an impact on the northern novice hurdle scene, at least.

POINTS TO NOTE:
Probable Best Distance	-	**2m 4f**
Preferred Going	-	**Good/Soft**

Connection's Comments: "He is such a laid back sort of horse, you didn't know what to expect but when you give him a squeeze he goes – Brian Harding said that with another couple of furlongs he would have won by twice as far." Nicky RICHARDS at Kelso (22/3/14)

GOING:	R	W	P	TRACK:	R	W	P
Good	1	1	0	Left Handed	1	1	0
				Tight/Undul.	1	1	0
TRIP:	R	W	P	JOCKEY:	R	W	P
2m	1	1	0	B.Harding	1	1	0

SPECIAL CATCH (IRE)

7 b g Catcher In The Rye (IRE) – Top Quality (Simply Great (FR))
OWNER: MIKE BROWNE & WILLIAM McKEOWN
TRAINER: K.REVELEY. Lingdale, Cleveland.
CAREER FORM FIGURES: 3 – 3513 – 11455 - 43130
CAREER WINS: 2011: Dec CATTERICK Soft NHF 2m: 2012: Dec CATTERICK Soft NH 2m
3f: 2013: Jan CATTERICK Heavy NH 2m 3f: 2013: Dec HAYDOCK Soft HH 2m 4f

Keith Reveley has trained some useful novice chasers since taking over the reins from his mother Mary at Groundhill Farm in 2004. Ungaro won the Feltham Novices' Chase at Kempton on Boxing Day 2006, Tazbar won three out of four starts over fences during the 2009/2010 campaign with his sole defeat, ironically, coming in the same Grade 1 event behind Long Run, Benny Be Good also won three and Victor Hewgo scored twice at Doncaster last season.

The former Rose Dobbin trained Special Catch has always been regarded as a prospective chaser since joining the Lingdale based operation. From the family of high-class jumper and dual Grade 2 winning chaser Simply Dashing, the Catcher In The Rye gelding reached a mark of 134 over hurdles. A dual novice winner the previous season, he was a ready two lengths winner of a handicap hurdle at Haydock in December. Prior to that, he had only finished three and a quarter lengths behind subsequent World Hurdle winner More of That over the same course and distance in November. Admittedly, Special Catch was receiving twelve pounds from Jonjo O'Neill's charge but it was still a fair performance. He also finished third in the Morebattle Hurdle at Kelso when possibly finding the trip on the sharp side.

A big, tall scopey gelding, Special Catch has recorded three wins from four visits to Catterick during his career already, so expect to see him at the North Yorkshire venue at some stage this winter. A strong traveller, it will be disappointing if he doesn't develop into one of the North's brightest chasing prospects. A step up to three miles may bring about even more improvement.

POINTS TO NOTE:

Probable Best Distance	-	2m 4f +
Preferred Going	-	Soft

Connection's Comments: "He's a nice horse and is closely related to Simply Dashing, who was a useful chaser. That will be his game." Keith REVELEY

GOING:	R	W	P	TRACK:	R	W	P
Heavy	2	1	0	Left Handed	13	4	5
Soft	6	3	2	Right	2	0	0
Good/Soft	4	0	1	Galloping	4	0	2
Good	3	0	2	Tight	6	1	2
				Tight/Undul.	5	3	1

TRIP:	R	W	P	JOCKEY:	R	W	P
2m	5	1	2	J.Reveley	12	4	3
2m 1f	2	0	1	M.Ennis	1	0	0
2m 2f	1	0	1	G.Lee	2	0	2
2m 3f	3	2	0				
2m 4f	3	1	1				
2m 5f	1	0	0				

STELLAR NOTION (IRE)

6 b or br g Presenting – Green Star (FR) (Green Tune (USA))
OWNER: R.S.BROOKHOUSE
TRAINER: T.R.GEORGE. Slad, Gloucestershire.
CAREER FORM FIGURES: 2112
CAREER WINS: 2013: Dec BANGOR-ON-DEE Good/Soft NHF 2m 1f: 2014: Jan NEWCASTLE
Heavy NH 2m

Tom George had a particularly productive second half of the 2013/2014 season with Module (Grade 2 Game Spirit Chase), Parsnip Pete (Red Rum Chase), Chartreux (Punchestown Festival) and God's Own (Grade 1 Ryanair Novice Chase) all winning big prizes. Hopes will be high at Down Farm outside Stroud that it will be more of the same this winter. Stellar Notion, who retains his position in the *Top 40 Prospects*, appears one of the yard's most interesting novice chasers.

Runner-up in his only Irish point at Bartlemy in May 2013 when trained by Willie Codd, he was bought by Roger Brookhouse for £140,000 at the Brightwells Cheltenham Sale ten days later. Stellar Notion made an excellent start to his Rules career with a two lengths victory in a bumper at Bangor in mid December. Travelling strongly throughout, he claimed the scalp of Desoto County (won twice since and rated 123 over hurdles) with the pair ten lengths clear of the remainder. A big, tall scopey gelding, he was sent hurdling the following month and made virtually all in a two mile novice event at Newcastle. Picking up well after the last, the Presenting gelding readily saw off the 114 rated Another Mattie. While unable to carry his penalty to victory at Doncaster, there was no disgrace in finishing eight lengths second behind Kim Bailey's Un Ace conceding six pounds. Built to jump fences, Stellar Notion gives the impression he will come into his own over two and a half miles plus.

Rated 121 over timber, Tom George has the option of targeting a 0-125 novices' handicap chase, in which he would be hard to beat. Either way, Stellar Notion has the potential to develop into a very useful chaser. Owner Roger Brookhouse looks very strong in the novice chase department with Champagne West, Wuff and, of course, Stellar Notion.

POINTS TO NOTE:

Probable Best Distance	-	2m 4f
Preferred Going	-	Good/Soft

Connection's Comments: "He's a very athletic horse, he will be a lovely chaser." Paddy BRENNAN at Newcastle (15/1/14)

GOING:	R	W	P	TRACK:	R	W	P
Heavy	1	1	0	Left Handed	3	2	1
Soft	1	0	1	Galloping	2	1	1
Good/Soft	2	1	1	Tight	1	1	0

TRIP:	R	W	P	JOCKEY:	R	W	P
2m	2	1	1	P.Brennan	3	2	1
2m 1f	1	1	0	R.P.McNamara	1	0	1
3m	1	0	1				

TELL US MORE (IRE)

5 b g Scorpion (IRE) – Zara's Victory (IRE) (Old Vic)
OWNER: GIGGINSTOWN HOUSE STUD
TRAINER: W.P.MULLINS. Bagenalstown, Co.Carlow.
CAREER FORM FIGURES: 11
CAREER WINS: 2013: Dec TATTERSALLS FARM Yielding/Soft 4YO Mdn PTP 3m: 2014: Mar GOWRAN PARK Soft NHF 2m 2f

Cheltenham Festival and Grade 1 winning amateur rider Jamie Codd partnered five winners at the Louth Foxhounds' meeting at Tattersalls Farm on Sunday 8th December. The star of the show was undoubtedly aboard his brother Willie's Tell Us More, who won the four year old maiden by three lengths. The trainer said afterwards: **"I always thought he was a hell of a horse."**

The Scorpion gelding went under the hammer at the Brightwells Cheltenham Sale five days later and, not surprisingly, he attracted a lot of attention. Bought for £290,000 on behalf of Gigginstown House Stud, Harold Kirk, representing Willie Mullins at the sale, said afterwards: **"He's a gorgeous horse and he won his point very well. He's by an exciting young sire and he would be the first one we've had by him. He should make a smashing chaser – he's a big-framed, scopey type."**

Tell Us More made his Rules debut in the same point-to-point bumper at Gowran Park in March, which First Lieutenant won in 2010. Willie Mullins wrote in his *Racing Post* column beforehand: **"He's a really good sort, a fine big five year old and we're looking forward to seeing him in action."** He certainly didn't disappoint either winning hard held by a dozen lengths under Patrick Mullins (champion amateur rider in Ireland for the seventh successive year). Conceding seven pounds to the runner-up Grand Isola (won his point by a distance), he readily pulled clear passing the two marker and looked a hugely exciting prospect. Irish point expert Declan isn't in any doubt either that Tell Us More is very much a horse to follow saying: **"One of the premier graduates from the pointing season: apart from possessing a striking physical presence, he indicated that he had the fight in him that makes a proper horse. This was on display at Tattersalls (Yielding/Soft) in December, where he looked the real deal. Coasting along throughout, Jamie Codd was almost caught out by the fact the second last fence was being by-passed...he had to snatch up his horse, knock him out of stride, and meander his way around the dolled off fence....losing four or five lengths in the process. Codd then had to get serious on Tell Us More, and the gelding responded by powering over the final fence and surging to the lead on the run in. It was an authoritative victory in the face of disaster. Gigginstown House Stud secured him for £290,000 at Brightwells December Sale: rehoused with Willie Mullins, he won the point confined bumper at Gowran laughing at the opposition. Gigginstown had previously won that race with First Lieutenant and, of all the point horses from 2013-2014, this son of Scorpion looks the banker to win a Graded race and more than likely Grade 1 chases in due course. Raced on yielding and soft, I think he may be happy on any ground except firm."**

Willie Mullins has won the Neptune Investments Novices' Hurdle three times in the last seven years (Fiveforthree (2008), Mikael d'Haguenet (2009) & Faugheen (2014)) and he may have a prime candidate for the 2015 renewal in the unbeaten Tell Us More.

POINTS TO NOTE:

Probable Best Distance	-	2m 4f +
Preferred Going	-	Soft

Connection's Comments: "He did that very nicely. For him to come and do that first time was very impressive." Willie MULLINS at Gowran (8/3/14)

GOING:	R	W	P	TRACK:	R	W	P
Soft	1	1	0	Right	1	1	0
Yield/Soft	1	1	0	Tight/Undul.	1	1	0

TRIP:	R	W	P	JOCKEY:	R	W	P
2m 2f	1	1	0	P.Mullins	1	1	0
3m	1	1	0	J.J.Codd	1	1	0

UP FOR REVIEW (IRE)

5 br g Presenting – Coolsilver (IRE) (Good Thyne (USA))
OWNER: ANDREA & GRAHAM WYLIE
TRAINER: W.P.MULLINS. Bagenalstown, Co.Carlow.
CAREER FORM FIGURES: 3 - 1
CAREER WINS: 2014: Feb KNOCKANARD Soft/Heavy 5YO Mdn PTP 3m

Andrea and Graham Wylie have enjoyed considerable success with former Irish pointers in recent seasons. Back In Focus, Briar Hill and Shaneshill have all graduated from racing 'between the flags' to winning at the highest level. There is every reason to believe the twice raced Up For Review may eventually do likewise, judged on his most impressive win at Knockanard in February. A six lengths winner, the five year old maiden point has been won by the likes of Keen Leader (2001) and Missed That (2004).

Pointing expert Declan Phelan reports: **"A towering son of Presenting, he is closely rated to Graded winning chaser Turpin Green. He raced once as a four year old for the Costello family in April 2013 but was too green and failed to cope with the bends at Quakerstown (Left handed) before keeping on late to place third. Was hobdayed and filled out considerably before reappearing at Knockanard (Soft/Heavy) in February. Prominent from the beginning, he extended his raking stride on the steady uphill climb from the second last and won with plenty up his sleeve, in the process defeating two proper rivals in Pulled Mussel and Private Malone. This bay with a white face was purchased by Graham Wylie and his style of running reminds one plenty of his Gold Cup runner up On His Own. He could win a bumper by a wide margin and Mullins could opt to switch him straight over fences with him as he could readily become a player next winter in the top bracket of three mile novices, if heading that way. If he improves and assuming his breathing is regulated by the hobdaying, then he is the type that one day may line up in a Gold Cup. Difficult to predict how he would manage on lively ground, his pounding stride may relate a negative to that question."**

POINTS TO NOTE:

Probable Best Distance	-	2m 4f +
Preferred Going	-	Soft

Connection's Comments: "This fellow cost €25,000 as a foal and he did a proper piece of work on the Curragh before Christmas." John COSTELLO (Owner/Trainer) at Knockanard (16/2/14)

GOING:	R	W	P	TRACK:	R	W	P
Soft/Heavy	1	1	0	Left Handed	1	0	1
Good/Yield	1	0	1	Right	1	1	0
TRIP:	R	W	P	JOCKEY:	R	W	P
3m	2	1	1	M.O'Connor	1	1	0
				J.J.King	1	0	1

URBAN HYMN (FR)

6 b g Robin Des Champs (FR) – Betty Brune (FR) (Dark Stone (FR))
OWNER: Mr & Mrs G.CALDER
TRAINER: J.M.JEFFERSON. Norton, North Yorkshire.
CAREER FORM FIGURES: FU1 - 12117
CAREER WINS: 2013: Mar LARKHILL Good Mdn PTP 3m; Nov HUNTINGDON Good/Soft Mdn PTP 2m; Dec HAYDOCK Heavy NH 2m 4f: 2014: Jan DONCASTER Soft Grade 2 NH 3m

"He's a big raw horse with a lot of ability, who we think will be even better over fences," predicted Brian Hughes after partnering Urban Hymn to victory in the Grade 2 River Don Novices' Hurdle at Doncaster in January. Indeed, it proved a career best season for the Irishman with 86 winners.

Featured in last year's *Top 40 Prospects*, Urban Hymn developed into a smart staying novice hurdler winning three of his five races under Rules. A winning pointer for Richard Barber, the Robin Des Champs gelding ran out an impressive seven lengths winner of a bumper at Huntingdon in November, making all and never looking like relinquishing his advantage. Sent hurdling soon afterwards, he found the talented Spirit of Shankly too strong in the latter stages at Haydock before gaining ample compensation over the same course and distance in late December. Once again, Malcolm Jefferson's charge made all the running and galloped his four rivals into submission before registering a twenty lengths victory. Urban Hymn then recorded his biggest success to date at Town Moor with a typically gutsy display. Despite slipping going into the first and not jumping with his usual fluency thereafter, he showed a terrific attitude to get the better of the 136 rated Blakemount in a prolonged duel. A short head separated the pair with a dozen lengths back to the third, Warden Hill. The four times winning hurdler Sausalito Sunrise was beaten over sixteen lengths in fifth. It was a gruelling contest run in atrocious conditions.

Although beaten fifty lengths, Urban Hymn ran respectably in the Grade 1 Albert Bartlett Hurdle at the Cheltenham Festival finishing seventh. A big strong gelding, his future lies over fences though and he is a cracking novice chase prospect. I contacted his owner Graham Calder in late August and there is every chance the six year old will drop back to two miles because he isn't short of speed. With that in mind, don't be surprised to see the son of Robin Des Champs making his chasing bow at somewhere like Carlisle. There is a two mile beginners' chase at the Cumbrian venue on Thursday 23rd October – Pendra won the race last year from Eduard. Either way, Urban Hymn could be very good over fences.

POINTS TO NOTE:
Probable Best Distance   -   2m – 2m 4f
Preferred Going   -   Good/Soft
Connection's Comments: "Urban Hymn will be some horse when he is a chaser." Malcolm JEFFERSON at Haydock (30/12/13)

GOING:	R	W	P		TRACK:	R	W	P
Heavy	1	1	0		Left Handed	4	2	1
Soft	3	1	1		Right	1	1	0
Good/Soft	2	1	0		Galloping	2	2	0
Good	2	1	0		Stiff/Undul.	1	0	0
					Tight	2	1	1

TRIP:	R	W	P		JOCKEY:	R	W	P
2m	1	1	0		B.Hughes	5	3	1
2m 4f	2	1	1		W.Biddick	3	1	0
3m	5	2	0					

VALYSSA MONTERG (FR)
5 b m Network (GER) – Mellyssa (FR) (Panoramic)
OWNER: Mrs S.RICCI
TRAINER: W.P.MULLINS. Bagenalstown, Co.Carlow.
CAREER FORM FIGURES: 111
CAREER WINS: 2013: Sept MACHECOUL APQS NHF 1m 4f; Oct LES SABLES Soft APQS NHF 1m 5f; Nov ANGERS APQS NHF 1m 7f

Having finished second behind Jetson in the Grade 1 Ladbrokes World Series Hurdle at the Punchestown Festival, the curtain came down on the wonderful career of top-class mare Quevega. The daughter of Robin Des Champs won the David Nicholson Mares' Hurdle at the Cheltenham Festival for a record breaking sixth time in March. In total, Willie Mullins' ten year old won 16 of her 24 races, including the aforementioned World Series Hurdle on four occasions, and earned £749,280 in prize-money.

Ireland's champion trainer now faces the unenviable task of seeking a replacement. Annie Power is making a good fist of it by winning 11 of her 12 career starts to date and more big race successes beckon for the Shirocco mare. Quevega also won three APQS Flat races in France before joining Mullins in late 2007 and a new incumbent of Closutton with a similar profile is the unbeaten Valyssa Monterg. Like Allez Colombieres, she was trained across the English Channel by Alain Couetil and the five year old is a half-sister to Paul Nicholls' winning hurdler Tonic Mellysse and from the family of the useful Hulysse Royal.

The Network mare was a comfortable winner on her debut at Machecoul in September before producing a smart performance to take a 'winners' bumper at Les Sables. A three lengths winner, the form has been subsequently franked with the runner-up Val De Law (has been sold to the UK since) winning twice and the third has also won. It was a similar story on Valyssa Monterg's final outing at Angers in November as she registered another three lengths win. Bought by Rich Ricci soon afterwards, she looks a tremendous prospect for this season in mares' novice hurdles and beyond.

POINTS TO NOTE:
Probable Best Distance	-	2m – 2m 4f
Preferred Going	-	Soft

TRIP:	R	W	P		R	W	P
1m 4f	1	1	0	1m 7f	1	1	0
1m 5f	1	1	0				

VAUTOUR (FR)

5 b g Robin Des Champs (FR) – Gazelle De Mai (FR) (Dom Pasquini (FR))
OWNER: Mrs S.RICCI
TRAINER: W.P.MULLINS. Bagenalstown, Co.Carlow.
CAREER FORM FIGURES: 22 - 11111
CAREER WINS: 2013: Dec NAVAN Good/Yielding Mdn Hdle 2m: 2014: Jan PUNCHESTOWN Soft/ Heavy Grade 2 NH 2m; Feb LEOPARDSTOWN Soft/Heavy Grade 1 NH 2m 2f; Mar CHELTENHAM Good/Soft Grade 1 NH 2m; May PUNCHESTOWN Good/Yielding Grade 1 NH 2m 4f

"That shows he is a bit above average, but I thought Vautour's performance was hugely exceptional. He looked to be in a different league. It blew me away," was Willie Mullins' response when he was supposed to be discussing Faugheen's four and a half lengths win in the Neptune Investments Novices' Hurdle at the Cheltenham Festival. Vautour is arguably the most exciting prospect in National Hunt racing at present following a fantastic campaign in novice hurdles last season.

Runner-up in both starts for Guillaume Macaire, the Robin Des Champs gelding joined Mullins last summer and swept the board with five victories, including three at the highest level. The highlight, of course, came at Cheltenham in March when winning the Sky Bet Supreme Novices' Hurdle by six lengths and, in doing so, breaking the course record, which had stood for fourteen years when Istabraq won his third Champion Hurdle. It was a devastating display of relentless galloping and magnificent jumping. Ireland's champion trainer said afterwards: **"I thought it was extraordinary how much in control of the race he was from the very beginning. Once he got into his stride, he was on a different level. He screams chaser to me. He was idling the whole way up the straight. If he can perform like that jumping wise over fences, he could be very good. I was surprised how much better he was than the field – I thought it was a good Supreme Novices' Hurdle but he treated them like a bunch of maidens. I thought it was all over going out passing the stands, if he kept jumping. It was an awesome performance."** Prior to the Festival, Vautour had beaten dual Grade 1 winner The Tullow Tank in the Deloitte Hurdle at Leopardstown, making all and toying with the opposition.

His three and a half lengths victory in the Grade 1 Tattersalls Ireland Champion Novice Hurdle at the Punchestown Festival did not see Vautour at his best. However, he was found to be suffering with a nasal discharge at the start of the week, hence he raced over two and a half miles on the Friday of the meeting rather than the Grade 1 over the minimum trip on the opening day. It therefore speaks volumes regarding his ability that he was still able to beat Graded winners Apache Stronghold, Lieutenant Colonel and Lac Fontana comfortably. The five year old's two least impressive performances both came at Punchestown and, while it is early days to be making conclusions, it is possible Vautour is a much better horse racing left-handed. Either way, he is a hugely exciting prospect for novice chasing this winter and may provide his trainer with his first win in the Arkle Trophy.

POINTS TO NOTE:
Probable Best Distance   -   2 miles
Preferred Going   -   Good/Soft
Connection's Comments: "I'd say he's a chaser. He looks a chaser and was bought as a chaser. He quickened off the bend and pinged the last – he was brilliant. Jesus, he's a good horse." Ruby WALSH at Cheltenham (11/3/14)

GOING:	R	W	P	TRACK:	R	W	P
Heavy	2	0	2	Left Handed	4	3	1
Soft/Heavy	2	2	0	Right	3	2	1
Good/Yield	2	2	0	Galloping	5	4	1
Good/Soft	1	1	0	Stiff/Undul.	1	1	0
				Tight	1	0	1

TRIP:	R	W	P	JOCKEY:	R	W	P
2m	3	3	0	R.Walsh	4	4	0
2m 1f	2	0	2	P.Townend	1	1	0
2m 2f	1	1	0	B.Lestrade	2	0	2
2m 4f	1	1	0				

YOUNG MR GORSKY (IRE)

5 b g High Chaparral (IRE) – Elizabeth Tudor (IRE) (Supreme Leader)
OWNER: J.P.McMANUS
TRAINER: J.J.O'NEILL. Temple Guiting, Gloucestershire.
CAREER FORM FIGURES: U21
CAREER WINS: 2014: Jan KILFEACLE Heavy 5YO Mdn PTP 3m

A half-brother to six times winners Oscar Hill and Thunderstorm, Mr Young Gorsky is another potentially very smart recruit from the Irish pointing field in training with Jonjo O'Neill. Described as the best horse he has ever trained by his former handler Kevin O'Sullivan, the High Chaparral gelding won at the third attempt before being acquired by the Jackdaws Castle team for £190,000 at the Cheltenham January Sale.

Following his one and three quarters of a length victory under Mikey O'Connor at Kilfeacle, the Co.Cork trainer said: **"This is a really nice horse. He's such a good moving type we were half afraid of the bad ground today, but he handled it well. He definitely has the class to win a bumper."** Pointing expert Declan Phelan believes: **"A very strong bodied gelding, who will never have difficulty carrying big weights: ran in three points in the depths of winter: was in the process of learning the ropes when unseating his rider at halfway on his Curraheen debut: at Ballindenisk (Good) in December, he was again waited with towards the rear, he used plenty of gas to close a twenty lengths gap on the all the way winner Oficial Ben, and his run flattened out between the final two fences, as he went down by six lengths. In the New Year at Kilfeacle (Heavy), ridden much closer to the action, he pounced running to the final fence and showed his raw talent as he commanded the contest to win by a nonchalant length and a half. Jonjo O'Neill was prepared to pay £190,000 at Brightwells January Sale for this son of High Chaparral, and those close to the horse in Ireland felt he had a bright future. He could certainly win a bumper and could be an above average participant in staying novice hurdles this winter. There is a better than average chance he can become a Grade 1 or 2 chaser."**

POINTS TO NOTE:
Probable Best Distance	-	2m – 2m 4f
Preferred Going	-	Soft

Connection's Comments: "He's won a point-to-point, but he'll have no problem over two miles. He'll go on to do big things." Former trainer Kevin O'SULLIVAN

GOING:	R	W	P	TRIP:	R	W	P
Heavy	1	1	0	3m	3	1	1
Soft	1	0	0				
Good	1	0	1				

OWNERS' ENCLOSURE
RICH & SUSANNAH RICCI

There can be little doubt that owners **Rich** and **Susannah Ricci** have the most exciting team of National Hunt horses on either side of the Irish Sea at the moment. With around 50 horses in training with nine times Champion Irish trainer Willie Mullins, 20 of which have yet to race in the famous pink and green silks, they have a lot to look forward to. Last season's star novice hurdlers Faugheen and Vautour created a big impression at Cheltenham in March and already prominent in the various ante-post lists to do likewise once again next spring. Mikael D'Haguenet provided the Ricci's with their first ever Grade 1 victory in the Barry & Sandra Kelly Memorial Novice Hurdle at Navan in December 2008. Twenty eight more have followed since, including ten last season. In an exclusive interview, Rich has kindly passed on his thoughts on his stars, plus his hopes for his new recruits from France, the Irish pointing field and former smart Flat racers.

ADRIANA DES MOTTES (FR) 4 br f Network (GER) – Daisy Des Mottes (FR)
Placed over hurdles at Auteuil before we bought her, she had a very good season winning twice, including the Grade 1 mares' novice hurdle championship final at Fairyhouse's Easter Festival. The ground was too fast for her at Punchestown on her final run. We always felt anything she achieved over hurdles was a bonus because she has chaser stamped all over her. She loves soft ground and, while she will probably start off over two miles, she is unbeaten over two and a half miles. The Grade 3 mares' chase at Clonmel (13th November) could be a possibility – it is a race I have won in the past with Blazing Tempo.

ALLEZ COLOMBIERES (FR) 4 b g Sageburg (IRE) – Paricolombieres (FR)
A very exciting prospect we bought at the Arqana Sale in France last Autumn. Previously trained by Alain Couetil, he won three of his four APQS bumpers and was the leading three year old bumper horse in France when we purchased him. Willie (Mullins) has been very pleased with him and has purposely given him plenty of time. He had a couple of racecourse gallops last winter and went very well. We have high hopes for him and hopefully he will be competitive in the top novice hurdles this season.

ANNIE POWER (IRE) 6 ch m Shirocco (GER) – Anno Luce
She had another very good season winning four out of five, including the Grade 1 Mares' Champion Hurdle at the Punchestown Festival. Her only defeat came in the World Hurdle at Cheltenham when she was beaten by a top-class horse (More of That). Rated 162, she has summered well and I love her to bits. I have always viewed her as a chaser in the making (16.2hh) but there is a difference of opinion in the camp regards which route she should take. The mares' hurdle route is an option, given the Cheltenham race is now a Grade 1, and since Quevega has retired, and then races like the Aintree Hurdle come into the equation. There is also the possibility of continuing down the World Hurdle route. She was quite keen at Cheltenham but there is no doubt she stayed the trip and she will settle better as she gets older. There is still plenty of drinking and thinking to be done between now and the Autumn.

ARBRE DE VIE (FR) 4 b g Antarctique (IRE) – Nouvelle Recrue (FR)
A new recruit, he could be anything. He raced twice on the Flat in France finishing second at Le Mans in November. Switched to hurdles, he finished a length third in a good race at Auteuil in March. There was a lot of interest in the race and the fact he is a maiden is a bonus. Trained in France by Philippe Peltier, he was also responsible for Arvika Ligeonniere, who won four Grade 1 chases for us and is now retired following an injury in the spring.

AU QUART DE TOUR (FR) 4 b g Robin Des Champs (FR) – Qualite Controlee (FR)

He won his only Irish point at Dromahane in April for Pat Doyle. A five lengths winner, he looked very good and is another who fits into the 'could be anything' bracket. I would imagine he will run in a bumper.

BABYLONE DES MOTTE (FR) 3 b f Blue Bresil (FR) – Nellyssa Bleu (FR)

I am hoping she may prove to be the 'value for money' acquisition of the year. She ran in three French bumpers, finishing second twice before winning by five lengths at Le Lion-D'Angers over an extended thirteen furlongs in late July. A well bred filly being out a winning mare, she has pleased Willie since joining him.

BALLYCASEY (IRE) 7 gr g Presenting – Pink Mist (IRE)

A good horse, who won twice over fences last season, including the Grade 1 Dr P.J.Moriarty Chase at Leopardstown in February. Unlucky not to win the Powers Gold Cup at Fairyhouse over Easter when falling at the second last, he didn't quite get home over three miles at Cheltenham and Punchestown. Two and a half miles is his trip and, if he is ready in time, he could be one for the Grade 2 chase at Down Royal (1st November). Rated 153, we are hoping he will develop into a Ryanair Chase horse in the spring.

BLOOD COTIL (FR) 5 b g Enrique – Move Along (FR)

He ran some very good races over hurdles the previous season, winning a Grade 3 at Auteuil and finishing second in a Grade 1 at the same track. Due to the fact he was late coming back into work last season, he didn't reappear until January. He was all set to win on his chasing debut at Cork but fell at the second last. We then decided to switch him back to hurdles because there was no point losing his novice status so late in the campaign. Tenth in the Boylesports Hurdle at Leopardstown, he didn't get the smoothest of runs that day. The plan is for him to go back over fences with two and a half miles on soft ground being his optimum conditions. Rated 140 over hurdles, I am hoping he will make a useful novice chaser.

BORDINI (FR) 4 b g Martaline – Didinas (FR)

A very good looking horse, who finished third in his only Irish point-to-point for Aidan Fitzgerald. Only beaten three lengths, he would have finished closer but for a mistake at the last. A scopey athletic sort, he is another who will run in a bumper.

CHAMPAGNE FEVER (IRE) 7 gr g Stowaway – Forever Bubbles (IRE)

A dual Festival winner, he was denied by a head in the Arkle Trophy in his attempt to make it three successive victories at Cheltenham. He is rated 156 over fences and the intention is to step him up in trip with the Cheltenham Gold Cup in mind. We are going to ride him differently this season, too. It is possible Willie will look for a 'winners' of one' chase or we could consider a race like the John Durkan Memorial Chase at Punchestown (7th December).

CHILDRENS LIST (IRE) 4 b g Presenting – Snipe Hunt (IRE)

He won the first four year old maiden point of the year at Belharbour (2m 4f) in February when trained by Pat Doyle. A half-brother to dual Grade 1 winner Schindlers Hunt, there was a lot of interest in him afterwards and we have high hopes for him. I would expect him to run in a bumper.

CLONDAW COURT (IRE) 7 br g Court Cave (IRE) – Secret Can't Say (IRE)

Unbeaten in four career starts, we thought he was better than Faugheen as a bumper horse a couple of years ago. Unfortunately, he has been delicate and has only raced three times during the last two seasons. If we can keep him sound, he has incredible potential. He appreciated the step up in trip at Thurles in February winning by eighteen lengths. We thought he had a huge chance in the Albert Bartlett Novices' Hurdle at the Festival but he incurred a setback and was forced to miss the rest of the season. We are hoping he will develop into an RSA Chase horse this season.

DANEKING 5 b g Dylan Thomas (IRE) – Sadie Thompson (IRE)

It took a while for the penny to drop over hurdles and, following a few near misses, he came good in the second half of the season, winning at Navan and Fairyhouse. He tends to be quite hard on himself in his races and is best fresh. We have kept him to two miles over hurdles but I think he will improve when stepped up to two and a half miles. He will continue in handicap hurdles, although I wouldn't rule out a trip to Royal Ascot next summer because he isn't badly treated on the Flat.

DJAKADAM (FR) 5 b g Saint Des Saints (FR) – Rainbow Crest (FR)

A Grade 2 winner over fences last season at Leopardstown, I think he would have gone close in the Jewson Novice Chase at Cheltenham. He, unfortunately, fell at the fourth last when still going well. We have got a lot of confidence in him and we are expecting more improvement when stepped up to three miles plus this season. He has enjoyed a good summer and his first main target is the Hennessy Gold Cup at Newbury (29th November) and, in all likelihood, he will go there first time out. We are hoping he is one for the premier staying chases and it would be nice to think he could develop into a Cheltenham Gold Cup horse.

DOUVAN (FR) 4 b g Walk In The Park (IRE) – Star Face (FR)

An interesting horse who was trained in France by Philippe Peltier, he raced twice over hurdles finishing second on his debut at Saint-Malo before winning by two and a half lengths at Compiegne in June. He remains a novice for this season and, while he appears to have the speed for two miles, there is plenty of stamina on the dam's side of the pedigree.

FAUGHEEN (IRE) 6 b g Germany (USA) – Miss Pickering (IRE)

Unbeaten in seven career starts, he had a fantastic season over hurdles winning all five races, culminating in impressive victories at Cheltenham and Punchestown. A four and a half lengths winner of the Neptune Investments Novices' Hurdle at Cheltenham, he won decisively, despite some indifferent jumping late on. Dropped back to the minimum trip in the Grade 1 Champion Novice Hurdle at the Punchestown Festival, he was even more impressive winning by twelve lengths. Following those victories, we are strongly considering going down the Champion Hurdle route, although Willie has other horses in the yard which could go down the same path, including Un De Sceaux, who is also unbeaten. I think he deserves a crack at the Champion Hurdle but there is a lot of competition with the likes of Jezki, who I was incredibly impressed with last season, and The New One. A lot of noodling still to do on him.

FULHAM ROAD (IRE) 4 b g Shantou (USA) – Bobomy (IRE)

Still in contention when falling two out in his only point-to-point at Punchestown (2m 4f) in February, we bought him out of Colin Bowe's yard in the spring. He has a good National Hunt pedigree and is bred to stay well over hurdles/fences. He is another who will run in a bumper and then we will take it from there.

KALKIR (FR) 3 b g Montmartre (FR) – Kakira (FR)
By a sire I like, he has a very good French pedigree and finished a promising fourth on his only run over hurdles at Auteuil in April when trained by Guillaume Macaire (same source as Vautour). Only beaten three lengths, the form of his race looks strong, too, with the third (Bonito Du Berlais) winning his two subsequent starts in Listed hurdles at the same track. I bought him shortly afterwards and we have high hopes for him in juvenile hurdles.

LIVELOVELAUGH (IRE) 4 b g Beneficial – Another Evening (IRE)
From the family of Operation Houdini, he was an emphatic six lengths winner of his only point-to-point at Oldcastle in April for Mark O'Hare. The runner-up (Mount Haven) has won a bumper by sixteen lengths since for David Pipe and the time was very good, being the fastest race on the card. The race also included Birch Hill, who fell at the third last but won next time before being sold for €160,000. He is an exciting prospect.

LONG DOG 4 b g Notnowcato – Latanazul
An eight lengths winner of his only race on the Flat when trained by Andy Oliver, he beat Thomas Edison in a ten furlongs maiden at Sligo in August last year. The runner-up has gone on to win two good handicaps at the Curragh this year, plus the Galway Hurdle in July. Once arriving at Willie's, he was gelded and given a break and allowed to develop and mature. He will start off in a maiden hurdle and we are hoping he will emerge as a good novice hurdler. We will let him progress through the ranks but he is a horse to look forward to.

MAX DYNAMITE (FR) 4 b g Great Journey (JPN) – Mascara (GER)
He was campaigned at the highest level on the Flat in France last year, finishing eighth in the Prix du Jockey Club behind Intello and he also ran in the Group 1 Grand Prix de Paris at Longchamp. A winner over eleven furlongs at Fontainebleau, we bought him at the Arqana Sale in October and have given him time. There is plenty of stamina in the pedigree so he won't have any trouble staying two miles. He is an interesting prospect for novice hurdles.

MOYLE PARK (IRE) 6 ch g Flemensfirth (USA) – Lovely Present (IRE)
A three times winner, his only defeat came in Grade 1 company at Leopardstown over Christmas when racing too keenly before finishing third behind The Tullow Tank. A horse with a lot of potential, he was still immature last year and we are expecting him to improve. I would think he will follow a similar route to Zaidpour, when he was younger, and contest two and two and a half mile conditions/Graded hurdles. It will also be interesting to see what mark he is given.

PONT ALEXANDRE (GER) 6 b g Dai Jin – Panzella (FR)
He is a horse I love. A winner over hurdles in France, he won the Grade 1 Navan Novice Hurdle on his first run for us in December 2012 before following up at Leopardstown in a Grade 2. Despite being beaten by a very good horse at Cheltenham in the Neptune Investments Novices' Hurdle, he wasn't right that day and suffered an injury subsequently, which prevented him from running last season. It wasn't a catastrophic injury but enough to keep him off the track and he is too good to risk. I think he is an incredibly exciting prospect for novice chasing and Willie is very enthusiastic about him. He has summered well and is going well at home. The RSA Chase is his ultimate target.

PYLONTHEPRESSURE (IRE) 4 b g Darsi (FR) – Minnie O'Grady (IRE)
He was bought at the Cheltenham May Sales following a five lengths win in his only point-to-point at Laurencetown. He made all and the runner-up (Cracked Rear View) won a bumper at Sligo next time before being subsequently sold for £130,000. By a promising sire, Willie knows the family well and he is another interesting prospect for bumpers this season.

ROYAL CAVIAR (IRE) 6 b g Vinnie Roe (IRE) – Blackwater Babe (IRE)

A six and a half lengths winner of a bumper at Fairyhouse in November, he followed up in a Grade 2 event at Navan but was subsequently disqualified. It was a very disappointing decision and one which I don't feel was justified. He suffered a problem soon afterwards and missed the rest of the season. Back in work, he will go novice hurdling over two and a half miles plus.

SEMPRE MEDICI (FR) 4 b g Medicean – Sambala (IRE)

A stunning looking horse who is an exciting prospect for novice hurdles. A nine furlongs winner at Longchamp as a two year old, he also finished fourth in the Group 1 Criterium de Saint-Cloud. Placed four times as a three year old, he chased home Vancouverite in a Listed event at Compiegne last summer. Bought last Autumn, he was gelded soon afterwards and has benefited from a good break. He is a gorgeous horse, who will be suited by two and two and a half miles.

THOMAS HOBSON 4 b g Halling (USA) – La Spezia (IRE)

A progressive horse on the Flat last season for John Gosden, he won four times and is rated 101. He has a good pedigree, he handles soft/heavy ground and clearly has a big engine. He has the right profile but I was reluctant to start with because he cost a lot of money. However, Willie has such a good track record with this type of horse. Gelded soon after arriving, he has purposely not been rushed and the plan was always to wait until this season before going jumping.

TOTALLY DOMINANT (USA) 5 b g War Chant (USA) – Miss Kilroy (USA)

A progressive horse in bumpers, we have realised he doesn't want soft or heavy ground. A dual winner at Punchestown and Bellewstown during the summer, he also finished third on the Flat at Wexford. He may have another run in a bumper before going hurdling over two and two and a half miles.

TURCAGUA (FR) 4 gr g Turgeon (USA) – Acancagua (FR)

Third in a valuable sales bumper at Fairyhouse in April, he is from a good family and has plenty of size and scope. I will be disappointed if he doesn't win a bumper before going novice hurdling.

VALYSSA MONTERG (FR) 5 b m Network (GER) – Mellyssa (FR)

Unbeaten in three French bumpers for Alain Couetil, she is an exciting mare who could be very good. There is a good programme for mares in Ireland and we are looking forward to seeing her run over hurdles.

VAUTOUR (FR) 5 b g Robin Des Champs (FR) – Gazelle De Mai (FR)

He had a fantastic season winning all five of his races, including the Supreme Novices' Hurdle at Cheltenham. He then followed up at Punchestown over two and a half miles even though he has wasn't at his best and scoped badly on the lead up to the Festival. The intention was to run him over two miles but he wasn't right at the start of the week so we gave him another couple of days and he was able to run at the end of the week. The plan is to send him over fences because he jumps hurdles like a chaser. I think he has got a great future in front of him and, despite the fact we also had Faugheen, I thought he was our best novice hurdler last season. Effective over two and two and a half miles, the Arkle is his main target this season.

VESPER BELL (IRE) 8 b g Beneficial – Fair Choice (IRE)
I thought he ran well in the Grand National considering he made a bad mistake at Becher's Brook first time. He then ran a good race at Punchestown and I hope there is a big staying handicap chase in him this season. The National is the target, once again, and he may take in the Becher Chase en route, in which he, unfortunately, fell at the first in last season.

VIGOVILLE (FR) 5 b g Lavirco (GER) – Kadalville (FR)
A lovely unraced five year old we bought at the Derby Sale a couple of years ago. He was ready to run in a bumper last season but suffered a stress fracture, which sidelined him for the remainder of the campaign. A very nice, scopey horse, he is one to look out for in bumpers.

VIVEGA (FR) 5 ch g Robin Des Champs (FR) – Vega IV (FR)
A full-brother to Quevega, we were disappointed with his run in a bumper at Navan in February only finishing third. He has been given time to mature since and he has grown a lot during the summer. We are therefore hoping he has improved. I would expect him to run in another bumper before going hurdling.

VROUM VROUM MAG (FR) 5 b m Voix Du Nord (FR) – Naiade Mag (FR)
Twice a winner in France, including over hurdles at Toulouse in September last year, she also finished second at Auteuil in March. Beaten four lengths by a stablemate, the winner has subsequently won over fences by fifteen lengths. A half-brother to a promising three year old trained by Nick Williams (Brise Vendeenne), she is no longer a novice over hurdles and therefore could go mares' novice chasing. However, she has only run twice over hurdles so Willie may decide to give her more experience before going chasing. Either way, she is a very nice mare and one to look forward to.

ZAIDPOUR (FR) 8 b g Red Ransom (USA) – Zainta (IRE)
He gained his third Grade 1 victory of his career in the Christmas Hurdle at Leopardstown last season. Runner-up in the Boyne Hurdle at Navan in February, his main target this season is Auteuil in November. We will take it race by race thereafter.

RICH RICCI'S HORSE TO FOLLOW: ALLEZ COLOMBIERES

ANDREA & GRAHAM WYLIE

Leading owners **Andrea** and **Graham Wylie** tasted more big race glory last winter with four Grade 1 winners, thanks to Boston Bob (twice), Briar Hill and Shaneshill. Third in the owners' championship in the UK during the 2013/2014 campaign and fourth in the Irish equivalent, three of the four Grade 1 wins were gained across the Irish Sea and yet the Wylies finished higher in the British table. Admittedly, that was largely due to the fact On His Own finished runner-up in the Cheltenham Gold Cup but it is surely also an indication of how strong the Irish scene is competing against the likes of J.P.McManus, Gigginstown House Stud and Rich & Susannah Ricci. Hopes are high though that Andrea and Graham will have another lucrative season with a host of promising youngsters combined with established household names.

Trained by champions Paul Nicholls and Willie Mullins, Graham has kindly sent me the latest news on a selection of his horses.

Willie MULLINS

Cheltenham Festival winner **BACK IN FOCUS** missed the whole of last season due to injury. The nine year old is back in training and will be aimed at the Grand National. Triple Grade 1 winning chaser **BOSTON BOB** will be targeted at either the Ryanair Chase or Cheltenham Gold Cup in March. Staying novice hurdles are on **BLACK HERCULES**'s agenda, having finished fourth in the Festival bumper at Cheltenham. **BRIAR HILL** suffered multiple fractures of his cheekbone when falling in the Albert Bartlett Novices' Hurdle in March. Thankfully, the Shantou gelding is OK now with the World Hurdle his prime objective. **SHANESHILL** was arguably the best bumper horse on either side of the Irish Sea last season, winning the Grade 1 championship event at the Punchestown Festival and, in doing so, turning the tables on Silver Concorde, who had beaten him at Cheltenham the previous month. The five year old will start off this season in two mile novice hurdles. Graham bought three potentially exciting recruits during the spring/summer including **BELLSHILL**. A four year old by King's Theatre who is a full-brother to John Quinn's bumper winner Chieftain's Choice, he finished second in his only point-to-point at Maralin (Soft/Heavy) for Wilson Dennison and Colin McKeever. **NICHOLS CANYON** is rated 111 on the Flat and the son of Authorized won 3 of his 10 races for John Gosden. A dual Listed winner, the four year old was also runner-up in the Group 3 St Simon Stakes at Newbury last October. His record on soft/heavy ground is 1121. He could develop into a top-class novice hurdler this winter. **UP FOR REVIEW** is another ex-Irish pointer who was previously trained by John Costello. A five year old by Presenting, he finished third on his debut at Quakerstown (Good/Yielding) last year before winning by six lengths on his reappearance at Knockanard (Soft/Heavy) in February.

Paul NICHOLLS

ALCALA (FR) 4 gr g Turgeon (USA) – Pail Mel (FR)
Runner-up over hurdles at Auteuil prior to us buying him, he ran well in the Adonis Hurdle at Kempton in February. Still a big baby and quite backward last season, we purposely put him away after that and he has strengthened up since. He is a nice type for novice hurdling.

KATGARY (FR) 4 b g Ballingarry (IRE) – Kotkira (FR)
Runner-up in the Fred Winter Juvenile Hurdle at the Cheltenham Festival in March, he has strengthened up during the summer. In all likelihood, he will start off in a handicap hurdle and then, depending on how he gets on, we will decide whether to go chasing.

MR DINOSAUR (IRE) 4 ch g Robin Des Champs (FR) – Miss Generosity
A huge horse who won his point-to-point very easily for Tom Lacey. We bought him during the spring/summer and it is possible he will have a run in a bumper. Otherwise, he will spend this season in novice hurdles. However, anything he achieves this year will be a bonus because he is a three mile chaser in the making.

SIMON SQUIRREL (IRE) 4 b g Robin Des Champs (FR) – Misty Heather (IRE)
Another new horse by Robin Des Champs, he was an impressive winner of his only bumper at Chepstow in April when trained by Charlie Brooks. Related to Rock On Ruby, he will make a very nice chaser eventually but, in the meantime, he will run in another bumper before going novice hurdling this season.

VAGO COLLONGES (FR) 5 b g Voix Du Nord (FR) – Kapucine Collonges (FR)
He has been sidelined for a year, due to an injury, but the time off has done him the world of good. Still only five, he will go novice hurdling having finished second in a Listed bumper at Newbury behind Oscar Rock before filling the same position in the Grade 2 event at Aintree's Grand National meeting.

TALKING TRAINERS

Harry FRY

Stables: Manor Farm, Seaborough, Beaminster, Dorset.
2013/2014: 34 Winners / 117 Runners 29% Prize-Money £302,748
www.harryfryracing.com

ACTIVIAL (FR) 4 gr or ro g Lord Du Sud (FR) – Kissmirial (FR)

I was delighted with the progress he made last season having arrived from France during the Autumn. Runner-up at Newbury's Hennessy meeting, he produced a very good performance to win the Grade 2 Adonis Hurdle at Kempton in February. He found the ground too lively at Aintree and he was taken out of his comfort zone. The softer the ground the better for him and the plan is to keep him to two miles for the time being. I think he is on a very fair mark (137) and, provided the ground is soft, we are keen to aim him at races like the Greatwood Hurdle at Cheltenham (16th November) and the Ladbroke Hurdle (20th December).

ASSAM BLACK (IRE) 6 b g Oscar (IRE) – Contrasting Lady

Placed on his first two starts in bumpers, he won nicely at Taunton before taking his chance at the Cheltenham Festival. He faced a tough task there but he wasn't knocked about and his rider looked after him. He has plenty of ability and I am hoping he will make his mark in novice hurdles this season. We have done a lot of schooling with him and, while he will probably start off over two miles, he will stay further in due course. I was pleased with his progress last year. He wouldn't want bottomless ground.

AYALOR (FR) 4 b g Khalkevi (IRE) – Physicienne

A new recruit from France, he won his only start over hurdles in the Provinces in good style. Still a novice until the end of October, he is in work now and looks a nice horse.

BITOFAPUZZLE 6 b m Tamure (IRE) – Gaelic Gold (IRE)

A lovely big strong mare, who won a point-to-point before joining us. Unbeaten in two bumpers last season, including a Listed event at Huntingdon, she suffered an injury soon afterwards hence she didn't run again. She is fine now and we may aim her at the Listed mares' bumper at Cheltenham this side of Christmas before going hurdling. A real galloper, she did it well at Huntingdon and enjoyed the conditions. I think soft/heavy ground was important for her in bumpers because she is a stayer who won a three mile point-to-point. I therefore don't think it will be quite so important over hurdles when she steps up in trip. She is a very nice prospect.

BLUE BUTTONS (IRE) 6 b m King's Theatre (IRE) – Babet (IRE)

A tough, genuine mare who was unfortunate to fall twice last season. However, she progressed nicely winning at Exeter and Taunton and was also narrowly touched off at the latter venue in a Listed hurdle in December. Versatile in terms of ground and trip, we are going to aim her at the same handicap hurdle at Wincanton (8th November) we won last year with Highland Retreat. We are keen to try her over two mile six again and see how she gets on. Officially rated 126, I think that's fair.

DASHING OSCAR (IRE) 4 b g Oscar (IRE) – Be My Leader (IRE)

A nice unraced four year old we bought at the Land Rover Sale in Ireland last year. Unable to race last term, due to a minor setback incurred during the winter, he is a nice stamp of a horse. We are still learning about him but I am hoping to have him ready for a bumper in September/October.

FLETCHERS FLYER (IRE) 6 b g Winged Love (IRE) – Crystal Chord (IRE)

He provided us with a fantastic day at the Punchestown Festival when winning a bumper. Runner-up at Uttoxeter prior to that in a race which has worked out well, he did it the hard way at Punchestown and I was delighted with him. We made plenty of use of him because he stays well and is a galloper. A winning Irish pointer, he jumps well and he will be going novice hurdling over two and a half miles plus. I don't think he wants extremes of ground but I am hoping he will develop into a nice staying novice hurdler this winter.

GENERAL GINGER 4 ch g Generous (IRE) – Nuzzle

I thought he ran a very promising race on his debut in a bumper at Exeter during the spring. He appeared to be travelling like the winner turning for home before his lack of experience told late on. Only four, we are going to keep him to bumpers for the time being and I will be disappointed if he can't win one. A tall leggy individual, he has improved a lot for the experience at Exeter.

HENRYVILLE 6 b g Generous (IRE) – Aquavita

Despite winning at Fontwell in March and running consistently for most of last season, he was a shade frustrating. However, he returned from his summer break to win a valuable handicap hurdle at Newton Abbot in August and I hope he will continue to progress. He didn't appear to stay three miles at Doncaster in December so we will keep him to trips around two and a half and two miles six.

HIGHLAND RETREAT 7 b m Exit To Nowhere (USA) – St Kilda

She has been a star and showed further improvement last season winning three of her four races, including a Grade 2 hurdle at Ascot in January. She benefited from a wind operation and the plan is to send her novice chasing this winter. Rated 144 over hurdles, it would be nice to think she will be competitive against the boys at some stage during the season. We will start her off in a mares' only novice chase and see how far she can progress. She loves the mud and three miles is her optimum trip.

JOLLYALLAN 5 b g Rocamadour – Life Line

A very nice horse who we hoped would run well on his debut at Wincanton in a bumper. He certainly didn't let us down and I was very taken by his performance winning by fifteen lengths. The horse who finished fourth won next time and therefore proved the race had some substance. We then threw him in at the deep end in the Grade 1 championship bumper at the Punchestown Festival. He wasn't disgraced in sixth and was only beaten fourteen lengths behind some of the best bumper horses in Ireland. He travelled well but lacked experience during the latter stages. He is a lovely horse and we are delighted to be training him for J.P.McManus. We will start him off in a two mile novice hurdle, although he will stay further.

JOLLY'S CRACKED IT (FR) 5 b g Astarabad (USA) – Jolly Harbour

A half-brother to Crack Away Jack, he was previously trained by Gary Moore before joining us last season. He won a bumper at Wincanton in January in good style with the first two pulling a long way clear of the remainder. We planned to run him in one of the better bumpers during the spring but he had a minor niggle and therefore hasn't raced since. He is 100% now though and there is every chance we will aim him at the Listed bumper at Cheltenham's Paddy Power meeting (16th November). We won the race four years ago with Rock On Ruby. Then, all being well, he will go novice hurdling. Two miles on soft ground will suit because he likes the mud. Two and a half miles on better ground should be OK, too.

KARINGA DANCER 8 b g Karinga Bay – Miss Flora

A winner over hurdles at Aintree in October, he then found the ground too soft when only fifth in the Elite Hurdle at Wincanton. Switched to fences soon afterwards, he won on his chasing debut at Doncaster. We were disappointed when he finished third next time at the same track but it turned out to be good form because Western Warhorse won the race. A non stayer over two mile five at Cheltenham in April, he did it well over an extended two mile three at Exeter the following month under A.P.McCoy. He really warmed to his task that day and the plan is to drop him back in trip this season. It won't be easy off a mark of 145 but we have the option of running him in Graduation Chases before going back down the handicap route.

KING'S ENCORE (IRE) 4 b g King's Theatre (IRE) – Royal Nora (IRE)

We bought him at the Tattersalls Derby Sale last year and he is currently in work. It is early days to say how much ability he possesses but I would like to run him in a bumper during the Autumn.

LADY OF LAMANVER 4 b f Lucarno (USA) – Lamanver Homerun

Unraced, she was in pre training last season and is in work at the moment. She is a nice stamp of a mare and her dam won races. All being well, she will run in a mares' bumper before Christmas.

MENDIP EXPRESS (IRE) 8 b or br g King's Theatre (IRE) – Mulberry (IRE)

A three times winner over fences last season, including a handicap in atrocious conditions at Cheltenham on New Year's Day. Indeed, I think that race took its toll and he was never at his best thereafter. I would be inclined to forget his run at Newbury in February and then he didn't stay in the Scottish National. He must go left-handed and I think he appreciates better ground. He is rated 144 and we will be looking towards the decent three mile handicap chases from the end of October onwards.

MISTER TREBUS (IRE) 5 b g Beneficial – Kiltoome Scot (IRE)

A winner on his pointing debut for Richard Barber, he ran out next time but he is a horse with ability. He will be aimed at a bumper in the Autumn.

OPENING BATSMAN (IRE) 8 b g Morozov (USA) – Jolly Signal (IRE)

He endured a more than frustrating season last year, having done so well the previous campaign. At least he showed more on his final start in the Bet365 Gold Cup at Sandown. Fitted with blinkers for the first time, we decided to ride him positively and he showed much more enthusiasm before being swallowed up around the Pond fence. There is no doubt he is well handicapped on his old form. His first target is the Badger Ales Chase at Wincanton (8th November).

POLAMCO (IRE) 5 b g Old Vic – Shanesia (IRE)

I must admit he surprised us a bit when winning a bumper at Taunton on his third start. We decided to operate on his wind following his debut run at Ascot. Fifth next time at Stratford, he improved a lot to win at Taunton. I think the ground helped him and we will send him hurdling in the Autumn. I would expect him to want a trip over jumps.

POPULAR OPINION (IRE) 4 b f Oscar (IRE) – Jeu de Dame

From the family of Harchibald, she was in pre training last year and we will start her off in a mares' bumper during the Autumn. It is too early to say how much ability she has.

PURE OXYGEN (IRE) 6 br g Presenting – Katday (FR)
A half-brother to Best Mate, he failed to settle over hurdles at Doncaster and joined Richard Barber to go point-to-pointing soon afterwards. He won his first two races for Richard, jumping very well in the process, but then the ground caught him out on his third start. We are going to send him novice chasing over two and two and a half miles on decent ground.

RENE'S GIRL (IRE) 4 b f Presenting – Brogella (IRE)
Another lovely unraced filly we bought at the Derby Sales in Ireland last year. She is from a good family, although we haven't done a lot with her yet. She is a nice stamp of a mare and is another for mares' bumpers.

ROCK ON RUBY (IRE) 9 b g Oscar (IRE) – Stony View (IRE)
We tried him over fences last season and, although he won twice at Plumpton and Doncaster, he got found out against the better novices in the Arkle. We therefore decided to stick at what he's best at and I was delighted with his run in the Aintree Hurdle over two and a half miles. Only beaten a head, The New One may not have been at his best but he still ran a very good race. He will be a year older and there is a really good crop of hurdlers at present but I am hoping he will be able to hold his own in the best two and two and a half mile races this season. The ground is very important to him though because he wants decent ground, having had two wind operations during his career.

SIR IVAN 4 b g Midnight Legend – Tisho
Third on his only start in a bumper at Taunton in April, he travelled well until his lack of experience took its toll late on. The first three were nicely clear of the remainder and I don't think it was a bad race. We will try and win a bumper before turning his attentions to hurdling.

SUMERIEN 3 b g Califet (FR) – Suzuka (FR)
A lovely unraced three year old who hails from a decent family. We haven't done a great deal with him but the plan is to run him in a bumper in the New Year.

THOMAS BROWN 5 b g Sir Harry Lewis (USA) – Tentsmuir
A dual winning pointer, I thought he ran well on his Rules debut in a bumper at Chepstow, despite showing signs of greenness. He then won in good style in a similar event at Newbury's Hennessy meeting and we decided to go down the same route as Oscar Rock the previous year. However, we were scratching our heads when he finished a tailed off last in the Listed bumper at Newbury in February. He was never travelling and I put it down to the ground. It was horrendous conditions and barely raceable. Thankfully, he bounced back next time at Bangor and won nicely. We hold him in high regard and, being a winning pointer over three miles, he will be aimed at two and a half mile plus novice hurdles.

TRIANGULAR (USA) 9 b g Diesis – Salchow (USA)
A new arrival last season, he finished second at Doncaster in January before winning next time at Kempton. Despite a five pounds rise, he remains potentially well treated on his best form. We were unable to run him again, due to a minor setback, but he is back in work now and we will target three mile plus handicap chases.

VIVANT POEME (FR) 5 b g Early March – Hasta Manana (FR)
He won his second point-to-point for Richard Barber before joining us. Disappointing in a bumper at Towcester, he was too keen and was probably over the top having been on the go for a long time. He is better than he showed that day and I will try and win a bumper with him before going hurdling.

VOIX D'EAU (FR) 4 b g Voix Du Nord (FR) – Eau De Chesne (FR)
We bought him at the Arqana Sale in France in July and he looks an interesting recruit. Successful in the latest of his three starts over hurdles, he could be aimed at a novice handicap chase in November onwards.

VUKOVAR (FR) 5 b g Voix Du Nord (FR) – Noraland (FR)
He has done very well during the summer and we are looking forward to seeing him run again. He is a good horse who won impressively at Newbury. We then took him to Cheltenham for the Jewson Novice Chase but he was almost brought down at the first and was playing catch up thereafter. We have given him a good break since and, with an official rating of 152, we will look towards the good handicaps and even Graduation Chases. He only arrived in October last year and will be fully acclimatised now. Effective over two and two and a half miles, he loves the mud and is at his best when ridden prominently. He has a very high cruising speed and is a terrific jumper.

ZULU OSCAR 5 b g Oscar (IRE) – Loxhill Lady
A dual bumper winner last season at Wincanton and Kempton, he will go novice hurdling this time. If we can keep him in one piece, he has the potential to be a nice horse. We will start him off over two miles.

TRAINER'S HORSE TO FOLLOW: BITOFAPUZZLE

Warren GREATREX

Stables: Uplands, Upper Lambourn, Berkshire.
2013/2014: 43 Winners / 192 Runners 22% Prize-Money £251,100
www.wgreatrexracing.com

ALPHABET BAY (IRE) 4 b g Kalanisi (IRE) – A And Bs Gift (IRE)

He has always shown plenty of ability at home and did it nicely on his debut in a bumper at Worcester in May. A big raw horse, he is not really a bumper type and will have learned a lot from his first run. J.P.McManus kindly bought him afterwards and we will see what he and his team would like to do before making plans. It is possible he could have another run in a bumper before going hurdling but his long-term future lies over fences. He will be suited by a step up to two and a half miles over hurdles.

ALZAMMAAR (USA) 3 b g Birdstone (USA) – Alma Mater

Rated 73 and placed three times on the Flat for Charlie Hills, we bought him at the Newmarket July Sales. He was recommended to me and is a lovely looking horse. He has plenty of size and, all being well, he will be running in juvenile hurdles early on.

BABY MIX (FR) 6 gr g Al Namix (FR) – Douchka (FR)

He is unlikely to be in action before Christmas but I think he is a very nice horse when he is at his best. An impressive winner over fences at Kempton, it was the only occasion we had him spot on last season and he showed what he is capable of, breaking the course record in the process. I was very disappointed when he was unable to run in the novices' handicap chase at the Cheltenham Festival because he was in terrific form beforehand and I am convinced he would have run a huge race. Unfortunately, he had a foot problem, which resulted in an infection in his bone and he missed the remainder of the season. He is OK now and he remains a lightly raced horse capable of winning a good prize over fences. Two and a half miles on decent ground on a flat track are his optimum conditions. We tried him over two mile five at Ascot in December and he didn't get home. However, that was on soft ground and we may try him over further in time.

BALLYCULLA (IRE) 7 b g Westerner – Someone Told Me (IRE)

I was delighted with him last season winning two staying handicap hurdles at Exeter and Ffos Las. I was also chuffed with his final run at Cheltenham in April finishing second behind a well handicapped winner of Henry Daly's (Kingsmere). It was arguably a career best performance. We decided to ride him a bit differently at Cheltenham and it seemed to suit him. We are going to send him over fences and I think he will make an even better chaser. He jumps very well, handles any ground and stays three miles thoroughly. He isn't ungenuine in any way but we decided to put cheekpieces on him at Cheltenham on his final start because it helps him concentrate. I wouldn't have thought we will keep them on over fences to begin with, but it is something we can consider again later on.

BELLS 'N' BANJOS (IRE) 4 b g Indian River (FR) – Beechill Dancer (IRE)

A half-brother to Masquerade, he is a horse I really like. An impressive winner on his debut in a bumper at Bangor in April, he then finished fourth under a penalty at Southwell. Despite his defeat, I still think he was the best horse in the race. He got further back than is ideal and may have found the track a bit sharp. The form looks OK and I may give him another run in a bumper because he looks capable of defying his penalty. He has improved physically during the summer and will be at home over two and a half miles over hurdles on a galloping track.

BLUE ATLANTIC (USA) 3 b g Stormy Atlantic (USA) – Bluemamba (USA)
I am delighted to be training for Roger Brookhouse this season. He has kindly sent me two horses, including this 74 rated ex-Flat horse. A winner over a mile and a half at Beverley in April for Mark Johnston, he will go juvenile hurdling.

BOUDRY (FR) 3 b g Crossharbour (FR) – Lavande (FR)
Unraced, he is a three parts brother to Sprinter Sacre. We bought him at the Doncaster May Sales and has only just been broken in. He looks well and the plan is to run him in a bumper during the spring.

CAITYS JOY (GER) 4 b f Malinas (GER) – Cassilera (GER)
I think she is quite an exciting filly, who won with a lot more in hand than the winning margin suggested at Fakenham in a bumper. She has improved out of all recognition since and hails from a good family. Her victory wasn't a surprise because she had been showing up nicely in her work. She possesses plenty of speed and we may aim her at a Listed mares' bumper before going over hurdles. There is a suitable one at Cheltenham's Paddy Power meeting, which may be a possibility.

CHALK IT DOWN (IRE) 5 b g Milan – Feedthegoodmare (IRE)
A four times winner, including over hurdles at Newton Abbot and Market Rasen in May and August respectively, it took a while for him to get his head right and he has been a bit quirky. However, he is learning to settle and I think there is more to come from him. A well bred horse, he appreciated the step up trip at Market Rasen. A four lengths winner, the handicapper put him up fourteen pounds and he finished second next time at Newton Abbot. He doesn't want soft ground and will have a mid winter break once the ground changes.

CHASE THE WIND (IRE) 5 ch g Spadoun (FR) – Asfreeasthewind (IRE)
I have always held him in high regard and, while he can be a bit of a character and race keenly, he gets on extremely well with Gavin (Sheehan) and the hood appears to have made a big difference, too. Two out of two since we fitted it, we also decided to ride him a bit handier and it has helped as well. Capable of further improvement over hurdles, I think he could be fairly smart. He possesses a very good cruising speed and is suited by flat tracks. While he has the speed for two miles, I am sure he will stay further in time and will jump fences eventually.

CHESTERTERN 7 ch g Karinga Bay – My Tern (IRE)
A lovely horse who has yet to run for us, having arrived last season from Jennie Candlish. We decided to pull the plug on him when he first arrived and he looks well, having benefited from a break. I like him and he appears to be on the right side of the handicapper at the moment. A maiden over fences, we could aim him at a novices' handicap chase. Beaten less than seven lengths by Pendra and Eduard at Carlisle last season, he didn't jump particularly well that day but, if we can get that sorted out, he looks capable of winning races.

COLE HARDEN (IRE) 5 b g Westerner – Nosie Betty (IRE)
He is a very exciting horse who has summered extremely well. Although not over big, he is strong and the plan is to keep him over hurdles this season. Rated 150, he only needs to improve around ten pounds to be mixing it with the big boys. Still quite green last season, he developed into a high-class novice hurdler winning twice at Fontwell and Newbury. Seventh in the Neptune Investments Novices' Hurdle at the Cheltenham Festival, we then stepped him up to three miles for the first time and he finished an excellent second in the Grade 1 Sefton Novices' Hurdle at Aintree. Running him in those races made a man of him. He came out of those two races absolutely bouncing and we were tempted to run him again. However, he is still only five and was always going to benefit from another summer on his back. He has built up a big fan base and I think that is largely due to the fact he wears his heart on his sleeve and

always gives his best. Gavin (Sheehan) was kicking himself after Aintree for not making more use of him but he still had most of the field in trouble with a circuit to run. It was a very good performance. He needs to go left handed and we may look at a race like the Silver Trophy at Chepstow (25th October). Otherwise, we could aim him at the West Yorkshire Hurdle at Wetherby (1st November). Effective on any ground, he will jump fences eventually but I hope there is more to come from him over hurdles in the meantime.

DETOUR AHEAD 6 ch m Needwood Blade – My Tern (IRE)
Like Chestertern, she arrived from Jennie Candlish's last season and won both her races over hurdles during the summer at Fontwell and Newton Abbot. She incurred a slight setback after her latest win and we have therefore given her a break. I actually rode her mother to victory over hurdles and she belongs to a very nice owner. I hope she remains fairly treated.

DOLATULO (FR) 7 ch g Le Fou (IRE) – La Perspective (FR)
A cheap buy, he has been a cracking horse and never lets us down. Even though he isn't over big, he is a better horse over fences and he paid his way again last season winning twice at Lingfield and Stratford. Slightly better racing left-handed, we haven't got any ambitious plans but I hope he will continue to be competitive in decent handicap chases.

ELLNANDO QUEEN 6 b m Hernando (FR) – Queen of Spades (IRE)
A lovely mare from a very good family. She wasn't the easiest to train early on and I was disappointed when she finished third on her hurdles debut at Ludlow in October. However, we operated on her wind and she hasn't looked back, winning a jumpers' bumper at Kempton and both her starts over hurdles at Plumpton since. She is a smart mare who will stay three miles in time. She will jump fences one day but I am keen to keep her over hurdles for the time being and gain some black type. She has strengthened up since last season and has everything you look for in a good mare.

GLADSTONE (FR) 3 b g Mizzen Mast (USA) – Bahia Gold (USA)
A nice type we bought out at the Arqana Sale in France in July. He won twice on the Flat for Jean-Claude Rouget and I liked the manner of his latest success. We have gelded him since arriving and I think he will benefit from that. I was keen to buy a few juvenile hurdlers and I will be disappointed if he doesn't win races.

GOING FOR GOLD (FR) 4 ch g Gold Away (IRE) – Sleeping Doll (FR)
He made a winning start to his career with a comfortable success in a bumper at Uttoxeter in late July. A nice horse from a good family, he will only improve and is capable of winning another bumper before going jumping. I think he will get better and better and is a potentially exciting horse. He jumps well.

HANNAH'S PRINCESS (IRE) 5 b m Kalanisi (IRE) – Donna's Princess (IRE)
We have some very good mares and I think she is one of the best. A winner on her debut at Market Rasen for Brian Storey in August, we bought her soon afterwards and she won in good style at Lingfield in November. Given a break, I thought she would win the Listed mares' bumper at Aintree because her work beforehand had been exceptional. I have been associated with a lot of good mares over the years, including when working at David Nicholson's, I think she is right up there. She finished sixth at Aintree and it transpired she had pulled a shoe off. Gavin (Sheehan) thought she would win turning for home and I am sure she is better than her finishing position suggests. We decided to give her a run over hurdles at Worcester and she finished second. It looked a strong race and the winner has won four on the trot. Gavin wasn't hard on her and the experience she gained will stand her in good stead. She will continue in mares' novice hurdles and, while she will stay further, she certainly isn't slow and we will keep her over two miles for the time being.

HORSTED VALLEY 4 gr g Fair Mix (IRE) – Kullu Valley
A lovely four year old who overcame greenness to make a winning debut in a bumper at Southwell in the spring. He finished off his race well and I think he is above average. We aren't going to rush him and he has developed during the summer. I would expect him to have another run in a bumper before we send him jumping. Two and a half miles will suit him over hurdles.

INTERIOR MINISTER 4 b g Nayef (USA) – Sister Maria (USA)
He joined us from Jonjo O'Neill in July, having disappointed over hurdles. Rated 79 on the Flat and 94 over hurdles, we will see how he gets on over jumps. If it doesn't work out, then we can always run him on the all-weather on the Flat.

KNIGHT BACHELOR 4 ch g Midnight Legend – Fenney Spring
A very likeable horse who didn't surprise us when winning a bumper on his debut at Market Rasen. He came out of the race well, so we purposely left him off and have given him time to mature. He is a very, very good jumper but I would like to run him in another bumper before turning his attentions to novice hurdles.

MA DU FOU (FR) 4 b or br g Le Fou (IRE) – Belle Du Ma (FR)
I think of all our youngsters, he is the one I am most excited about. He is a very exciting horse with loads of class. An impressive winner on his only start in a bumper at Wetherby, there were still a few horses in contention around three out but, by the time he crossed the line, he had pulled ten lengths clear. He is a very nice horse and has been bought by Dai Walters and James Potter since. Despite the fact he has schooled brilliantly, I am keen to run him in another bumper and, provided that goes to plan, he could be saved for better bumpers in the second half of the season. When the time comes to go hurdling, he possesses more than enough speed for two miles. I think he is one of those horses for whom the trip or ground doesn't really matter. He has summered exceptionally well and looks great.

MADNESS LIGHT (FR) 5 b g Satri (IRE) – Majestic Lady (FR)
Ex-French, he won twice over hurdles at Lingfield and Uttoxeter, but we were always a bit concerned about his breathing last season. Having disappointed on his last two runs at Cheltenham, we decided to operate on his wind and I think it will make a big difference. He tended to be quite keen early on but I think that was due to his breathing. He jumps well and we are going to send him over fences. Unfortunately, he isn't a novice having won a chase in France, prior to joining us. However, I think he will make a nice chaser over two and a half miles, although I am sure he will stay three miles. He handles most types of ground and has done well physically during the summer.

MASQUERADE (IRE) 5 b g Fruits of Love (USA) – Beechill Dancer (IRE)
A consistent sort, he won over hurdles at Bangor last season but is bred to be a chaser. Physically, he has improved since last year and we may give him another run over hurdles before going over fences. I don't think he quite stayed two and a half miles last season but I am hopeful he will in future, especially having strengthened during the summer. He doesn't want the ground too soft though.

MERCOEUR (FR) 3 gr g Archange D'Or (IRE) – Erivia (FR)
Another we bought at the Arqana Sale in July. He has already got plenty of experience over hurdles being placed twice in four starts. All being well, he will be running in September and I think there could be a fair bit of improvement in him.

MISS ESTELA (IRE) 4 b f Tobougg (IRE) – Simply Divine (IRE)

A very likeable mare, who won both her starts in bumpers last season, prior to being bought by Mr Brookhouse at the Cheltenham April Sales. He has kindly sent her back to us and she is a very nice prospect for mares' novice hurdles. I wasn't surprised when she made a winning debut at Taunton and then she did it very well under a penalty at Cheltenham in April. A filly with a good attitude, she will want a trip over jumps.

MISSED APPROACH (IRE) 4 b g Golan (IRE) – Polly's Dream (IRE)

Successful in his only Irish point, we bought him at the Cheltenham May Sale. We haven't done a great deal with him but I think he will improve on better ground. He appears a straightforward horse who could run in a bumper before going hurdling. I suspect he will want a trip over jumps.

ROYAL MOLL (IRE) 7 b m King's Theatre (IRE) – Moll Bawn (IRE)

Another new arrival, she won a bumper at Sligo and over hurdles at Galway for Willie Mullins last season. She has only raced four times during her career and is an interesting prospect.

ONE TRACK MIND (IRE) 4 b g Flemensfirth (USA) – Lady Petit (IRE)

A big raw horse, he won the first division of the two bumpers at Wetherby in April (Ma Du Fou won the other division). Still quite gawky, he is not really a bumper horse but he still won in good style by six lengths. I must admit I was slightly surprised when he won so well. Very much a three mile chaser in the making, we won't see the best of him for a couple of years. He may have another run in a bumper before going novice hurdling.

PAINT THE CLOUDS 9 b g Muhtarram (USA) – Preening

He was the first horse I bought and he has been an absolute star. Not the easiest to train, he has won five out of five over fences, including three hunter chases during the spring. An eight lengths winner of the Foxhunters Champion Hunters' Chase at Stratford last time, he will continue in that sphere next year with the Foxhunters' at Cheltenham his ultimate target. Twice a winner at the track in the past, he will have a couple of runs beforehand. He appreciates decent ground and I think he has the ideal profile for the race. He has done really well throughout his career because he has had leg problems and broken his pelvis.

RELENTLESS PURSUIT (IRE) 3 b g Kodiac – Dancing Debut

We recently acquired him out of Ger Lyons' yard in Ireland. An early type for juvenile hurdles, he has been schooled and jumps well. A winner on the Flat at Dundalk in May, he appears to be enjoying his new job.

SHANTOU BOB (IRE) 6 b g Shantou (USA) – Bobset Leader (IRE)

A tough horse who won his only Irish point before we bought him in January. He has had a few problems since arriving but I thought he won well at Ffos Las in May. He jumps very well and I am tempted to send him straight over hurdles because he is six years old. A strong horse, he isn't without speed and will probably start off over two miles and step up in trip as the season goes on. He enjoys soft ground.

SKY WATCH (IRE) 7 b g Flemensfirth (USA) – The Shining Force (IRE)

Bought at Doncaster Sales last year, he is a half-brother to Shining Gale and I think he will make a better chaser. Placed four times last season, I was disappointed he didn't win over hurdles. He has summered well and we will be looking towards a novices' handicap chase off his mark of 118.

STONEY SILENCE 6 b g Generous (IRE) – Stoney Path

From the family of Hurricane Lamp, he took time to come to himself but was a dual winner in point-to-points for Marcus Foley last spring. We bought him at the Doncaster Sales and I hope he will provide his new owner with plenty of fun. A chaser in the making, he could start off in a novice hurdle.

TEOCHEW (IRE) 6 b m Shantou (USA) – Papal Princess (IRE)

Previously trained in Ireland, I thought she was unlucky not to win over hurdles last season. Runner-up at Sandown and Bangor, she didn't run a bad race and I think we have got something to work with this time. Two and a half miles on soft ground or three miles on better ground is ideal.

TOP DANCER (FR) 7 b g Dark Moondancer – Latitude (FR)

An impressive winner of an amateur riders' handicap chase at Newbury's Hennessy meeting, he reappeared a week later at Sandown under a penalty but only finished fifth. With hindsight, we should have ridden him handier because it developed into a sprint and it didn't suit him. Unfortunately, he suffered an injury soon afterwards and missed the remainder of the season. Back in work in August, I am hoping to have him ready for the same race at the Hennessy meeting. I think he is on a fair mark and it wouldn't surprise me if he developed into a National horse of some description. He handles most types of ground, jumps well and has the right profile.

TSAR ALEXANDRE (FR) 7 b g Robin Des Champs (FR) – Bertrange (FR)

A winning pointer, I thought he produced a very good performance at Uttoxeter on his final start in May. A tall horse who jumps well, he will make a better chaser. We will probably start him off over two and a half miles but he stays three and is a galloper.

UMADACHAR (FR) 6 gr m Turgeon (USA) – Intelectuelle (FR)

We are going to try and get her back this season, having missed the whole of last term due to a degenerative problem. She is a fine big mare with some good form. The plan is to send her over fences because she jumps very well and has a lot of ability.

VIRTUOSE DU CHENET (FR) 5 b g Irish Wells (FR) – Lili Bleue (FR)

We bought him in France in July and he has shown a good level of form, winning over hurdles at Nantes in March. He loves heavy ground. He had a minor back issue but he has been vetted and it has been remedied. We can't believe we acquired him for such a reasonable price. I think he is real value and sure to win plenty of races for us.

WARRANTOR (IRE) 5 b g Turtle Island (IRE) – Pixie Dust (IRE)

Demoted to second in his only Irish point-to-point having crossed the line in front, we bought him at the Cheltenham Festival Sale. He was a very impressive winner at Towcester in a bumper. We then ran him at Aintree but they went a slow gallop and he found himself too far back. As a result, he used a lot of energy making up ground and then had nothing left late on. He will go novice hurdling and I think he is smart. A good traveller and jumper, he has plenty of speed and may be best suited by softer ground.

WESTWARD POINT 7 ch g Karinga Bay – Hottentot

A very talented horse, he has only raced twice over fences, including an impressive eight lengths victory at Wetherby in December. An injury soon afterwards means he hasn't run since but he should be back in action by October. From a late maturing family, he will appreciate a step up to three miles in time. Quite gasey early on in his career, he is learning to settle and handles most types of ground. There should be plenty more to come from him over fences.

TRAINER'S HORSE TO FOLLOW: MA DU FOU

Nicky HENDERSON

Stables: Seven Barrows, Lambourn, Berkshire.

2013/2014: 124 Winners / 514 Runners 24% Prize-Money £2,019,935

ACT ALONE 5 b g Act One - Figlette

He was placed in a couple of bumpers before making a winning debut over hurdles, and an impressive one at Doncaster in January. He was placed in two more competitive novice events, producing solid performances. It seems the further he went, the better he got. Whether to go chasing this year will be the first decision, but I think he has got more to offer over hurdles.

ADMIRAL MILLER 4 b g Multiplex – Millers Action

Another of Henry Ponsonby's 'Miller' family and a particularly nice one, and almost certainly the biggest we have had of this line. For a big horse, he showed us quite a bit in the spring before finishing third in a bumper at Wincanton. He has strengthened up over the summer and is likely to go straight over hurdles.

ALTIOR (IRE) 4 b g High Chaparral (IRE) – Monte Solaro (IRE)

He was one of several High Chaparral's we bought last summer and I am pleased to say they seemed to be a pretty talented bunch. This four year old was almost certainly one of our best bumper horses in the spring and, although he only had one run at Market Rasen, he won by twenty lengths without coming off the bridle. He is a very exciting prospect for novice hurdles.

AREA FIFTY ONE 6 b g Green Desert (USA) – Secret History (USA)

Anthony Bromley bought him in October as a prospective hurdler, but we decided to give him a couple of runs on the Flat during the spring and he duly won the Doncaster Shield in late March, which was a great start. Despite that, I think he had endured quite a long summer the previous year and he wasn't moving as well as I would have liked, so we decided to give him a break. Sixth on his only run over hurdles, he has schooled very well since and is ready to resume his National Hunt career.

BARKIS 5 ch g Selkirk (USA) – Batik (IRE)

He is another we bought at the Horses in Training Sale last Autumn, having previously won three times on the Flat in Italy. Rather like Area Fifty One, he looked in need of a holiday and I consequently put him away. He has returned a completely different horse and may have a run on the Flat before going hurdling. He has schooled very well.

BEAT THAT (IRE) 6 b g Milan – Knotted Midge (IRE)

One of last season's revelations, even though we liked him a lot as a bumper horse. He began by winning his maiden at Ascot and, in fairness, should have won the Grade 2 Neptune Investment Winter Novices' Hurdle at Sandown. Still big and backward, Cheltenham was never on the agenda last season. However, we sent him to Aintree for the Grade 1 Sefton Novices' Hurdle and he ran out a very impressive winner. The step up to three miles suited him and then he headed to Punchestown, where he produced another very professional performance beating Cheltenham Festival winner Don Poli in the Grade 1 Irish Daily Mirror Novices' Hurdle. Only six, it would have been interesting to see how far he could go over hurdles but, with his size and scope, novice chasing beckons.

BIG HANDS HARRY 5 b g Multiplex – Harristown Lady

An Irish point-to-point winner, who Anthony Bromley bought on behalf of Alan Spence on the same day he purchased Josses Hill, too, at the Brightwells Cheltenham Sale. He wasn't the easiest to start with but, as soon as the ground softened up, life definitely became easier. Runner-up behind Royal Boy at Ascot in December, he then won impressively at Newbury on heavy ground. He found the track too tight at Bangor on his next start before running respectably in a competitive handicap hurdle at Haydock. Chasing is on his agenda this season and I hope he will have a productive career over the larger obstacles.

BIRCH HILL (IRE) 4 b g Kalanisi (IRE) – Miss Compliance (IRE)

Bought at the Goffs Sale during Punchestown Festival week, he won one of his two point-to-points. A gorgeous looking horse, I don't know much about him at the moment, but I am certainly looking forward to finding out. He looks the part.

BIVOUAC (FR) 3 b g Califet (FR) – Pazadena (FR)

A grand big three-year-old, who arrived from France during the summer, having won an APQS Flat race before pulling up over hurdles at Auteuil in April. He looked a big, overgrown baby when he arrived, but he has benefited from a good holiday. Hopefully, we have a very exciting prospect to look forward to.

BLUE FASHION (IRE) 5 b g Scorpion (IRE) – Moon Glow (FR)

He had some high class form in France the previous year and we debated whether to go straight over fences. However, we decided to aim him at a competitive handicap hurdle at Haydock in November, where he was a highly encouraging second behind More of That. However, things went against him thereafter. He had lameness by a DVT and then, by the time we had overcome that, his wind had deteriorated and it was necessary to call stumps to rectify that. He is a gorgeous, big horse by Scorpion with chaser written all over him. I am really looking forward to seeing him over fences and I sincerely hope he could be top class.

BOBS WORTH (IRE) 9 b g Bob Back (USA) – Fashionista (IRE)

It was obviously disappointing to see him lose his Gold Cup crown but I am sure he will fight his way back to the top. One of the difficulties of last season was over where he would reappear. Stamina is undoubtedly his strong suit and we feel he is at his best going left-handed on good ground. The *Betfair* Chase at Haydock has always been a bête noire, but the fact the race was being run on the outer track encouraged us to let him take his chance. Unfortunately, he didn't fire but it wasn't due to a lack of fitness. With the King George at Kempton off the agenda, we took him to Ireland for the Lexus Chase, hopeful rather than confident. He produced a fantastic performance to beat his old rival First Lieutenant again. In the Gold Cup, it appeared to be between him and Silviniaco Conti going to the last but, for the first time during his career, he didn't come up the hill with his usual relish. We had no explanation for it and a full MOT revealed nothing dramatic, apart from some fine tuning. He is not the most robust, but he has come back looking as well as I have ever seen him. The dilemma, once again, is where to start. We haven't ruled out the possibility of running him in a three mile hurdle because there are so few opportunities which fit his criteria.

BRINGITHOMEMINTY 5 gr g Presenting – Rosie Redman (IRE)

Quite a backward horse, he was a bit too keen for his own good to start with. Despite being beaten on his debut at Ffos Las, he was very impressive when beating a big field of bumper horses at Kempton in February. He didn't live up to expectations in the Aintree bumper, but I will be very disappointed if he doesn't make a high class novice hurdler.

BROXBOURNE (IRE) 5 b m Refuse To Bend (IRE) – Rafting (IRE)

We bought her at the Horses in Training Sale last year, mainly due to the fact I had seen her contest a lot of the good staying handicaps on the Flat. She had endured a busy couple of years on the Flat and, although she jumped really well, we decided to wait until this year to now commence her National Hunt career. I hope she can develop into a high class prospect, particularly with all the new mares' novice hurdles.

CALL THE COPS (IRE) 5 b g Presenting – Ballygill Heights (IRE)

He won a bumper first time out at Southwell before winning twice over hurdles last season. He started off being a rather buzzy character and it has taken him time to learn his job. However, he had a good season over hurdles and, in all likelihood, he will go straight over fences.

CANUWEST (IRE) 5 b g Westerner – High Court Action (IRE)

A five-year-old we bought at one of the Brightwells Sales at Cheltenham after he won an eighteen runner maiden point in Ireland. He spent the summer with his new owner Dai Walters and looks very sharp and is an exciting prospect. We will have to see where we start, although he looked as if he would make a bumper horse. Otherwise, he will go straight over hurdles.

CAPTAIN CONAN (FR) 7 b g Kingsalsa (USA) - Lavandou

He ran a good race first time out in the Tingle Creek at Sandown in December when third behind Sire De Grugy. Things did not go well through the winter though with niggling problems but he made it to Cheltenham for the Queen Mother Champion Chase. Unfortunately, Barry (Geraghty) was never happy with him and pulled him up knowing something had gone badly wrong. It transpired he had two separate fractures to his pelvis and it took us some time to get him back home. It has been a long summer of remedial work and there is still some way to go but, as he showed the previous year when winning three Grade 1 novice chases, he is a top class horse we have always thought the world of.

CARDINAL WALTER (IRE) 5 b or br g Cape Cross (IRE) – Sheer Spirit (IRE)

He joined us in the summer with a view to going hurdling, having had a year off with a leg problem. He was undoubtedly a talented horse over a mile and a half on the Flat and I have been very pleased with what we have seen so far. He is a horse I like a lot.

CHAPEL HALL (IRE) 4 b g Arcadio (GER) – Auction Hall

He came from last year's Derby Sale and we always thought he was near the top of last year's bumper crop. Unfortunately, just before he was due to run, he cut his knee and sadly could not make his debut. However, we knew what we had and there is a huge amount to look forward to.

CLEAN SHEET (IRE) 5 b g Oscar (IRE) – High Park Lady (IRE)

He is a lovely Oscar gelding who won his only point-to-point for JP (McManus) and Enda Bolger. He was coming along nicely when a frustrating injury necessitated time off and he returned to Martinstown Stud in Ireland to recuperate. He is back now and in terrific shape and, being only five years old, he remains a very exciting prospect.

CLONDAW BANKER (IRE) 5 b g Court Cave (IRE) – Freya Alex

We bought him after he won a point-to-point in Ireland and, I have to say, it was no surprise when he won his first bumper at Kempton on one of their 'bumpers for jumpers' days. He showed a really good attitude and turn of foot before going back there for an ordinary bumper but was beaten by his penalty. He was disappointing when we ran him in the Grade 2 Aintree bumper in the spring, but he was still quite a weak horse. He has summered well and I would be disappointed if he did develop into a high class novice hurdler.

CLOSE TOUCH 6 ch g Generous (IRE) – Romantic Dream

Having won the EBF Final at Sandown the previous season, I thought he would be our star novice chaser but a small, but significant, injury meant we had to put him away for the season and his chasing career was put on hold. Touch wood, he will be ready to go straight over fences this season. Still only six, he loves soft ground and, having only been beaten once in his career so far, I think he is a horse with an enormous future.

COCKTAILS AT DAWN 6 b g Fair Mix (IRE) – Fond Farewell (IRE)

He had won a point-to-point in Ireland before embarking on a novice hurdle career. He has always shown us a huge amount of ability at home but things haven't always been plain sailing. He was fourth at Newbury on his debut over hurdles, but an hour later he completely seized up and it was a year later before he came out again, starting with a third at Cheltenham in December. He then ran in the Neptune at Cheltenham, which was probably a bit ambitious at that stage of his career, but he then came out at Kempton and showed his true colours by winning extremely easily. I had to run him again under a penalty at Chepstow, as he was due a massive hike in the ratings and, as is always the case, these things have a habit of backfiring, and he was beaten. However, he is only a six-year-old and built like a chaser, so I will be disappointed if he doesn't go a long way in that sphere.

CUP FINAL (IRE) 5 ch g Presenting – Asian Maze (IRE)

A young horse of JP's (McManus), who I like a lot. He began his hurdling career by bumping into Irving at Taunton, when finishing second. Unfortunately, another horse galloped into the back of him and the injury took months to repair. We couldn't get him back until the Dovecote at Kempton, where he again was beaten by Irving. He then finished tenth in the Neptune Novice Hurdle at the Festival. Consequently, he is still a maiden and, being out of that great mare Asian Maze, the further he goes the better he will be. Only a five-year-old, another season over hurdles should be very productive.

DAWALAN (FR) 4 gr g Azamour (IRE) – Daltawa (IRE)

He is a beautifully bred horse, being a half-brother to Daylami amongst others. He was placed twice on the Flat in France for the Aga Khan and began his hurdling career with three runs at Newbury, finishing fourth in a very hot maiden first time out and then winning his next two starts comfortably. He was always a cheeky horse who we gelded on arrival, but he still treated life as a big game and I don't think we have seen the best of him yet. His wind wasn't perfect at the backend when finishing mid division in the Fred Winter Hurdle, but that has now been rectified. I hope there is a lot of improvement to come.

DAYS OF HEAVEN (FR) 4 b or br Saint Des Saints (FR) – Daramour (FR)

A very nice young horse we found in Ireland and he had one run in a bumper at Taunton. He was very much on the weak side last season and, having looked like winning comfortably a furlong out, he didn't get home. It was still a very creditable run and he has come back looking twice the horse and is something to look forward to this autumn.

DIFFERENT GRAVEY (IRE) 4 b g High Chaparral (IRE) – Newtown Dancer (IRE)

A lovely four-year-old by High Chaparral, who won his only point-to-point in April. I was a bit bemused to start with how a horse could have anything to do with gravey. In Ireland, 'different gravey' is a compliment of the highest order, let's hope they are right.

FOREVER FIELD (IRE) 4 b g Beneficial – Sarahs Reprive (IRE)

An attractive four-year-old by Beneficial, who is one of two we bought for Robert Kirkland last season and both are full of potential. This fellow was actually the more backward of the two and he had one run in a bumper at Uttoxeter, which he won, despite being very green. There is any amount of improvement in him mentally and physically, and he has the makings of a high class novice hurdler.

FULL SHIFT (FR) 5 b g Ballingarry – Dansia (GER)

I hope he is a youngster with a big future. He won a point-to point emphatically and began last season by winning at Newcastle before finishing second at Newbury. He then won impressively at Kempton when stepped up to two miles five. He finished mid-division in the Martin Pipe Conditional Jockeys' Hurdle at Cheltenham, but never really got into the race. Now is the time for him to go novice chasing and I am sure he has a bright future.

GAITWAY 4 b g Medicean – Milliegait

We bought him at the Doncaster May Sales last year. He was an outstanding individual with a very good pedigree and, not surprisingly, his first objective was to win the Doncaster Sales Spring Bumper at Newbury and, with the first two well clear, he won readily. Christopher and Jenny Powell were of the same opinion that there was no need to go further down the bumper route, so we put him away to go novice hurdling for this season. He has had an incredible summer at Juliet Minton's, where he was consigned in the first place. He is something to look forward to.

GRANDOUET (FR) 7 b or br Al Namix (FR) – Virginia River (FR)

Last season we sent him over fences, in which he was second twice in Grade 1 and Grade 2 novice chases and sixth in the Arkle Trophy at Cheltenham. However, one felt something was not quite right and we have pinpointed a number of issues with respiration being one of them. I hope we have corrected it and he can still become a high class chaser. Still only a seven-year-old, one has to be hopeful that he still has a considerable future.

HADRIAN'S APPROACH (IRE) 7 b g High Chaparral (IRE) – Gifted Approach (IRE)

He brought a wonderful close to what had been a frustrating season, but all the same a very good one, by winning the Bet365 (Whitbread) Gold Cup at Sandown. One felt he had gained his just rewards for everybody, particularly Richard and Lizzie Kelvin-Hughes and Barry, who gave him such a spectacular ride. It hasn't all been plain sailing with him but he has now won three chases, third in the RSA Chase, fifth in the previous year's Bet365, and runner-up in the Feltham Novices' Chase. We have had to work hard on his jumping, but it is effective, if a little untidy at times. Still only a seven-year-old, I think there is even more to come.

HEL TARA 5 b m Kayf Tara - Heltornic

She is a well-bred and homebred mare of Simon Hubbard-Rodwells, leased to the Racegoers Club. They took her over towards the backend of the season and came up trumps first time out when winning a bumper at Towcester in April. She is bred to stay and will almost certainly go straight over hurdles this season.

HERITAGE WAY 5 b g Tamayaz (CAN) – Morning Caller (IRE)

He is our new and exciting incumbent for Million in Mind this season. Million in Mind's success story needs no introduction and each year we are lucky enough to have a new inmate. I am particularly excited about this five year old Anthony (Bromley) bought off Stuart Crawford after he had won a useful looking bumper at Ayr in February on his only start. He is a grand individual, who is related to our own Ericht, and I imagine will go straight over hurdles. He is an exciting prospect.

HUNTERS HOOF (IRE) 5 b g Flemensfirth (USA) – Madgehil (IRE)

A horse I like a lot. He has been a bit backward all the way through, but made a pleasing debut in a bumper at Ascot and was then narrowly beaten at Doncaster in November. We ambitiously went to Aintree for the Grade 2 bumper on Grand National day, where he ran respectably. It is now time to get serious and I think he should make a very good novice hurdler.

HURRICANE HIGGINS (IRE) 6 b g Hurricane Run (IRE) – Mare Aux Fees

A high class Flat horse when trained by Mark Johnston, he has unfortunately had leg problems and had a year off. He has joined us with a National Hunt career in mind and has the size and scope for the game. He will take a bit of time to get ready, but could be an exciting staying hurdler, if not a chaser, one day.

IN FAIRNESS (IRE) 5 b g Oscar (IRE) – Dix Huit Brumaire (FR)

A lovely horse by Oscar who has needed a considerable amount of time. However, he has made steady progress, concluding in his last run at Sandown, when he won a two mile novice hurdle comfortably. He has taken all the time in the world but one day he will make a serious novice chaser.

JACK FROST 4 ch g Midnight Legend – Bella Macrae

A very likeable and strongly made home-bred of the Queen's out of a mare we used to train, Bella Macrae. He only came in after Christmas, with a view to having a run in a bumper, which he did and duly won comfortably at Ludlow in May. He then went straight back to Juliet Minton's for the summer, which has seen him develop considerably. We did plenty of schooling with him in the spring and I imagine he will go straight over hurdles.

JOSSES HILL (IRE) 6 b g Winged Love (IRE) – Credora Storm (IRE)

He won his bumper first time out for us at Ascot, and then won his novice before finishing second to Royal Boy in the Grade 1 Tolworth Hurdle. He was then second behind Vautour in the Supreme Novices' Hurdle before rounding off his season with a mightily impressive performance in the Grade 2 Top Novices' Hurdle at Aintree. He is a gorgeous horse with bags of scope and the big question is what to do next. He is undoubtedly a chaser in the making, but as he is only a six-year-old, one could be tempted to see how far he could go over hurdles. That division looks pretty strong at the moment, so maybe we might take the alternative route. We will see how his schooling goes before we decide. Either way, he has a very exciting future.

KENTUCKY HYDEN (IRE) 4 ch g Kentucky Dynamite (USA) – Cap Serena (FR)

He had a productive first season over hurdles, having been placed in three starts at Auteuil. Anthony Bromley bought him for Simon (Munir) and Isaac (Souede) and he gave them an exciting season, although it was rather littered with too many seconds. Having won at Sandown first time out, he was then beaten a neck at Cheltenham in December; second in the Finale at Chepstow; second in the Grade 2 Finesse Juvenile Hurdle at Cheltenham in January before a brilliant second to Tiger Roll in the Triumph Hurdle. He is a fine, big strong horse that one could easily see over fences. However, we might see how far he can go over hurdles before going chasing. He has summered exceptionally well and, with normal improvement, he could reach the top.

L'AMI SERGE (IRE) 4 b g King's Theatre (IRE) – La Zingarella (IRE)

An Irish bred by King's Theatre, Anthony (Bromley) bought him recently from Guillaume Macaire in France for Simon (Munir) and Isaac (Souede). He is the most gorgeous big horse and I couldn't believe what he achieved as a four-year-old given his size and scope. He has had six runs at Auteuil, finishing second three times and third twice. The great thing about him is the fact he is still a novice for this season and, indeed a National Hunt novice, which gives us a lot of opportunities. He is, undoubtedly, a very exciting prospect for this season and, hopefully, for many years to come.

LESSONS IN MILAN (IRE) 6 b g Milan – Lessons Lass (IRE)

He is a lovely big horse David Minton bought for Trevor Hemmings a year ago, having won his only Irish point. Unfortunately, we stumbled upon a problem and it was necessary for him to take a sabbatical. The little work we did with him suggests he is a nice horse in the making and the time off won't have done him any harm.

LOLLI (IRE) 4 b f High Chaparral (IRE) - Unicamp

She is a lovely big filly by High Chaparral, who always showed us a lot of potential throughout the spring and, like many of the others, had one bumper at the backend. Of all of them, I thought she was the most certain to win, and probably the only one that didn't. But even so, she ran a very promising race and I think she has enormous potential. Following a very good summer at grass, she has developed into a gorgeous mare.

LONG RUN (FR) 9 b g Cadoudal (FR) – Libertina (FR)

Last season proved a mixed bag, which did not start very well so we decided to give the Gold Cup a miss and concentrate on the Grand National. We found a lovely race for him in the Ivan Straker Memorial Chase at Kelso, which he won well and he then went into Aintree full of beans – may be a bit too full – as he set off round there with a lot of enthusiasm until he unfortunately disregarded Valentines and had a horrible fall. Luckily, both he and Sam (Waley-Cohen) survived and we went on to Ireland, where he ran a sound race finishing third behind Boston Bob. We then had an even more daring expedition to France for the Grand Steeple-Chase de Paris at Auteuil. Sam could not ride him, due to an absurd rule over there (which has since been rectified), and Ruby Walsh took over for the first time. For three quarters of the race, he travelled and jumped those fences really well but he emptied very quickly. The race proved a bridge too far at that time of the year, but I certainly would not mind having another crack at it, although the National is likely to be his prime objective, once again, this year. Unfortunately, he travelled back from France really badly and suffered some nasty injuries, so it has been a long summer of recuperation. He therefore won't be running early on.

MA FILLEULE (FR) 6 gr m Turgeon (USA) – Kadaina (FR)

She was a revelation, particularly in the second half of last season, when switching her to fences. When she first arrived here, she had already won three chases in France but was a novice over hurdles and we had a very lucrative novice hurdle campaign with her, winning a Grade 2 at Warwick. Her first steeplechase at Cheltenham proved to be a bit of a learning curve and she got a bit lost, but she soon bounced back to win a valuable race at Kempton on Boxing Day. She then finished a gallant second behind Holywell in the three-mile handicap at Cheltenham which, on reflection after he won at Aintree, showed it was an amazing performance. She is still only six, so it was quite a brave call to head for the Topham, but she has been such a good jumper all the way through that I was pretty confident she would enjoy the fences and, I have to say, she was absolutely brilliant and won very impressively. The problem is what to do next – as we have now reached the dizzy heights of a rating of 163 – which has effectively taken her out of handicaps and we will have to start to look at some very grown up races. She is still very young, but she doesn't show it. She has done fantastically well over the summer and seems to have grown and strengthened again.

MAESTRO ROYAL 5 b g Doyen (IRE) – Close Harmony

A good looking five year old out of a very good mare we trained for the Queen Mother. He is a half-brother to Barbers Shop and began his season with a very promising second in a bumper at Newbury before finishing fourth at Market Rasen. He was still growing at the time and we had an issue with his wind, which has hopefully been rectified. He undoubtedly has ability and I think he will make a very useful novice hurdler.

MAYFAIR MUSIC (IRE) 5 br m Presenting – Native Bid (IRE)

She won her only bumper the previous season and then went novice hurdling last year, following her run in a Listed bumper at Cheltenham in November. She won her maiden hurdle at Wincanton by seven lengths and we then stepped her up to three miles for the mares' Listed novice hurdle at Doncaster in March. She produced a fantastic performance and won comfortably. We thought it would lead us to some exciting projects during the spring, including the Albert Bartlett Novices' Hurdle at Cheltenham. Unfortunately, she got a stress fracture in a hind leg, which brought her season to an end. Thankfully, it was not a major injury and she is back in work and looking absolutely tremendous. She is from a great family.

MEGALYPOS (FR) 5 b or br g Limnos (JPN) – Bourbonnaise (FR)

A gorgeous big horse, who had hurdle and chase form in France before he joined us the year before last. He made his debut in England in the Finale Grade 1 Hurdle at Chepstow and finished a respectable third and, following a slightly disappointing run at Cheltenham, we put him away for last season. Unfortunately, he never raced last year, due to injury, but he is back in action now with a few repairs and looks a ready made novice chaser, who could go a long way.

MY TENT OR YOURS (IRE) 7 b g Desert Prince (IRE) – Spartan Girl (IRE)

He has summered very well following another very productive year, which he began by winning the Fighting Fifth at Newcastle and then beat The New One in a tremendous duel in the Christmas Hurdle. We used an all-weather jumpers' bumper at Kempton to prepare for the Champion Hurdle and all seemed set for what was billed as one of the great races of the season. It was, but JP's other horse, Jezki, trained by Jessie Harrington and ridden, ironically, by Barry Geraghty, beat us and AP (McCoy) by a neck. He, unfortunately, got into the habit of running far too freely, especially in the middle part of the race and, as AP said, it is amazing he finished a race at Cheltenham as well as he did, having pulled so hard. There was obviously no point taking on Jezki again in Ireland, so we went to Ayr for the Scottish Champion Hurdle but, once again, he was too keen before finishing third behind Cockney Sparrow. The dilemma is whether to stay over hurdles or try him over fences and I suspect the decision will have to be made on the schooling ground and we will see what AP thinks. He is hugely talented but I hope he will learn to settle a bit better.

MY WIGWAM OR YOURS (IRE) 5 b g Beneficial – Midnight Pond (IRE)

He followed up a promising bumper season the previous spring with an encouraging campaign over hurdles. He won his maiden very easily at Newbury in March following some promising efforts. It was his first attempt beyond two miles and it certainly made a big difference. With his size and scope, it will be disappointing if he does not make up in to a high class staying novice chaser.

NATIVE DISPLAY (IRE) 4 b g Presenting – Native Shore (IRE)

A very good looking four year old by Presenting, we thought highly of him in the spring and, rather than make his debut in a bumper for £1200, we ambitiously ran him in the valuable sales bumper at Punchestown. Unfortunately, things did not go to plan, but I think there was a genuine excuse and, having had a good summer out at grass, he has returned stronger and much more mature. He will go straight over hurdles.

NEWSWORTHY (IRE) 4 b g Presenting – Cousin Jen

He came to us in the spring from Ireland, where he had done a fair bit of work and Barry Geraghty had actually sat on him over there and recommended him to us. He is a really taking individual, not the most typical Presenting in the world, in that he is a very racy horse, all quality and looks ready made. He was in here for a very short time before he went out to grass for the summer. He has come back in looking the finished article and is an exciting prospect.

ONE FOR THE GUV'NR (IRE) 5 b g Oscar (IRE) – Wintry Day (IRE)

A horse I like a lot, he has always shown us a lot of promise at home. Successful in two of his three bumpers, he was beaten less than two lengths on the other occasion at Lingfield, conceding weight to the winner. He will go straight over hurdles and I think there is a lot to look forward to.

OSCAR HOOF (IRE) 6 b g Oscar (IRE) – New Legislation (IRE)

He has always shown us a lot of promise at home and won two of his three bumpers the previous year. He made his debut over hurdles in a Listed race at Haydock and was only beaten a length, before winning impressively at both Doncaster and Kempton. We resisted the temptation of going to Cheltenham and kept him for Aintree. He was running a very good race when falling at the penultimate flight in the Grade 1 novice hurdle. To add insult to injury, he fractured a bone in his off fore knee, which is taking time to mend. This means a later start to the season than one would have liked but, provided it comes right, he is potentially top class.

OSCAR WHISKY (IRE) 9 b g Oscar (IRE) – Ash Baloo (IRE)

He has been one of the stars of the show during the last five years, winning 16 of his 26 races. We switched to fences last season, following a hurdling career which included finishing third in the Champion Hurdle and winning the Aintree Hurdle in consecutive years. Two and a half miles has always been his optimum trip over hurdles and he had a very lucrative first season over fences. Following a respectable debut when runner-up to Taquin du Seuil, he won his next two starts at Cheltenham before landing the Grade 1 Scilly Isles at Sandown. Unfortunately, he had the first fall of his life in the Jewson Novices' Chase at the Festival and it came at the first fence. He finished off with a very good second in another Grade 1 novice at Aintree and is back in looking in great heart. We have operated on his wind during the summer and he is ready for another campaign.

OUT SAM 5 b g Multiplex – Tintera (IRE)

A good looking five year old by an up and coming stallion, he was runner-up in both his starts in the Irish point-to-point field in the spring. We toyed with the idea of running him in a bumper, but resisted the temptation and so a much stronger and more mature horse has returned to go novice hurdling this Autumn. He is a very good individual and showed us plenty of talent before we put him away.

PEGGY DO (IRE) 6 b m Pierre – So Marvellous (IRE)

She is a lovely big mare who Anthony Bromley bought at a Brightwells sale for Simon (Munir) and Isaac (Souede) after she had won her last two starts in Irish point-to-points. She was apparently very impressive. She can technically start anywhere we like, but whatever happens, I cannot believe it will be long before she goes over fences, considering her size and scope. We do not know much about her yet, but she looks an exciting prospect, for either hurdling or chasing.

POLLY PEACHUM (IRE) 6 b m Shantou (USA) – Miss Denman (IRE)

She began last season with a rating of 117 over hurdles, having won the Mares' Novice Handicap Hurdle Final, which was run at Kempton, the previous campaign, and ended it with a mark of 147. She won a Listed handicap hurdle at Cheltenham in April before finishing second in a similar event at Sandown on the final day of the season. Her improvement was dramatic and one can only hope that it might continue. She is a beautifully bred filly being out of a half-sister to Denman and Silverburn, and she will obviously have enormous value when she goes to the paddocks. She doesn't really have the physique for chasing, but there is really no need for that with the numerous opportunities for mares' nowadays.

QUIET CANDID (IRE) 5 b m Beneficial – Lady of Appeal (IRE)
A good looking filly who came to us in the Spring, having won a point-to-point in Ireland. She looked really well when she came over and we gave her two runs in bumpers before she went out for the summer. She was runner-up on both occasions, showing a lot of promise in the process. Being a five year old, she is ready to run over hurdles this season. She has the size and scope to jump a fence and that will probably be her job in a year's time.

RAJDHANI EXPRESS 7 br g Presenting – Violet Express (FR)
Not surprisingly, he found life tougher last season, following the successes of the previous year. He began with a creditable fifth in the Paddy Power Gold Cup but, due to the prevailing wet ground, he did not race again until the Ryanair Chase at the Festival when he finished third and was only beaten four lengths by Dynaste. He did not run to his best at Aintree, but I think we unearthed some reasons for that and he has certainly come in looking bigger and stronger than I have ever seen him before. He has never raced over further than two miles five, and we all feel it is only a matter of time before we try him over three miles. Sam (Waley-Cohen) gets on very well with him and he has got a good turn of foot. If he can use that in a three mile race, he could be in for an exciting season.

RIVER MAIGUE (IRE) 7 b g Zagreb (USA) – Minor Tantrum (IRE)
A very talented hurdler but, unfortunately, he has been plagued with troubles but hopefully they are behind him and we can get a full season out of him this time. He is rated 142 over hurdles, which is always a difficult area to be in, as far as the good handicaps are concerned. We may decide to turn his attentions to chasing because he came from the Irish point field originally. When at his best and he is sound, he is not far off being top class.

ROLLING STAR (FR) 5 b g Smadoun (FR) – Lyli Rose (FR)
He is a gorgeous looking horse and very talented, too. He began his English career by winning the Grade 2 Finesse at Cheltenham in January 2013 and, on the strength of that, he was made favourite for the Triumph Hurdle. He went on to finish sixth behind Our Conor, which was disappointing, but he began last season with a good win in a valuable conditions race at Haydock. It was followed by two disappointing runs in the Ladbroke Hurdle at Ascot and *Betfair* Hurdle at Newbury. Unfortunately, a hind leg injury was diagnosed, which has required an extended rest, but at least no surgery. He will hopefully be back in action before Christmas and still remains a fine prospect.

ROYAL BOY (IRE) 7 b or br g Lavirco (GER) – Quintanilla (FR)
He began last season in a novice chase at Kempton in November, which we rather hoped would be a formality, particularly as he had shown so much as a former point-to-pointer. However, his jumping went to pieces and we were forced to revert back to hurdles. He won over two miles six at Ascot, beating Big Hands Harry, before successfully dropping to two miles in the rescheduled Tolworth Hurdle at Kempton. Once again, he beat another of ours, Josses Hill. We prepared him for Cheltenham thereafter but Michael's (Buckley) torrid season hit another low when he was forced out through injury. It is proving quite a long road back, but we shall do everything to make sure we get there and he is still only a seven year old with stacks of potential.

ROYAL IRISH HUSSAR (IRE) 4 b g Galileo (IRE) – Adjalisa (IRE)
He joined us at the beginning of last season as a three year colt from Aidan O'Brien. He had won a maiden on the Flat over a mile and six but Aidan felt he would be suited by jumping and he made a very good start to his career, winning his first three races over hurdles. However, the crucial thing to him is the ground because he must have good or even faster. We therefore put him away for the winter. He came back for the Triumph and went to Punchestown but he was not quite the same horse in the spring. We have gelded him since, which I am sure will make a big difference. He is not big, but beautifully bred and he will have an Autumn campaign. I think he will find life more enjoyable as a gelding and I am sure there is much more to come from him.

SAINT CHARLES (FR) 4 b g Manduro (GER) – Tropical Barth (IRE)

He is a lovely big four year old we bought after he had won a point-to-point in England. He has shown us quite a lot and I think he is a very talented youngster. He was very impressive in his point-to-point and we did give him one run in a bumper. We would probably have been better to have put him in the field, but temptation overtook us and he ran well without winning at Ayr. The summer break has done him the world of good. A big baby, he looks really well and is ready to go straight over hurdles.

SCOLBOAQUEEN (IRE) 6 br m Lahib (USA) – Ladyrosaro (IRE)

A lovely looking mare, who won a point-to-point in Ireland during the spring of 2013. Unfortunately, she was beset by niggling problems throughout the whole of last season and we failed to get her on the racecourse. There was no single major problem, it was just one thing after another, but she has done very well for a summer out and looks fantastic. I hope she will reward her very patient owners this season. She is a lovely mare who will probably go straight over hurdles.

SIGN OF A VICTORY (IRE) 5 b g Kayf Tara – Irish Wedding (IRE)

Having been bought at the Doncaster Breeze Up Sale at Newbury the previous year, he had a great first season, winning a bumper easily at Ludlow in November, before winning his next three starts, including competitive novice hurdles at Doncaster and Newbury in impressive fashion. He rounded off his season in what is always a good novice at Ayr's Scottish National meeting, but just as it looked as if he was coming to win his race going to the last, the horse he joined, unseated its rider and carried him across the track on to the chase course. He has progressed physically through the summer and I would like to see how far he can go over hurdles before thinking about chasing. He appears a genuine two miler and I think he can go a long way.

SIMONSIG 8 gr g Fair Mix (IRE) – Dusty Too

Sadly, things went wrong for him last season before we even got to a racecourse. A splint problem arose, which had been sore for some time before he was lame on it and it was advised that it was best left alone. Luckily, it did not require surgery and he is back in now after a good summer. He has strengthened up and I still feel he is a horse with an enormous future. He won the Neptune as a novice hurdler and Arkle and I think, as a former point-to-pointer, we are more than likely to try over further rather than drop him in trip. The King George is a realistic objective. It will be great to see him back as he is undoubtedly top class and still has the potential to reach the very top.

SON DU BERLAIS (FR) 4 ch g Muhtathir – King's Daughter (FR)

A four year old who has arrived from France, where he raced twice over hurdles, winning his last start at Auteuil in March. That means he only remains a novice until the end of October, so we will give him a couple of runs before he goes handicap hurdling for the remainder of the season. He is a lovely big horse, typically a bit lean to start with, but he has had a very good summer at J.P.'s (McManus) Martinstown Stud in Ireland. He is a really imposing, strong individual who we are very much looking forward to and, hopefully, he will be one of our earlier runners, provided the ground is suitable.

SPARTAN ANGEL (IRE) 6 b m Beneficial – Greek Melody (IRE)

She has won three of her four starts, two of which were in bumpers the previous season. She raced twice over hurdles, winning on the second occasion at Worcester in June. Due to the fact she enjoys decent ground, she didn't race during the winter because it was too wet. She has had a short holiday at Crimbourne Stud and is now back and ready for an early season campaign before the ground turns soft. She is a gorgeous looking mare.

SPRINTER SACRE (FR) 8 b or br g Network (GER) – Fatima III (FR)

I am glad to say he has returned to the fray in fantastic condition. Last season's disappointments have been well documented and, I have to say, that I honestly do not know what caused his heart fibrillation at Kempton that day or, for whatever reason, why were not as happy as we should have been after that. He has had a fantastic summer at Juliet Minton's and has come back looking magnificent. We have to hope we can get him back to where he was. In his absence, Sire de Grugy has proved to be a highly talented champion and it will be fascinating if the two of them can get together and fight it out this season, because they are two top class horses. It would be marvellous for us all, particularly Caroline and Raymond (Mould), if he can come back to what he was before, which really was the most exciting horse we have ever had.

SUGAR BARON (IRE) 4 b g Presenting – Shuil Oilean (IRE)

He was another of our babies who didn't get to the racecourse last season, but we had seen plenty at home. He is another typical Presenting out of a Be My Native mare, with all the Presenting qualities – big, scopey, athletic and a really nice horse. However, he was on the big side and we did not run him, which was perhaps a blessing as he has done very well over the summer. He has returned a bigger and stronger horse that we saw last season. A really taking individual.

SUMMER STORM 4 b g Lucarno (USA) – Midsummer Magic

He was one of three homebreds of Her Majesty's who all managed to win a bumper at the back end of last season. He was not the most robust individual last year and one had to be careful. It was therefore a case of one run, but he did it well at Southwell and he has come back in considerably stronger and I would think more mentally aware. I would think he will go straight over hurdles in the Autumn.

TAYLOR (IRE) 5 b m Presenting – Britway Lady (IRE)

Not the biggest or most robust mare, she came from Ireland following a promising fourth in a Listed bumper at Navan. We gave her one run in a bumper at Cheltenham in April and a furlong out, it looked as if she would win comfortably, but she was still weak and in the end finished third of fifteen, which was a good run. She has come back in looking much bigger and stronger and will go straight over hurdles. While she hasn't grown much, she has developed quite considerably and is carrying twice the condition she had last year. I think she is a very exciting prospect for the mares' novice hurdle series.

THEINVAL (FR) 4 b g Smadoun (FR) – Kinevees (FR)

A new arrival from France, he has run a number of good races at the likes of Auteuil and Enghien and was only beaten narrowly at Strasbourg in March. The fact he remains a maiden is a bonus, plus he has a lot of experience. It is difficult to gauge, at this stage, what he is capable of, but he has had a good summer out and he is a very likeable character and seems straightforward. He will continue over hurdles for the time being before going chasing eventually.

TISTORY (FR) 7 ch g Epalo (GER) – History (FR)

He has been very consistent throughout his career, winning five of his nine races. However, it hasn't always been plaining sailing with him. He won his bumper first time out and began his novice hurdle career by winning two of his first three races. We then stepped him up in class and trip at Aintree in the Grade 1 Sefton Novices' Hurdle. Despite being Punchestowns' brother, the trip probably stretched him. However, his wind has never been quite 100% and we have re-adjusted his palate during the summer. I think it will prove beneficial and he will almost certainly go straight over fences this season.

TOP NOTCH (FR) 3 b g Poliglote – Topira (FR)

He has recently arrived from France, having won his only start over hurdles for Guillaume Macaire at Enghien in April. He is very robust, without being an enormous horse and is a ready made juvenile hurdler. He starts with some experience and I hope he will be running in the Autumn and we shall look forward to some of the better early juvenile hurdles. He is a horse that I think could be very exciting.

TOWERING (IRE) 5 b g Catcher In The Rye (IRE) – Bobs Article (IRE)

He is one of the horses we bought at the sales thinking he was going to be one of the really early types and, once again, the trainer got it wrong in that he did not see a racecourse until May. He was narrowly beaten in this bumper at Market Rasen, finishing third. At Christmas, he was working like a very good horse but he was still weak. He was actually Gaitway's work companion and I was anticipating great things, but we had to leave him alone for a while and wait until the backend to run him. He is a good jumper and I am looking forward to a reasonably early campaign this time round.

TRIOLO D'ALENE (FR) 7 ch g Epalo (GER) – Joliette D'Alene (FR)

He finished the previous season by winning the Topham Chase at Aintree and, with a prep race under his belt, won the Hennessy Gold Cup at Newbury last season. After the Topham, we thought the Grand National should be his objective and Barry (Geraghty) did everything to try and persuade us to avoid the Hennessy and protect his mark for the National. Rightly or wrongly, we settled for the Hennessy and he won it, which obviously took him to the top of the Grand National weights. By this time, we were having problems with his wind (which has been rectified this summer) and also the prospect of softish ground at Aintree. All Grand Nationals from now on are likely to have the word *soft* somewhere in the going description for good reasons but, for a horse like Triolo, who must have it good, it is never going to suit him. He is a top class chaser with a lovely character and, although he will be difficult to place from now on, we will remember the very good days and hope for more.

UNE ARTISTE (FR) 6 b m Alberto Giacometti (IRE) – Castagnette III (FR)

She has been a great servant over the last couple of years since Anthony (Bromley) bought her in France, winning eleven of her twenty two starts. She won a Grade 3 and two Listed novice hurdles the previous season and, although one can only call her small, we had to try her over fences and, once again, she came up trumps. Firstly, she won a good novice at Kempton and then, secondly, the Grade 3 John and Chich Fowler Memorial Novice Chase at Fairyhouse, which for obvious reasons was very special to us and she actually beat our own Nadiya de La Vega, who won the race the year before. She finished the season with another great performance in a Listed handicap at Punchestown finishing third.

VANITEUX (FR) 5 br g Voix Du Nord (FR) – Expoville (FR)

He came to us at the beginning of last season, having finished third and fourth in two point-to-points in Ireland, but immediately showed us he was not a typical pointer in that he had an abundance of pace. He won his first novice hurdle at Sandown comfortably but then got beaten on soft ground at Kempton. He soon bounced back to win easily at Doncaster and, having always thought Cheltenham was not for him this year, we finally succumbed and Barry (Geraghty) rode him to finish a highly respectable third in the Supreme Novice Hurdle just behind Josses Hill. He is only five, so the dilemma is, once again, whether to switch to fences or see what more he can achieve over hurdles. Whichever way he goes, he is a very exciting prospect.

VASCO DU RONCERAY (FR) 5 gr g Al Namix (FR) – Landza De Ronceray (FR)

He came to us having won an AQPS Flat race in France and immediately won his first novice hurdle at Hereford by thirty two lengths. He has not won since but he has been placed at Grade 2 level on three occasions. Last season was littered with problems, but he is a horse I like and have great faith in. I think novice chasing will bring out the best in him.

VOLNAY DE THAIX (FR) 5 ch g Secret Singer (FR) – Mange De Thaix (FR)

Anthony (Bromley) found him for Judy Wilson after he had won a hurdle race in the French Provinces. He began last season with facile victories at Kempton and Newbury before finishing second to Irving in a Grade 2 novice at Ascot. He came back to win another good hurdle race at Newbury before finishing a highly respectable fifth in the Grade 1 two and a half mile novice hurdle at Aintree. An out and out chaser, he is a gorgeous horse and, despite only being five, I think a switch to fences is imminent.

VYTA DU ROC (FR) 5 gr g Lion Noir – Dolce Vyta (FR)

He had been placed in a couple of hurdle races in France but, unfortunately, a few hiccups kept him off the track for a year. However, he returned in the spring and won comfortably at Uttoxeter and Hexham. He jumps and looks like a chaser and, having shown us what he is capable of, he is another exciting prospect for the Munir/Souede partnership.

WEST WIZARD (FR) 5 b or br g King's Theatre (IRE) – Queen's Diamond (GER)

He was the talking horse at the beginning of last season, having looked very special when winning his bumper at Kempton the previous March. We went back to Kempton in November for his debut over hurdles and I was mortified when he was beaten, but it turned out to be a blessing in disguise. Firstly, he was beaten by a high class horse in Sgt Reckless and, secondly, he returned with a knee problem that necessitated missing the rest of the season. It was depressing, to say the least, but it means he remains a novice over hurdles. I think because he was still a big, weak horse last season, his problems were no more than growing pains. Therefore I think we still have a most exciting young prospect to go novice hurdling with this season.

WHISPER (FR) 6 b g Astarabad (USA) – Belle Yepa (FR)

He was undoubtedly one of the stars of the show last season and, indeed, the one who got us out of trouble at Cheltenham in March. Minty bought him as a yearling in France for Dai Walters and he began his career with an easy bumper win and then an impressive victory over hurdles at Ffos Las. He went on to win two more novices the previous season and began last year with some very good performances, which led us to what was meant to be his prime objective, the Welsh Champion Hurdle at Ffos Las. At the time, I was bitterly disappointed when he was beaten a short head, but he got his just deserts when winning the Coral Cup at the Cheltenham Festival by a short head. I think both Dai and I were relying on Oscar Whisky, so this was a very special day, being Dai's first Festival winner and we bravely marched on to Aintree. He produced an ultra game performance to beat At Fishers Cross in the Grade 1 Liverpool Hurdle. Undoubtedly, the step up to three miles played to his strengths and, although there has been much debate over what to do next, it was only the fact that Oscar Whisky was going novice chasing last season, that we left Whisper over hurdles. Therefore, I think this fella will now and indeed should, make the transition to fences, and I am hoping he can reach the top.

Philip HOBBS

Stables: Sandhill, Bilbrook, Minehead, Somerset.
2013/2014: 106 Winners / 542 Runners 20% Prize-Money £1,583,307
www.pjhobbs.com

AL ALFA 7 ch g Alflora (IRE) – Two For Joy (IRE)
A very consistent and tough horse, he won at Stratford and Taunton last season and was placed on four other occasions. He is versatile in terms of trips because he is effective over two miles and stays three. However, he wants soft or heavy ground over the minimum trip. Rated 126, I think he is fairly treated and he should continue to be competitive off such a mark.

BALLYGARVEY (FR) 8 b g Laveron – Vollore (FR)
He ran very well at Cheltenham's Paddy Power meeting in November finishing fourth in a good two mile handicap chase. Unfortunately, he suffered a tendon injury soon afterwards and hasn't raced since. All being well, he will be back in action during the winter and he remains unexposed over fences. He likes soft ground.

BALTHAZAR KING (IRE) 10 b g King's Theatre (IRE) – Afdala (IRE)
A phenomenal horse, he won four times last season, including the Cross Country Chase at the Cheltenham Festival. He also won the Listed Cross Country Chase at Craon in France in September and it was one of the best days of our racing life. They even played the National Anthem after the race – it was unbelievable. The plan is to go back to Craon in September and then aim him at the Cross Country race at the Paddy Power meeting again. He ran a fantastic race in the Grand National last season finishing second and the plan is to aim him at the race again, though he is higher in the handicap now. Best fresh, we may go straight to Aintree after his run in November rather than aim him at the Festival again in between. Then, all being well, he will run at Le Lion-d'angers in May. He fell there earlier this year. The ground is important to him though because he doesn't want it too soft.

BIG EASY (GER) 7 b g Ransom O'War (USA) – Basilea Gold (GER)
We were planning to run him in the Ascot Stakes in June but he got balloted out. The plan is to run him in the Cesarewitch Trial at Newmarket in late September and then we will decide whether to stay over hurdles or try him over fences. He hasn't had a lot of racing during the last couple of seasons, largely due to bad luck. I thought he ran well at Aintree in April but then found the ground too soft at Haydock last time.

BINCOMBE 6 gr g Indian Danehill (IRE) – Siroyalta (FR)
A three times winner at Wincanton, Newbury and Haydock, he had a good season and I hope he will continue to improve. Still only six, he handles most types of ground and two and a half miles appears to be his trip.

BROTHER TEDD 5 gr g Kayf Tara – Neltina
Bred by his owner, it wasn't a total surprise when he made a winning debut at Huntingdon in a bumper. Fifth next time under a penalty on heavy ground at Wincanton, he will appreciate two and a half miles plus over hurdles this season.

CAPTAIN CHRIS (IRE) 10 b g King's Theatre (IRE) – Function Dream
Third in the Peterborough Chase at Huntingdon on his reappearance, he produced two very good performances in his subsequent starts at Kempton and Ascot. A twenty three lengths winner of a Listed chase at the former, he was very impressive in the Grade 1 Ascot Chase next time. Unfortunately, he suffered a tendon problem shortly afterwards and missed the remainder of the season. He is most unlikely to run before Christmas and I would imagine his first start will be in the Ascot Chase again in February.

CARA CARLOTTA 5 br m Presenting – Dara's Pride (IRE)

She ran very pleasingly on her debut in a bumper at Taunton finishing third. We then took her to Cheltenham in April for another mares' only bumper but she was disappointing and we don't know why. In all likelihood, she will go straight over hurdles and be aimed at mares' only events. She has the ability to win races.

CATHERINES WELL 5 b m Kayf Tara – Dudeen (IRE)

A nice mare who ran well in a bumper at Taunton during the spring. Runner-up that day, we may give her another run in a mares' bumper, if there is a suitable race in the Autumn. She will then go novice hurdling over two and a half miles.

CHAMPAGNE WEST (IRE) 6 b g Westerner – Wyndham Sweetmarie (IRE)

A very nice horse who showed progressive form last season winning three times over hurdles. Even though he had an inclination to jump to his left, it didn't stop him winning well at both Wincanton and Ascot. He did race a shade keenly on occasions but he is a lovely horse who I think will be even better over fences. Three miles on soft ground are his optimum conditions. Indeed, he ran well to finish fourth in the Grade 1 Albert Bartlett Novices' Hurdle at the Festival but he found the ground too quick. He will go novice chasing straight away.

CHANCE DU ROY (FR) 10 ch g Morespeed – La Chance Au Roy (FR)

He has been a great horse who has provided us with a lot of fun over years. He produced a very good performance to win the Becher Chase at Aintree before finishing sixth in the Grand National. The plan is to aim him at the Becher Chase, once again, and he is likely to go straight there because he is best fresh. He is obviously higher in the ratings but, granted soft ground, I don't see why he won't run well again.

CHELTENIAN (FR) 8 b g Astarabad (USA) – Salamaite (FR)

He won a novice hurdle at Uttoxeter before running well in defeat in the *Betfair* Hurdle at Newbury finishing fourth and filling the same position at Aintree. Third at Punchestown on his final outing, he will go novice chasing this season. He tends to be rapid over his hurdles and I think he will show fences more respect. Although he has the speed for two miles, Richard Johnson said he stays two and a half miles well and may get even further. I would think he will start off over two miles over fences.

CLOUD CREEPER (IRE) 7 b g Cloudings (IRE) – First of April (IRE)

An easy winner over hurdles at Southwell in March, he is a winning Irish pointer and will go chasing this season. I think he should do well over fences with two and a half miles being his trip.

COLOUR SQUADRON (IRE) 8 b g Old Vic – That's The Goose (IRE)

Placed in all three starts last season, he was runner-up in both the Paddy Power Gold Cup and Byrne Group Plate at Cheltenham. He didn't get the rub of the green in the former, having met interference after the second last. Rated 152 over fences, he must be the best third season novice chaser in training. Owned by J.P.McManus, I will speak to his racing manager Frank Berry regarding plans but I would imagine they will be keen to win a novice chase before going back down the handicap route.

DE LA BECH 7 ch g Karinga Bay – Vallis Vale

When he is at his best, he is a decent horse and proved it when winning at Chepstow last season. A strong stayer, he possibly doesn't want the ground too soft. We will continue to aim him at three mile handicap chases.

DUKE OF LUCCA (IRE) 9 b g Milan – Derravaragh Native (IRE)
Runner-up at Ascot in November, the conditions came right for him at Aintree on Grand National day and he won a valuable handicap chase. He then ran very well in the Cross Country Chase at the Punchestown Festival but didn't quite stay. The plan is to take him to Craon in September, along with Balthazar King, and then we will consider all the Cross Country Chases at Cheltenham. The Grand National is a possibility, although the trip is a concern. He seemed to really enjoy jumping the cross country fences at Punchestown.

DUNRAVEN STORM (IRE) 9 br g Presenting – Foxfire
He had a good season over hurdles, winning twice at Ascot and Taunton. Despite his age, we are likely to send him novice chasing this time. He suffered an injury to a hind leg earlier in his career and has done well to come back. He has always had plenty of ability though. I would think he will start off over two miles, but two and a half on good ground is ideal.

FILBERT (IRE) 8 b g Oscar (IRE) – Coca's Well (IRE)
He looked good when winning a decent handicap chase over two miles at Newbury's Hennessy meeting. Despite that, I think he wants two and a half miles now and we will be stepping him up in trip this season. He is another who had problems with a hind leg a couple of years ago but he has bounced back.

FINGAL BAY (IRE) 8 b g King's Theatre (IRE) – Lady Marguerrite
I was delighted with him last season winning the Pertemps Final at the Cheltenham Festival. Fifth last time in a Grade 1 hurdle at the Punchestown Festival, we haven't decided whether to stay over hurdles or go chasing. I suspect his owner will be keen to stay hurdling but I think he could develop into a very good chaser. He hasn't run over fences since that peculiar day at Exeter when he jumped badly to his left and ran through the wing. He suffered a tendon injury soon afterwards and missed the remainder of that season. Prior to that, he had jumped very well at both Chepstow and Cheltenham. If he stayed over hurdles, I suppose a race like the West Yorkshire Hurdle at Wetherby (1st November) is a possibility. Otherwise, if he goes back over fences, those Graduation Chases will be ideal.

GARDE LA VICTOIRE (FR) 5 b g Kapgarde (FR) – Next Victory (FR)
He had a good season over hurdles winning three times, including on his final run at Cheltenham in April. Only five, he is still progressing and we will keep him over hurdles for the time being. A race like the Silver Trophy at Chepstow (25th October) looks a suitable target and we will see how he gets on there before deciding whether to go chasing later on. He is not the most natural jumper of hurdles but he will go over fences at some stage.

GOLDEN DOYEN (GER) 3 b or br g Doyen (IRE) – Goldsamt (GER)
He raced five times on the Flat in France as a two year old, winning on his final start at Compiegne in October. We bought him soon afterwards and he has a jumping pedigree. Rated 81 on the Flat, he will be going juvenile hurdling and I hope he is a nice prospect.

HANDSOME HORACE (IRE) 4 br g Presenting – Paumafi (IRE)
I was surprised when he was made favourite for his debut in a bumper at Exeter in April. I don't think it was the greatest of races but he ran well and was a bit unlucky not to finish closer. Still green, he will improve for the experience and may have another run in a bumper before going hurdling. I think he will want a trip over jumps.

HELLO GEORGE (IRE) 5 b g Westerner – Top Ar Aghaidh (IRE)

I hope he is a very nice horse. Placed in his first two bumpers, he won in good style at Sandown in November but hasn't run since. There has been nothing wrong with him though. He was only four at the time so we purposely gave him time to mature and then considered running him in the good bumpers during the spring but decided against it. The time off has benefited him because he has come back stronger and he could be a very nice novice hurdler this season. He will stay two and a half miles but he is inclined to be a shade keen and he certainly isn't short of speed. We will therefore start him off over two miles over hurdles. The plan is to have him ready to run in October.

HE'S A BULLY (IRE) 5 b g Westerner – Kitty Maher (IRE)

A winning English pointer, he was runner-up in a bumper at Fontwell when trained by Polly Gundry. We bought him at the Cheltenham April Sale and he looks a nice prospect. We haven't decided whether he runs in another bumper or goes straight over hurdles.

HORIZONTAL SPEED (IRE) 6 b g Vertical Speed (FR) – Rockababy (IRE)

A very consistent horse, he had an excellent season winning four times and finishing second on two other occasions. Indeed, his only disappointing run came in the EBF Final at Sandown in March. The ground was soft but he copes with it and we don't know why he underperformed. Thankfully, he returned to form at Haydock and won nicely. He will be going novice chasing with two and a half miles being his trip. I hope he will make a lovely chaser.

IF IN DOUBT (IRE) 6 b g Heron Island (IRE) – Catchers Day (IRE)

A winner on his reappearance at Towcester, he then ran two very good races at Kempton and Exeter, including in the Lanzarote Hurdle at the former. He ended the season by finishing ninth in the Pertemps Final at Cheltenham. I thought he ran up a bit light that day and I feel he is better than he showed. In fact, he is a big, tall narrow horse who has always been quite backward. With that in mind, I don't think he has achieved yet what he is capable of and is therefore open to further improvement. He could improve enough to win a decent handicap hurdle before going chasing. Two and a half miles plus is his trip and he ought to make a smashing chaser in time.

INK MASTER (IRE) 4 b g Whitmore's Conn (USA) – Welsh Connection (IRE)

A big, strong gelding with a very good temperament, he was placed in his two Irish points for Tom Keating. Aidan Murphy bought him at the Punchestown Festival Sale in the spring and he is going well at the moment. All being well, he will be in action around October time and will either start off in a bumper or go straight over hurdles.

IRISH BUCCANEER (IRE) 7 b g Milan – Supreme Serenade (IRE)

He looked useful when winning his bumper on his debut at Chepstow but hasn't progressed over hurdles in the manner we expected. Having said that, he has had one or two issues and he won on his final start in May at Ludlow. I would think he will go novice chasing and hopefully that will bring out the best in him.

LAMB OR COD (IRE) 7 ch g Old Vic – Princess Lizzie (IRE)

Three times a winner over fences during the spring/summer at Cheltenham, Fakenham and Newton Abbot, he remains a novice until the end of October. We will therefore run him again before going handicapping from November onwards. It won't be easy though off a mark of 144 but he stays well and handles most types of ground.

LORD PROTECTOR (IRE) 7 b g Oscar (IRE) – Warts And All (IRE)

A big horse, he was still weak last year but still managed to win over hurdles at Sandown and Chepstow. Fences ought to bring about further improvement and he will go novice chasing over two and two and a half miles.

MEETMEATTHEMOON (IRE) 5 gr m Flemensfirth (USA) – Valleya (FR)

Her form improved as she gained in experience. She is a thorough stayer and appreciated the galloping track at Chepstow to win on her third start in bumpers. She will be aimed at mares' only novice hurdles with the final at Newbury in the spring her ultimate target.

MENORAH (IRE) 9 b g King's Theatre (IRE) – Maid For Adventure (IRE)

He came right on the final day of the season, winning a Listed chase at Sandown in emphatic fashion. We then decided to run him on the Flat and he wasn't disgraced in the Group 3 Henry II Stakes at the same track. We considered running him in the Queen Alexandra Stakes at Royal Ascot but the ground was too quick. He is probably capable of winning a good race on the Flat but we are going to concentrate on his jumping career and aim him at the Charlie Hall Chase at Wetherby (1st November). We were going to run him in the race last season but he had a problem with a knee, hence he didn't reappear until the King George. He doesn't want the ground too soft though.

MILOSAM (IRE) 7 b g Milan – Lady Sam (IRE)

A sound tough horse who improved markedly last year winning four times. He was most progressive and I hope he has more to offer. Ideally, he doesn't want the ground too soft and is suited by three miles plus.

MOUNTAIN KING 5 b g Definite Article – Belle Magello (FR)

Despite still being green and lacking experience, he did well winning a bumper and twice over hurdles at Ludlow and Ascot. Admittedly, he was a fortunate winner on the latter occasion but remains open to further improvement. We will keep him over hurdles for the time being, but he won't have any trouble jumping fences later on. Two miles is his trip at the moment but he will stay further, if necessary.

NECK OR NOTHING (GER) 5 b g Intikhab (USA) – Nova (GER)

A bumper winner for Tom Hogan in Ireland, he was bought by Roger Brookhouse in November. He is inclined to be keen and things didn't go to plan in the Festival bumper at Cheltenham. Runner-up at Wincanton on his final run in April, he needs to learn to settle. Otherwise, he will hopefully make a nice novice hurdler.

ONENIGHTINVIENNA (IRE) 5 b g Oscar (IRE) – Be My Granny

A consistent horse who won a bumper at Taunton in February before finishing third over hurdles last time. He is slow in a nice way and has a very good attitude. His long-term future lies in three mile chases but we will give him another run or two over hurdles. He is capable of winning one and then we may have a look at a novices' handicap chase and use his hurdles rating.

PERSIAN SNOW (IRE) 8 b g Anshan – Alpine Message

He has been an unhealthy horse in the past and has had his fair share of problems. However, he had a clean run last season and did well winning twice at Warwick and finishing sixth at the Cheltenham Festival in the novices' handicap chase on the opening day. He is a likeable horse who always tries his best. Two miles on soft ground is OK for him but otherwise he wants two and a half miles on better ground. Rated 137, he could sneak into the Paddy Power Gold Cup in November and that is an option.

PRINCELY PLAYER (IRE) 7 b g King's Theatre (IRE) – Temptation (FR)
He will continue to run over hurdles and fences, but he wants good ground and will therefore continue to run in the Autumn before having a winter break. A winner over fences at Ludlow last season, he also won over hurdles at Worcester in June. Trips around three miles are ideal but it won't be easy off his mark.

QUICK DECISSON (IRE) 6 b g Azamour (IRE) – Fleet River (USA)
Despite winning over hurdles at Wincanton in January, I was a bit disappointed with him last season. However, I think he will make a better chaser and we will go down the novices' handicap route off his mark of 119. I always thought he wanted two and a half miles but I think two miles is his trip.

RETURN SPRING (IRE) 7 b g Vinnie Roe (IRE) – Bettys Daughter (IRE)
I was delighted with him last season winning twice at Cheltenham, including a Listed handicap hurdle at the Paddy Power meeting. Runner-up a couple of times, too, he isn't over big but the plan is to send him chasing. He stays well and handles most types of ground.

RIVER DEEP (IRE) 5 ch g Mountain High (IRE) – Testaway (IRE)
A bumper winner at Huntingdon on his second start, he won on his hurdles debut at Newton Abbot in May and did it nicely. He is still a novice for this season and I think he will improve as he gains in experience.

ROALCO DES FARGES (FR) 9 gr g Dom Alco (FR) – Vonaria (FR)
Having missed the whole of the previous season, he came back well to win at Newbury in March. Things didn't work out in his subsequent two starts though in the Scottish National and Bet365 Gold Cup. However, I think we have got his trip wrong because we thought he wanted a long distance but that's not the case. He is not devoid of speed and we will be dropping him back in trip this season and may even consider something like the Grand Sefton Chase over the National fences at Aintree because he is a good jumper.

ROCK THE KASBAH (IRE) 4 ch g Shirocco (GER) – Impudent (IRE)
A very promising youngster who ran well on his debut in a bumper at Chepstow. The race was won by Simon Squirrel, who has been subsequently bought by Paul Nicholls. Our horse certainly wasn't wound up and was still quite green. We like him a lot and, only being a four year old, he will probably have another run in a bumper before going hurdling. Two miles will be his trip over jumps to start with because he has plenty of pace.

ROYAL PLAYER 5 b g King's Theatre (IRE) – Kaydee Queen (IRE)
He won twice over hurdles at Exeter and Warwick last season. His future lies over fences and he will be going novice chasing. I think he is crying out for a trip because he stays well.

ROYAL REGATTA (IRE) 6 b g King's Theatre (IRE) – Friendly Craic (IRE)
He made a very good start to his hurdling career winning at Aintree and Leicester. Unfortunately, things didn't go to plan thereafter and he had a disappointing end to his novice hurdle campaign. We thought he was quite well handicapped and aimed him at the Martin Pipe Conditional Jockeys' Handicap Hurdle at the Festival but he didn't finish off his race. I suppose there are one or two doubts about him now but he was still quite a tall, narrow horse who will hopefully strengthen up as he gets older. We will keep him over hurdles for the time being and have a look at suitable two and a half mile handicaps.

SADDLERS ENCORE (IRE) 5 br g Presenting – Saddlers Leader (IRE)

I was pleased with him during the spring showing progressive form. Still quite green, he won over hurdles at Wincanton and Exeter and is open to more improvement. He stays three miles well and we will give him another couple of runs over fences before we start thinking about chasing.

SAUSALITO SUNRISE (IRE) 6 b g Gold Well – Villaflor (IRE)

He did very well over hurdles winning on four occasions, including an impressive victory at Perth on his final start. He appreciated the step up to three miles and he is still progressing. A winning Irish pointer, we are going to send him over fences and I hope he will develop into a very nice staying novice chaser. He handles soft ground well.

STERNRUBIN (GER) 3 b g Authorized (IRE) – Sworn Mum (GER)

A new arrival, he only raced three times on the Flat for Peter Chapple-Hyam before being bought by Terry Warner. Runner-up at Thirsk over a mile and a half last time, he is rated 77 and is a nice prospect for juvenile hurdles. He should be in action in October.

THE SKYFARMER 6 br g Presenting – Koral Bay (FR)

A three times winner over hurdles during the first half of the season, he didn't really progress during the second half of the year. He is a very genuine horse but I was a bit disappointed with him in the Martin Pipe Conditional Jockeys Handicap Hurdle. He is another who will be going novice chasing and is effective over two and two and a half miles.

TRICKAWAY (IRE) 6 b g Stowaway – Rosie's Trix (IRE)

A former Irish pointer, he won a bumper at Exeter in February before finishing third in both his hurdle races in the spring. Rated 109, we may aim him at a novices' handicap hurdle or we could go straight over fences and use his hurdles mark. He will certainly go chasing at some stage this season and I don't think he will be badly treated over fences.

UNCLE JIMMY (IRE) 7 b or br g Alderbrook – Carrabawn

He isn't very big but tries hard and won a Pertemps qualifier at Warwick in January. Disappointing in his next two races, he will have another run over hurdles before going chasing. He is a good jumper and stays three miles.

WESTERN JO (IRE) 6 b g Westerner – Jenny's Jewel (IRE)

He had an issue with a hind leg last season hence he only raced three times. I was pleased with his run at Doncaster though finishing second. He will jump fences one day, even though he isn't over big, but we will keep him over hurdles for the time being.

WISHFULL THINKING 11 b g Alflora (IRE) – Poussetiere Deux (FR)

A fantastic horse over the years and, once again, he showed a good level of form last season winning a valuable handicap chase at Cheltenham in January. Rated 162, we will be looking towards a similar programme with handicaps and condition chases on the agenda. I am still not sure what his best trip is but he is very effective over two and two and a half miles.

TRAINER'S HORSE TO FOLLOW: SAUSALITO SUNRISE

Alan KING

Stables: Barbury Castle Stables, Wroughton, Wiltshire.
2013/2014: 75 Winners / 444 Runners 17% Prize-Money £1,112,822
www.alankingracing.co.uk

AVISPA 5 b m Kayf Tara – Ladylliat (FR)
A very progressive mare who has always shown plenty of ability. She won in good style at Huntingdon and I thought she had a big chance in the Listed mares' bumper at Sandown in March. Unfortunately, the ground was very soft and she got bogged down in it and finished fourth. She came good at Aintree though in another Listed bumper and it wasn't a surprise. We have schooled her over hurdles and she is an exciting prospect. She spent the summer with her breeder Robert Chugg and has done well. We will start her off over two miles, although she will stay further.

BALDER SUCCES (FR) 6 b g Goldneyev (USA) – Frija Eria (FR)
He had a marvellous season over fences winning five times, culminating in victory in the Grade 1 Maghull Novices' Chase at Aintree on Grand National day. We then took him to Punchestown but we got the tactics wrong and made too much use of him. He is an exciting horse and, while he stays two and a half miles, I am keen to stick to two miles and hope he can develop into a Queen Mother Champion Chase horse. Possible starting points include the Haldon Gold Cup at Exeter (4th November) or the Shloer Chase at Cheltenham's Paddy Power meeting (16th November). He has summered very well and I am delighted with him.

BILLY BISCUIT (IRE) 6 b g Presenting – Native Novel (IRE)
Runner-up a couple of times over hurdles during the spring, he has been quite a slow learner. His season was somewhat interrupted because he made a noise at home, which meant we hobdayed him and therefore he didn't get started until late on. However, I thought he ran well at Uttoxeter and looked like winning until making a mistake at the third last, which probably cost him the race. I hope he can win over hurdles before ultimately developing into a three mile chaser.

BULFIN ISLAND (IRE) 5 b g Milan – Tournore Court (IRE)
A winning Irish pointer for Gary Aherne, we did some work with him during the spring and I was pleased with him. I would imagine he will go straight over hurdles and we will look towards a two and a half mile novice event to start with.

CARRAIG MOR (IRE) 6 b g Old Vic – Lynrick Lady (IRE)
He looked a very decent horse on his hurdles debut at Uttoxeter but things went wrong after that. He made a bad mistake at the third last at Ascot next time and then a few of my horses weren't right. We took him to Punchestown at the end of the season but he loves soft ground and it had dried out a bit. He has had a good break since and has strengthened up a lot and seems more relaxed. We are going to send him chasing and we will probably start him off over two and a half miles. Ultimately, he will want three miles and he loves to use his stride and bowl along in front.

CHATEZ (IRE) 3 b g Dandy Man (IRE) – Glory Days (GER)
He has done very well on the Flat winning three times, including the Silver Bowl at Haydock in May. The key to him is the ground because he must have ease underfoot. He wouldn't let himself down on the ground at Newmarket last time. We have given him a break with a view to bringing him back for a valuable handicap at Ascot on Champion's day (18th October). The plan is then to send him juvenile hurdling. He has schooled well and is a horse with plenty of ability.

CHOSEN WELL (IRE) 5 b g Well Chosen – Killmaleary Cross (IRE)
Showed progressive form in Irish points winning on his latest start before we bought him at the Cheltenham April Sale. We did a fair bit with him in the spring and I like him. He is likely to go straight over hurdles.

DAYDREAMER 3 b g Duke of Marmalade (IRE) – Storyland (USA)
He has been running well on the Flat this summer for William Haggas, winning twice on the all-weather at Lingfield. Too keen at Newmarket last time, he is due to join us later in the year with a view to going juvenile hurdling.

DESERT JOE (IRE) 8 b g Anshan – Wide Country (IRE)
Missed the whole of last season, having won over hurdles at Chepstow the previous year. He is back now and could be a decent prospect for staying novice chases.

DUNDEE 6 ch g Definite Article – Gardana (FR)
The plan is to send him novice chasing. He progressed over hurdles last year winning on his final start at Uttoxeter. Prior to that, he didn't have the best of luck because he was hampered one day at Newbury when finishing second and then he was mounting a challenge at Ayr when a horse fell in front of him at the second last. He stays three miles well.

FIRST MOHICAN 6 ch g Tobougg (IRE) – Mohican Girl
Despite winning on his hurdles debut at Doncaster, he had a frustrating season because I thought he would develop into a very good novice. Fourth a couple of times at Kempton, he has also had a few runs on the Flat since. We have given him a break and will bring him back for the November Handicap before going back over hurdles. Two miles is his trip and I would like to think he is on a fair mark over jumps.

GABRIELLA ROSE 4 b f Kayf Tara – Elaine Tully (IRE)
A half-sister to Rule The World, she is a fine big filly who was still weak last year. We gave her a couple of runs in bumpers but she took time to get organised. She appears to have plenty of stamina and we may try her in another bumper before going hurdling.

GODSMEJUDGE (IRE) 8 b g Witness Box (USA) – Eliza Everett (IRE)
He ran some very good races last season considering he was wrong for most of the year. I was delighted with his reappearance at Cheltenham but he disappointed in his subsequent two runs at Sandown and Doncaster. However, he bounced back and ran two tremendous races in the Scottish National and Bet365 Gold Cup. He has spent the summer with David Dennis, doing some pre-training, and I would imagine everything will be geared towards the Grand National. We haven't made any plans regarding where he may run beforehand.

GONE TOO FAR 6 b g Kayf Tara – Major Hoolihan
He won well first time out over hurdles at Wetherby but I was a bit disappointed with him thereafter. He tended to race too keenly, so we fitted him with a hood on his final run at Huntingdon and he settled better and finished second. Having spent the summer at Martinstown Stud, he has come back looking well and we will more than likely send him novice chasing. He stays further but I would think he will start off over two miles over fences.

GRUMETI 6 b g Sakhee (USA) – Tetravella (IRE)
I was very pleased with his victory over fences at Bangor in May and it was a real confidence booster following a few hard races over hurdles. It was a smashing performance. He jumped very well and we are looking forward to running him in the good two mile novice chases. He has summered well.

HURRICANE VIC 4 b g Mount Nelson – Fountains Abbey

A huge horse, I am surprised we managed to get one run into him let alone three last season. I thought he ran well in the circumstances because he is still learning. He will go straight over hurdles and we will probably start him off over two miles.

INNER DRIVE (IRE) 6 b g Heron Island (IRE) – Hingis (IRE)

I like him a lot and I think he could be very useful. A winning pointer for Don Cantillon, he also finished second in a bumper before we bought him at the Cheltenham December Sale. Runner-up on his first start for us at Lingfield in an all-weather bumper, it was disappointing that he didn't win but it wasn't the end of the world. He had a few minor niggles thereafter, hence he didn't run again but I have been pleased with him during the summer. He will go novice hurdling.

KAREZAK (IRE) 3 b g Azamour (IRE) – Karawana (IRE)

A smashing horse who we bought during the summer from John Oxx. Rated 88 on the Flat, he was runner-up on three occasions and has taken well to jumping at home. It is possible we will give him another run on the Flat before making his jumping debut possibly at one of the early Chepstow meetings in October.

KOTKIRI (FR) 5 b g Ballingarry (IRE) – Kakira (FR)

A big backward horse who had one run in a bumper at Ascot in November, he scoped badly afterwards so we turned him away. I haven't spoken to Dai (Walters) regarding plans but he will either have another run in a bumper or go straight over hurdles.

L'AMIRAL DAVID (FR) 4 b or br g My Risk (FR) – Mme La Vicomtesse (FR)

He disappointed me in his three runs last season because, judged on his homework, I thought he was our best bumper horse. We have given him a good break and he has done tremendously well during the summer. He will go novice hurdling and I certainly haven't lost faith in him.

L'UNIQUE (FR) 5 b m Reefscape – Sans Tune (FR)

She has done very well during the summer and we are going to stay over hurdles with the David Nicholson Mares' Hurdle at the Festival her main target. She ran a tremendous race in it last year finishing third and Quevega has been retired. We lost her a bit during the first half of the season but she bounced back and won at Sandown. She was past her best by the time she ran at Haydock and I wouldn't be against trying her over three miles again at some stage.

MALDIVIAN REEF (IRE) 6 ch g Reefscape – Spirited Soul

I like him. I thought he ran well on his debut at Taunton finishing third in a bumper. He then fractured a pastern, which required surgery and he missed the rest of the season. There is no doubt he has ability and we will try him in another bumper before going hurdling.

MANYRIVERSTOCROSS (IRE) 9 b g Cape Cross (IRE) – Alexandra S (IRE)

He has been a grand horse over the years and he had a good season over fences winning at Exeter and Ascot and finishing second in the Grade 1 Scilly Isles Novices' Chase at Sandown. He has been away doing his roadwork during the summer and we will aim him at the big handicaps over two and two and a half miles.

MCCABE CREEK (IRE) 4 b g Robin Des Pres (FR) – Kick And Run (IRE)

I like him very much and he ran well on his first start at Newbury finishing second behind a highly regarded horse of Gary Moore's (Puisque Tu Pars). We then ran him in the championship bumper at Aintree, which gives everyone an idea of what I think of him, but he was too buzzy and didn't settle. I think he will settle better over hurdles and he has plenty of speed for two miles.

MEDERMIT (FR) 10 gr g Medaaly – Miss D'Hermite (FR)

We nursed him back following nearly two years on the sidelines. He lacked match practice on his first couple of runs back but I was delighted with his run at Punchestown. He stayed on well in the Grade 1 Punchestown Gold Cup and there was a lot of encouragement to be taken from it. He will continue down the three mile chase route and the Charlie Hall Chase at Wetherby (1st November) is a possible starting point.

MEDINAS (FR) 7 b or br g Malinas (GER) – Medicis (FR)

I think he paid for his success the previous season last year. Runner-up on his reappearance in the West Yorkshire Hurdle at Wetherby, he struggled thereafter. We may run him at Wetherby again and then decide about his future. He is probably too small for fences and, if things didn't go well at Wetherby, we may retire him because there is no point carrying on when he isn't enjoying it or being competitive.

MIDNIGHT PRAYER 9 b g Midnight Legend – Onawing Andaprayer

He had a tremendous season over fences winning three times, including the National Hunt Chase over four miles at the Cheltenham Festival. His first main target is the Welsh National because he handles soft ground. In all likelihood, he will have one run beforehand.

MILES TO MEMPHIS (IRE) 5 b g Old Vic – Phillis Hill

A smashing horse who we planned to send hurdling last season but he made a noise and we hobdayed him. He bolted up on his debut in a bumper at Kempton and then followed it up with another win in what is traditionally a strong bumper at Ayr's Scottish National meeting. He has spent the summer with Annabel Murphy and is an exciting prospect for two mile novice hurdles. He travels strongly in his races and that will stand him in good stead over jumps.

MIRKAT 4 b g Kalanisi (IRE) – Miracle

A full brother to Katchit, he is better than he showed in two bumpers last spring. Fontwell didn't suit him first time out and then he finished third at Ffos Las. He is a horse I like and we might try and win a bumper before going hurdling.

MONTBAZON (FR) 7 b or br g Alberto Giacometti (IRE) – Duchesse Pierji (FR)

He ran very well in the County Hurdle finishing third but hasn't had a lot of luck with the weather since. He wants decent ground but it turned soft in the Swinton Hurdle and then again on the Flat at Haydock in June. Even in the Summer Hurdle at Market Rasen, it rained about two hours before the race and it changed the ground. We will probably give him another run on the Flat before going novice chasing. We haven't schooled him yet but I don't envisage any problems. I may step him up in trip as well because he is finding two miles a bit sharp nowadays.

NED STARK (IRE) 6 b g Wolfe Tone (IRE) – Last Moon (IRE)

A promising horse who ran well over hurdles at Exeter in November on his first start for us. He was then wrong for much of the season but I was very pleased with his win at Chepstow in late April. An ex-pointer, he has schooled well over fences and the intention is for him to go novice chasing. We will start him off over two and a half miles but he stays further.

NYANZA (GER) 3 b f Dai Jin – Nouvelle Fortune (IRE)

Twice a winner on the Flat at Kempton in the spring, she has been placed a couple of times since. We have schooled her over hurdles and she jumps very well. Following a break, she will have another run on the Flat before going juvenile hurdling. I would like to aim her at the Listed juvenile fillies hurdle at Aintree (6th December) with one run beforehand. L'Unique won the race for us a couple of years ago.

ORDO AB CHAO (IRE) 5 b g Heron Island (IRE) – Houldyurwhist (IRE)
A fine big horse, he looks very promising. Despite falling twice, he had shown plenty of ability in both his Irish points, prior to us buying him at the Doncaster November Sales. He looked very good when winning a bumper at Huntingdon and then finished fourth in the championship event at Aintree's Grand National meeting. A horse I like a lot, he will be a three miler eventually but we will be looking towards two and a half mile novice hurdles to begin with.

PAIN AU CHOCOLAT (FR) 3 b g Enrique – Clair Chene (FR)
Quite lean when he first arrived from France, he is a big rangy horse and doesn't look a typical juvenile hurdler. Placed on the Flat and over hurdles, he is still a maiden and we will be aiming him at three year old hurdles in the Autumn.

PIRATES CAY 7 b g Black Sam Bellamy (IRE) – Mistic World
He won his only Irish point-to-point but was off for nearly two years before finishing fourth over hurdles at Huntingdon in May. He has obviously had his problems but he has always shown a lot of promise at home. The plan is for him to continue in novice hurdles.

RIDGEWAY STORM (IRE) 4 b g Hurricane Run (IRE) – Hesperia
Placed three times on the Flat, he ran well behind Arod at Windsor in April and was only beaten a neck at Kempton in early July. He puts a lot into his races so we make sure we space them out. He will have another run or two on the Flat before going novice hurdling.

ROBERTO PEGASUS (USA) 8 b or br g Fusaichi Pegasus (USA) – Louju (USA)
An easy winner over hurdles at Worcester in June, he enjoys cut in the ground. He appreciated the step up in trip and I will be disappointed if he doesn't win more races. I think he could do OK over fences, too.

RONALDINHO (IRE) 4 b g Jeremy (USA) – Spring Glory
He ran some good races in defeat last season. Placed at Doncaster and Ascot, I don't think he quite got home in testing ground at Sandown on the final day of the season. Runner-up on the Flat at Windsor since, he has the ability to win races over hurdles. Two miles is his trip.

SEGO SUCCESS (IRE) 6 b g Beneficial – The West Road (IRE)
He didn't have the best of fortunes last year being brought down at Huntingdon and then I thought he was going to win at Exeter before falling at the second last. A winner at Southwell, he is a winning pointer and will be going novice chasing.

SIMPLY A LEGEND 5 b g Midnight Legend – Disco Danehill (IRE)
He can be his own worst enemy because he doesn't always settle in his races. However, he won twice in the spring when fitted with a hood. I thought Wayne (Hutchinson) gave him a very good ride at Ascot and then he followed up at Kempton. We are going to send him novice chasing having schooled well.

SMAD PLACE (FR) 7 gr g Smadoun (FR) – Bienna Star (FR)
He had a very good season over fences winning twice and finishing a neck second in the RSA Chase at Cheltenham in March. He won in good style at Newbury and did everything bar win at the Festival. We are going to aim him at the Hennessy Gold Cup (29th November) and go there first time out because he is good fresh. Effective on any ground, we won't over race him and, hopefully, he will have another good season over fences.

THE PIRATE'S QUEEN (IRE) 5 b m King's Theatre (IRE) – Shivermetimber (IRE)

A lovely mare who has changed owners during the summer (now owned by the Dunkley & Reilly Partnership). Placed four times last season, including in three Listed mares' hurdles, she remains a novice for this season and will continue in mares' events. She is effective over two and two and a half miles.

THE TOURARD MAN (IRE) 8 b g Shantou (USA) – Small Iron

Ex-Irish, he won two point-to-points and has been placed in a bumper and maiden hunter chase. He arrived in the spring but we haven't done a great deal with him. I would think he will start off in a novice hurdle.

TURN OVER SIVOLA (FR) 7 b g Assessor (IRE) – Notting Hill (FR)

Very consistent, he ran an excellent race in the Red Rum Chase at Aintree in April. We didn't want to lose his novice status late on so waited until May before he won at Huntingdon. I don't think he was at his best that day because it was at the end of a long season, plus the ground was plenty soft enough for him. We will aim him at the better two mile novice chases and I think he is suited by flat tracks such as Kempton. He ran at Cheltenham one day a couple of years ago and I don't think he came up the hill.

ULZANA'S RAID (IRE) 5 ch g Bach (IRE) – Peace Time Beauty (IRE)

A progressive horse who was quite a slow learner to begin with. He has grown again and has developed into a big, tall horse. Twice a winner over hurdles at Warwick and Ayr in the spring, we are going to keep him over hurdles for the time being. He doesn't want bottomless ground and is suited by two and a half miles plus. Long-term, I am hoping he will make an exciting chaser.

UXIZANDRE (FR) 6 ch g Fragrant Mix (IRE) – Jolisandre (FR)

He has returned from Martinstown Stud looking tremendous. He had a great season over fences winning a Grade 1 novice chase at Aintree and finishing three parts of a length second in the Jewson at Cheltenham. The fact he has to go left-handed limits our options a bit but there is a possibility he will come back in trip at some stage this season. A.P. (McCoy) feels he will be suited by dropping back in distance because he loves to dominate. There is a possibility though he will start off in a newly formed Intermediate Chase at Newton Abbot (10th October) over two mile five furlongs.

VALDEZ 7 ch g Doyen (IRE) – Skew

Another who had a good year over fences winning three times, including the Grade 2 Lightning Novices' Chase at Doncaster. He ran well in the Arkle finishing fifth but disappointed me last time at Ayr. He has a tendency to jump to his right but did it violently there and it transpired he was suffering from a kissing spine. He has undergone surgery since and I hope it will bring about further improvement. I think two and a half miles is his trip and we are going to aim him at the Paddy Power Gold Cup.

WEST END ROCKER (IRE) 12 b or br g Grand Plaisir (IRE) – Slyguff Lord (IRE)

Ran very well in the Midlands National finishing third, having been off for a year. He may be a twelve year old but his run at Uttoxeter proved he still retains plenty of ability. Once again, he will be aimed at the good long distance handicap chases.

WILDE BLUE YONDER (IRE) 5 b g Oscar (IRE) – Blue Gallery (IRE)

He is a bloody good horse but he was very unlucky last season. Having won his first two races of the season, we were disappointed when he fell at the last at Newbury's Hennessy meeting. When he did it again at Ascot next time, we were mortified. Thankfully, he bounced back and finished a good fifth in the Supreme Novices' Hurdle at the Festival. We stepped him up to two and a half miles at Aintree and I think it was more a case of him feeling the effects of a long season rather than the trip which beat him. The plan is to stay over hurdles and I wouldn't be against trying him over further again in future.

YANWORTH 4 ch g Norse Dancer (IRE) – Yota (FR)

A winner of his only bumper at Wincanton in May, I think it was a good race because Paul (Nicholls) likes the runner-up a lot and the pair were twenty eight lengths clear of the third, which is also well regarded. J.P.McManus has bought him since and he could be anything. His victory wasn't a surprise because he has always worked well at home. It is possible he will have another run in a bumper before going hurdling. I like him a lot.

ZIGA BOY (FR) 5 gr g Califet (FR) – Our Ziga (FR)

A big horse, he won over fences in France before joining us and had two starts at Newbury. He ran well on both occasions and we are going to try and win a novice hurdle before going back over fences. I think three miles will turn out to be his trip eventually.

TRAINER'S HORSE TO FOLLOW: MILES TO MEMPHIS

Charlie LONGSDON

Stables: Hull Farm Stables, Stratford Road, Chipping Norton, Oxon.
2013/2014: 78 Winners / 387 Runners 20% Prize-Money £496,742
www.charlielongsdonracing.com

A VOS GARDES (FR) 4 b g Kapgarde (FR) – Miscia Nera (FR)
He is a really exciting four year old. Despite winning both his starts in bumpers last season, he was still a baby. We purposely only ran him twice and he has grown and strengthened during the summer. Admittedly, he was receiving a lot of weight on his debut at Bangor but he beat one of Rebecca Curtis's who was very well fancied. He then won in good style at Ascot and we put him away for the summer. He does everything easily at home and the plan is to send him novice hurdling. Effective on soft ground, he will start off over two miles but will get further later on.

ATLANTIC GOLD (IRE) 4 b or br g Robin Des Pres (FR) – Marys Isle (IRE)
A new arrival, we bought him at the Cheltenham May Sale and he is a horse I like a lot. A very good looking horse, he ran in two Irish points winning on the second occasion. There was plenty to like about the performance. He looks a sharp sort and will run in a bumper in October.

BATTLE BORN 5 b g Kayf Tara – Realms of Gold (USA)
He is a lovely horse with a very good attitude. A smart bumper performer last year, he finished third on his Rules debut at Haydock in November. Noel (Fehily) felt we used the wrong tactics and he would have won had we ridden him more positively. He won his next two starts at Warwick and Bangor and then took his chance in the championship bumper at Aintree on Grand National day. Once again, Noel thought he should have gone quicker on him. Despite that, he still ran creditably in sixth. He has done well during the summer and is much stronger now. I think he will want a trip over hurdles but we may start him off over a stiff two miles. We have done well at Carlisle during the last couple of seasons and he may head there for their first meeting of the season (10th October).

BEST WORK (FR) 3 b g Network (FR) – Harmony (FR)
A very good looking horse we purchased in France during the summer. We haven't done a great deal with him but I will be disappointed if he doesn't win his bumper.

CADOUDOFF (FR) 4 gr g Davidoff (GER) – Hera Du Berlais (FR)
It was always going to be tough for him last season, having arrived from France during the summer and forced to carry a penalty. Runner-up a couple of times at Wetherby in the Listed Wensleydale Hurdle and Newbury, it ought to be easier for him this season. Every jockey who rode him last year said he wasn't a typical juvenile hurdler. He will appreciate a step up in trip and slow ground. The intention is to stay over hurdles for the time being but it may not be long before he goes chasing.

DEADLY MOVE (IRE) 5 b g Scorpion (IRE) – Sounds Attractive (IRE)
We bought him at the Cheltenham April Sale having finished second in his only point-to-point in Ireland for Sam Curling. He is a very nice horse with a lot of presence. I think of all the Irish pointers we have bought this spring/summer, he has the scope to be the best. A fine big strong horse, he is very much a three mile chaser in the making but he will start off in a bumper.

DROP OUT JOE 6 ch g Generous (IRE) – La Feuillarde (FR)
He proved a revelation last season winning twice at Uttoxeter and Carlisle and placed on another three occasions. We always thought he was a nice horse and purposely started him off early on last year. He will be going chasing this time and I can see him developing into a nice staying novice. A very good jumper, I think he will be a bold front runner and it wouldn't surprise me if he ended up in the four miler at the Cheltenham Festival.

ELY BROWN (IRE) 9 b g Sunshine Street (USA) – Browneyed Daughter (IRE)
He has been a superstar. A three times winner last season, he won the Grade 2 Towton Novices' Chase at Wetherby before finishing fifth in the Reynoldstown Chase at Ascot. He picked up an injury that day hence he never raced again. However, he is fine now and will be aimed at the big staying handicaps. We also have the option of Intermediate and Graduation Chases, although his owner's ultimate dream is the Grand National. It is possible he is best on flat tracks because Noel (Fehily) said he hated the downhill fences at Ascot in the Reynoldstown. Good or soft ground is ideal and he stays very well.

FRAMPTON (IRE) 5 b g Presenting – Drumavish Lass (IRE)
Placed in a bumper for Stuart Crawford before joining us, I thought he was unlucky not to win a similar event for us, finishing third at both Market Rasen and Fontwell. He will be running by late September/early October and will want two and a half miles over hurdles. I will be disappointed if he can't win a race or two over hurdles, especially on decent ground.

GERMANY CALLING (IRE) 5 b g Germany (USA) – Markir (IRE)
He is a talented horse who finished second behind Lac Fontana at Cheltenham in October before incurring a setback. By the time he came back, it was February so we decided to aim him at the good novice events and, if he didn't win, it meant he remained a novice for this season. Fifth in the Adonis Hurdle at Kempton, he ran creditably for a long way in the Supreme Novices' Hurdle at the Festival. An easy winner at Uttoxeter in early May, we have operated on his wind since and I think it will make a big difference. Rated 121, he is fairly treated in handicaps but I feel he is capable of winning another novice hurdle under a penalty. We may keep him to the minimum trip for the time being but I think he will improve when stepped up to two and a half miles. He has plenty of ability.

HARRISTOWN 4 ch g Bering – New Abbey
Bought for 15,000gns in August last year, he proved a good buy winning at Newton Abbot and Huntingdon. He loves soft ground and I think there is a decent handicap hurdle to be won with him this season. He has had his first proper break and has benefited from it. We will be looking to step him up in trip at some stage.

IZA OWENS (IRE) 5 b m Golan (IRE) – Luck Penni (IRE)
Third in her only Irish point, we bought her in March at the Newbury Sales. I don't know a great deal about her but she gives the impression she will stay well and is one for two and a half mile plus mares' novice hurdles.

JAVA ROSE 5 b m Ishiguru (USA) – Mighty Splash
A lovely, good looking mare, she ran well in both her races over hurdles at Fakenham and Warwick. I am hoping she will improve again and we will mix and match between the Flat and two and a half mile hurdles. I think she could be a fun horse for mares' events this season.

KILCOOLEY (IRE) 5 b g Stowaway – Bealaha Essie (IRE)
He is a very nice horse with a lot of ability. A bumper winner at Market Rasen, he won his first two starts over hurdles at the same track. Well held at Aintree last time, he didn't run his race and is a much better horse running from the front. Still only five, he beat some useful horses last season and I think he has got a bright future. I am going to keep him over hurdles this season. A lot of his sire's progeny are keen going types and he is the same, although he settles well at home. Running in handicaps will help because they will go quicker and it will give him a chance to settle better.

KILLALA QUAY 7 b g Karinga Bay – Madam Bijou
He is a good horse and thoroughly deserved his victory in the Grade 2 Winter Novices' Hurdle at Sandown in December. An excellent fourth in the Neptune Investments Novices' Hurdle at the Festival, he wasn't right next time at Aintree. We are going to send him novice chasing and he is an exciting prospect. We have done plenty of schooling with him and he jumps well. While we will start him off over two and a half miles, he will stay further later in the season.

KITENEY WOOD (IRE) 4 ch g Layman (USA) – She Runs (FR)
Bought at the Cheltenham March Sale, he won his second Irish point and looks a horse with plenty of speed. We are going to try and win a bumper during the Autumn with a view to going hurdling later in the season. He may not want extremes of ground but he looks a sharp sort.

LONG LUNCH 5 b g Kayf Tara – Royal Keel
Twice a winner at Market Rasen and Plumpton, he was consistent throughout last season. A half-brother to Hidden Keel, he is bred to stay further but is a keen going horse. It is possible we will operate on his wind at some stage, but I think he is fairly handicapped off 122.

LOOSE CHIPS 8 b g Sir Harry Lewis (USA) – Worlaby Rose
A winner over fences at Kempton and Huntingdon, he finished fifth in the Pendil Novices' Chase at Kempton in February. He had endured a lot of hard races, hence we gave him a break and he hasn't run since. We are going to space his races out this time but it won't be easy for him off a mark of 139. We will also consider Graduation and Intermediate Chases.

MAGNIFIQUE ETOILE 7 b g Kayf Tara – Star Diva (IRE)
He won over hurdles at Stratford in October but found it tough thereafter off a mark of 148. He is in good form at home though and will go novice chasing. I will be disappointed if he can't win races over fences. Two and a half miles is his trip.

MASTERPLAN (IRE) 4 b g Spadoun (FR) – Eurolucy (IRE)
Successful in his only Irish point-to-point, we bought him at the Cheltenham May Sale. A big raw horse, he is still backward and I am surprised he even ran in a point. We aren't in a rush with him because he is one for the long-term. It is possible he will run in a bumper but he will want two and a half mile plus over hurdles.

NO NO MAC (IRE) 5 b g Oscar (IRE) – Whatdoyouthinkmac (IRE)
A tough hardy horse who won twice over hurdles at Southwell and Market Rasen. We have operated on his wind during the summer, which will hopefully bring about further improvement. I think there is a handicap hurdle to be won with him before going chasing. Two and a half miles suits him at present but he will want further eventually.

NO NO MANOLITO (IRE) 4 b g High Chaparral (IRE) – Dawn Bid (IRE)

He is a smart horse who, despite being very green on his debut at Fontwell, won his bumper easily. We were beginning to run out of time but I was keen to run him and he was very impressive. We have always liked him and I know Gary Moore's (Puisque Tu Pars) was well fancied but he picked him up very easily and won going away. Even though he is bred for jumping, we may give him another couple of runs in bumpers with the Listed event at Cheltenham's Paddy Power meeting (16th November) the obvious target. Still only four, he is more than capable of winning under a penalty so I may even run him again in October beforehand. Richard Johnson rode him at Fontwell and he, too, was impressed.

NO NO ROMEO (IRE) 5 b g Scorpion (IRE) – Penny Brae (IRE)

Another promising bumper horse from last season, he won at Southwell before finishing second at Huntingdon and then seventh in the championship event at Aintree on Grand National day. We considered taking him to Punchestown but decided to give him a break. I think he is capable of winning a couple of novice hurdles, including under a penalty, before we have a look at some of the decent novice hurdles around Christmas time. He enjoys soft ground and, while he is quick enough to win over two miles, he will be even better over further.

OUR KAEMPFER (IRE) 5 b g Oscar (IRE) – Gra-Bri (IRE)

A lovely big rangy horse, he is another very nice prospect for novice hurdlers this winter. There is plenty to like about him and we have operated on his wind since his last run. His bumper form is very good winning at Worcester and finishing third behind Red Sherlock at the Paddy Power meeting in a Listed contest. I would be inclined to forget his run at the Festival because he had run his race beforehand. He bolted going to the start and got worked up. Fifth at Aintree last time, he was beaten less than six lengths and I was delighted with his run. I think he has got an exciting future and will want two and a half miles over jumps.

PENDRA (IRE) 6 ch g Old Vic – Mariah Rollins (IRE)

Having won twice over fences at Carlisle and Lingfield, I thought he was unlucky at the Cheltenham Festival in the novices' handicap chase. If he had jumped the last better, he would have gone very close. I think his lack of experience caught him out. It was his first run over two and a half miles over fences but I think he will want three miles eventually. I thought he ran a blinder in the Irish National but he got hampered and, ultimately, I don't think he quite got home. Races like the Paddy Power Gold Cup and December Gold Cup at Cheltenham are obvious targets but it may be worth considering the United Homes Handicap Chase at Ascot (1st November) over three miles. He is fairly treated off 139 and he will have learned a lot from his last two races. He has improved mentally since Cheltenham in March.

PIED DU ROI (IRE) 4 b g Robin Des Pres (FR) – Long Acre

A huge horse, I thought he ran well in his only bumper at Haydock because the race wasn't run to suit him. They went no pace and it turned into a sprint. He is a big strapping horse who is capable of winning a bumper before going hurdling. This will be very much a bonus year though because he is an out and out chaser in the making.

PROMANCO 5 b m Kayf Tara – Shelayly (IRE)

She is a nice mare who ran a good race on her debut in a bumper at Huntingdon. The form has worked out well with the winner going on to land the Listed mares' bumper at Aintree. I would ignore her next run at Towcester. She jumps nicely and is one for mares' only novice hurdles over two and a half miles. She has the ability to win races.

QUIETO SOL (FR) 3 ch g Loup Solitaire (USA) – First Wonder (FR)
A very nice unraced three year old we bought in France during the summer. He breezed very well and we put him out in the field for six weeks when he arrived. All being well, he will be aimed at a junior bumper in November.

READY TOKEN (IRE) 6 gr g Flemensfirth (USA) – Cool Tire (IRE)
An unlucky horse, he fell twice at Market Rasen and Warwick and it knocked his confidence. Placed in his two subsequent starts, he is still a novice but we have the option of running in a handicap because he could be well treated. The aim is to try and win a novice hurdle in October and take it from there.

SASSANOVA (FR) 4 b f Sassanian (USA) – Anglaise (IRE)
She made her debut in the DBS Spring Sales bumper at Newbury in March and ran respectably in sixth. While we will be aiming her at mares' only novice hurdles this season, I think she is capable of winning a bumper beforehand. Two and a half miles will suit her over jumps.

SERGEANT MATTIE (IRE) 6 b g Naheez (USA) – Glyde Lady (IRE)
He won on his reappearance over hurdles at Carlisle but got struck into hence he didn't run again until the spring. Successful again on his return at Plumpton, I thought he was unlucky not to make it three wins at the same track on his latest outing when conceding over a stone to the winner. He is a nice horse who will go novice chasing in October. Two and a half miles is ideal.

SHANTOU MAGIC (IRE) 7 b g Shantou (USA) – Supreme Magical
He has had a breathing operation during the summer and I hope it will make a big difference. Impressive early on last season, he beat the likes of Cole Harden easily at Fontwell before following up at Market Rasen. We stepped him up in class and ran him in the Grade 1 Challow Hurdle at Newbury but he finished very tired. It was a similar story in the Martin Pipe Conditional Handicap Hurdle at the Festival. I am hoping he will improve and we will find out if he is going to be competitive in handicaps over hurdles before going chasing. Two and a half miles suits him at the moment but I think he will stay three. He loves soft ground and wants good to soft at least.

SIMPLY THE WEST (IRE) 5 b g Westerner – Back To Stay (IRE)
Bought at the Cheltenham May Sales, he won the second of his two outings in Irish points and the form has worked out well. He will be running in two and a half mile novice hurdles and I think he is an interesting horse.

SPIRIT OF SHANKLY 6 ch g Sulamani (IRE) – Lago D'Oro
He is another we have operated on his wind. I thought he was well handicapped last season but each time at Kempton and Aintree he hit a flat spot before flying home at the finish. I will be disappointed if he can't win a decent handicap hurdle this season. He has always been a very good work horse and, while he stays two and a half miles, he certainly isn't short of speed.

ST JOHNS POINT (IRE) 6 b g Darsi (FR) – Dunsford Belle (IRE)
Successful in his only Irish point, we bought him cheaply at the Doncaster May Sales. I don't know a great deal about him but we may go straight over fences with him because he is a six year old.

UP TO SOMETHING (FR) 6 b g Brier Creek (USA) – Evane (FR)
He made a good start to his chasing career winning at Carlisle and finishing second on his two subsequent outings at Ascot and Wincanton. However, he was a bit disappointing thereafter. Noel (Fehily) said he would love to ride him over the National fences at some stage and, with that in mind, the Grand Sefton Chase at Aintree (6th December) is a possible target. He is a very good jumper and I feel he is on a fair mark.

VULCANITE (IRE) 7 b g Dubawi (IRE) – Daraliya (IRE)
He has been in great form during the spring/summer and has really benefited from a wind operation. A three times winner between March and June, he won in good style at Worcester under a very good ride from Ger Fox. He, unfortunately, unseated his rider early on in the Galway Plate. We will keep him going until the Autumn and then give him a mid winter break. He likes decent ground and will mix and match between hurdles and fences.

WADSWICK COURT (IRE) 6 b g Court Cave (IRE) – Tarasandy (IRE)
Twice a winner over hurdles at Huntingdon and Southwell, he also finished second at Ascot in February. We are going to see if he is competitive in handicaps before turning his attentions to chasing. I think the stronger gallop in handicaps will suit him because he is inclined to race keenly (too keen at Cheltenham in a Listed bumper in November). Provided he settles, he will also be suited by a step up to two and a half miles.

WELLS DU LUNE 3 b g Irish Wells (FR) – Pepite De Lune (FR)
A lovely big horse who ran twice over hurdles for Guillaume Macaire in France. A winner on his debut in the Provinces, he then finished second. We have gelded him since arriving and given him a good break. The plan is to run him under a penalty in a juvenile hurdle in October and then possibly aim him at the Wensleydale Hurdle at Wetherby or the juvenile hurdle at Cheltenham's Paddy Power meeting.

WILBERDRAGON 4 b g Kayf Tara – Swaythe (USA)
Seventh in his only bumper for Venetia Williams during the spring, we bought him at the Doncaster May Sales on recommendation. He didn't look wound up on his debut and I feel there is plenty of improvement to come. A well bred four year old, I would like to win a bumper with him before going hurdling.

Unnamed 5 b g King's Theatre (IRE) – Mariah Rollins (IRE)
Bred by Paul Murphy, he is a half-brother to Pendra and is potentially a very nice horse. He spent the summer in Ireland but the vibes about him are very good.

TRAINER'S HORSE TO FOLLOW: BATTLE BORN

Donald McCAIN

Stables: Bankhouse, Cholmondeley, Malpas, Cheshire.
2013/2014: 142 Winners / 775 Runners 18% Prize-Money £964,606
www.donaldmccain.co.uk

ABRICOT DE L'OASIS (FR) 4 b g Al Namix (FR) – La Normandie (FR)
A nice horse who won over fences in France in May for Guy Cherel. He has a similar profile to another of our ex-French horses, Volcanic. Still a novice over hurdles, he will go down that route to start with and see how he gets on.

ACROSS THE BAY (IRE) 10 b g Bob's Return (IRE) – The Southern (IRE)
He ran a massive race in the Grand National considering he was carried out by the loose horses passing the stands with a circuit to run. It obviously isn't going to be easy for him this season off his mark of 147 but we will follow a similar programme. The Becher Chase is likely to be his first main target followed by the National again.

AL MUSHEER (FR) 3 c Verglas (IRE) - Canzonetta (FR)
A winner on the Flat in France, we bought him at the Arqana Sale in July. A handy horse, he has schooled over hurdles and will be running early on in a juvenile event.

AMIRLI (IRE) 3 ch g Medicean – Amenapinga (FR)
We also bought him at the Arqana Sale in France during the summer. Previously trained by Alain De Royer-Dupre, he is a half-brother to Listed bumper winner Aminabad and he finished runner-up on the Flat at Dieppe in June. I thought he would have made more at the sales because he is from a good family of the Aga Khan's. However, he ran the day before the sale was a bit disappointing, hence his price. We have gelded him since arriving (he was a rig) and he will be running in juvenile hurdles in the Autumn.

AMYS CHOICE (IRE) 4 b f Craigsteel – Tanya Thyne (IRE)
She is a half-sister to Wymott who we bought at the Cheltenham May Sale. She ran in two Irish points winning on the second occasion. We will look for a mares' bumper in the Autumn.

ARDNAHOE (IRE) 4 b f Brian Boru – Queen Sophie (IRE)
She joined us in the summer, having won a bumper for David Kiely at Limerick in March. Fourth next time at Cheltenham the following month, she is a nice filly who will be aimed at mares' only novice hurdles.

ASKAMORE DARSI (IRE) 5 b g Darsi (FR) – Galamear
A former Irish pointer, he won a bumper at Uttoxeter and over hurdles at Wetherby last season. We may give him one more run over hurdles but it won't be long before he goes over fences. I think he will develop into a hard knocking northern long distance novice chaser but he doesn't want the ground too soft.

BALLYBOKER BREEZE (IRE) 6 b g Gold Well – Ballyboker Lady (IRE)
He is one of a number of Irish pointers we purchased during the spring/summer. An older pointer, we bought him at the Doncaster May Sales. A big attractive gelding, he won his latest start and appears to want soft ground. It is possible he will run in a bumper before going hurdling. He is one for long distance novice hurdles.

BEATU (IRE) 5 b g Beat All (USA) – Auntie Bob
A half-brother to Irish Cesarewitch winner Dani California, he ran in a couple of Irish points before we bought him. A good winner at Catterick in December, I thought he would run well in the Aintree Championship bumper but he received a nasty bump and came back with a hairline fracture of his pelvis. He will be going novice hurdling and, while he isn't slow, he will stay a trip, too. He is a nice horse.

BIG BAD DUDE (IRE) 5 ch g Blueprint (IRE) – Cathedral Ave (IRE)
A nice type of horse who we bought at the Cheltenham May Sales. A four lengths winner of his only Irish point, he will probably start off in a bumper before going hurdling.

BILLY BUFF 4 b g Multiplex – Shanxi Girl
Bred by Richard Kent, I know the family well and I am a fan of the sire and feel he is underrated. He didn't join Colin Bowe until quite late and, having run well on his debut finishing second in a point-to-point, he won by three lengths a week later. We bought him four days later at the Cheltenham May Sale and he looks a nice horse for the future. He is another who will probably run in a bumper before we send him novice hurdling.

CARRIGEEN LANTANA (IRE) 5 b m Beneficial – Carrigeen Lily (IRE)
A full-sister to Carrigeen Lechuga, she comes from a very good Irish chasing family. She was an impressive four lengths winner of her only point-to-point before we bought her at the Doncaster May Sale. A running on third in a slowly run bumper at Market Rasen in August, there are plenty of opportunities for mares and I hope she makes her mark under Rules before possibly one day being a broodmare.

CLASSIC MOVE (IRE) 5 b g Flying Legend (USA) – Jennylee (IRE)
A three times winner last season, including twice over hurdles at Bangor and Catterick, we then ran him in the EBF Final at Sandown but he got very upset beforehand and lost the plot. A faller at the second last, I shouldn't have run him again at Haydock because he had had enough by that stage. However, I didn't want him to end his season with a fall. A winning pointer, he is going over fences and I think he could be exciting over two and two and a half miles. He likes to get on with it and it is possible he won't want much further than two miles over fences. His two hurdle wins were on soft or heavy ground but he handles better ground, too.

CLONDAW DRAFT (IRE) 6 b g Shantou (USA) – Glen Ten (IRE)
He won twice over hurdles at Worcester and Bangor during the Autumn before finishing third at Cheltenham in October. Forced to miss the rest of the season due to injury, he is back in work and will be going novice chasing.

CLONDAW KAEMPFER (IRE) 6 b g Oscar (IRE) – Gra-Bri (IRE)
I was delighted with his victory at Aintree in April because he is a horse we have always thought a lot of. His novice hurdle career was cut short, due to injury, and it was great to see him back to his best at Aintree. We thought he would run well in the Coral Cup but we made too much use of him and he didn't get home. Rated 147, we haven't decided whether to aim him at the good handicap hurdles, once again, or go novice chasing. Yet to be schooled over fences, he isn't short of speed but it wouldn't surprise me if he stayed three miles one day. I think he will make a very nice chaser when the time comes.

CORRIN WOOD (IRE) 7 gr g Garuda (IRE) – Allstar Rose (IRE)
He developed into a very useful chaser last season winning his first three races. We then ran him in the RSA Chase at Cheltenham but things didn't go to plan. He has done well during the summer and we will be aiming him at the good staying chases. The Charlie Hall at Wetherby (1st November) could be a possible starting point and I think he could be an Aintree horse one day, although not necessarily this season. Despite winning twice on soft/heavy ground last season, I have always thought he would be better on nicer ground.

COURT DISMISSED (IRE) 4 b g Court Cave (IRE) – Carramanagh Lady (IRE)
A nice little horse who ran twice in point-to-points for Sean Doyle in Ireland. Third on debut, he won next time and we bought him a week later at the Newbury March Sale. He isn't over big and I hope he will make a decent novice hurdler following a run in a bumper.

COURT OF LAW (IRE) 6 b g Court Cave (IRE) – Divine Dancer (IRE)
I purchased him cheaply at the Doncaster May Sales and he is mine at the moment. A tall horse, he won the final of his four Irish points by ten lengths for Denis Murphy in May. He is a solid horse who looks to be improving.

CRACKED REAR VIEW (IRE) 4 gr g Portrait Gallery (IRE) – Trip To Knock
An exciting new recruit we bought at the Cheltenham May Sale. By the same sire as Beeves, I loved him in his point-to-points and then he won his bumper at Sligo, which made him more expensive. He has a great way about him and he is a lovely big, tall horse. Still immature, he will possibly run in another bumper before we go novice hurdling with him.

DEEP MARGIN (IRE) 5 b g Scorpion (IRE) – Deep Supreme (IRE)
A lovely, big unraced gelding owned by Mr Hemmings. He is a half-brother to Heath Hunter but he won't be in action until later on due to a little setback. I like him.

DESOTO COUNTY 5 gr g Hernando (FR) - Kaldounya
He had a good season winning three times, including twice over hurdles and never finished out of the first two in six races. Despite that, I don't think he showed what he is capable of. Still immature, he doesn't do a lot when hitting the front and he doesn't want the ground too soft. We could run him in a handicap hurdle before going chasing. He tends to be quite careful over his hurdles and I think he will jump fences better. He has plenty of speed but he ought to stay further in due course.

DIAMOND KING (IRE) 6 b g King's Theatre (IRE) – Georgia On My Mind (FR)
He won two of his three races over hurdles at Wetherby and Doncaster but missed most of the second half of the season, due to a couple of minor niggles. We could have got him back for Aintree but he is a very smart horse and not one to risk if he isn't 100%. He will make a chaser but there is a possibility he will have another run or two over hurdles beforehand. Two and a half miles is his trip at the moment but, if he settles, he will have no problem staying three miles.

DISPOUR (IRE) 4 ch g Monsun (GER) – Dalataya (IRE)
I was pleased with him last season winning three times, including a decent handicap hurdle at Sandown on the final day in April. We had been aiming him at the Fred Winter Juvenile Hurdle at Cheltenham but he didn't get in. We fitted him with blinkers for the first time on his previous start at Aintree but we didn't make enough use of him. His victory at Sandown therefore didn't surprise us and he handled the conditions well because we thought he wanted better ground. Still lightly raced, he will stay further than two miles and will continue to run in the good handicap hurdles.

DOYLY CARTE 6 b m Doyen (IRE) – Generous Diana
Runner-up a couple of times at Haydock and Doncaster last season, she chased home Annie Power in a Grade 2 hurdle at the latter. She looks great and we are looking forward to sending her over fences. Mares' only novice chases are few and far between so we will run her against the geldings, too. Two miles is her trip.

DRY YOUR EYES (IRE) 3 b f Shamardal (USA) – Kindling
A half-sister to Bayan, her owner Grant Mercer bought her back at the Newmarket July Sales with a view to going juvenile hurdling. A winner over twelve furlongs at Beverley for Mark Johnston in May, the ground was heavy, which bodes well for her jumping career. Only small, she has schooled nicely and is one for the early juvenile hurdles.

DUKE ARCADIO (IRE) 5 b g Arcadio (GER) – Kildowney Duchess (IRE)
By a sire I like, he is a smashing horse who we acquired at the Doncaster May Sales. A twelve lengths winner of a confined maiden point for Colin McKeever, it may not have been the strongest of races but he won well and is a nice prospect for bumpers and novice hurdles this season.

FEATHER LANE (IRE) 4 b g Court Cave (IRE) – Laffan's Bridge (IRE)
Unlucky not to win the second of his two Irish points, he looks a nice four year old. We will run him in a bumper and then decide whether to go novice hurdling.

FIVE FOR FIFTEEN (IRE) 5 b g Craigsteel – Gentle Eyre (IRE)
A good solid horse with a likeable attitude. We bought him at the Goffs Punchestown Sale in early May having run in two Irish points. Third on his debut, he won next time and didn't look overpriced.

FRANCISCAN 6 b g Medicean – Frangy
A useful horse on the Flat for Luca Cumani, he took well to hurdles winning four times. He won his final two races, including at Cheltenham in April. Better ground and blinkers helped him and he did it well at Cheltenham. Unfortunately, he sustained a bit of a knock afterwards and has had a break since. If he switches off, he could stay two and a half miles. It won't be easy off 139 but I hope he will continue to give a good account of himself in handicap hurdles.

GABRIAL THE GREAT (IRE) 5 b g Montjeu (IRE) – Bayourida (USA)
Another we bought out of Luca Cumani's yard at the Tattersalls October Sales last year. He was rated 93 on the Flat and is a horse with a big engine. Runner-up on his hurdles debut at Aintree in December, he has appreciated racing on better ground during the spring/summer winning three times very easily. We fitted him with a hood at Perth in early July and he made all and won by 46 lengths. He returned to the same track the following month but could only finish fifth in the Summer Hurdle. A 17hh son of Montjeu, he will jump fences in time and could be an exciting chaser one day.

GO CONQUER (IRE) 5 b g Arcadio (GER) – Ballinamona Wish (IRE)
He failed to complete in either of his Irish points but was holding every chance when departing on both occasions. We purchased him at the Cheltenham January Sale and he made all to win a bumper at Carlisle in the spring. The new hurdles track at Carlisle didn't suit him because it is very sharp but he still won well. A galloper, he will be aimed at two and a half mile novice hurdles. I think he is a nice horse by a good stallion.

GREENSALT (IRE) 6 b g Milan – Garden City (IRE)
A full brother to Raya Star, I can't believe he hasn't won a race yet. He hasn't finished out of the first three in all seven career starts. We have operated on his wind and he is every inch a chaser in the making. Rated 110 over hurdles, we will aim him at a novices' handicap chase. I have taken some heart from the fact Ballabriggs didn't win over hurdles, prior to going chasing.

HESTER FLEMEN (IRE) 6 ch m Flemensfirth (USA) – Hester Hall (IRE)
She is a massive mare we acquired at the Cheltenham Festival Sale in March. Trained in Ireland by Aidan Fitzgerald, she finished second on her debut in a point-to-point but improved a lot to win next time by a distance. She looks a lovely mare.

HILLS OF DUBAI (IRE) 5 ch g Dubai Destination (USA) – Mowazana (IRE)
A nice horse who won his only Irish point for Paul Cashman but was forced to miss the whole of last season due to a pelvic injury. He is fine now and is a smashing big horse who is likely to run in a bumper.

I NEED GOLD (IRE) 6 b g Gold Well – Coola Cross (IRE)
A dual winner over hurdles last season, he loves soft ground and stays all day. We purposely didn't over race him last time because his future lies over fences. I think he will make a nice staying northern novice chaser this winter. He wants three miles plus.

JONNY EAGER (IRE) 5 b g Craigsteel – Dishy (IRE)
From the family of Fiendish Flame and Will Be Done, I know his pedigree very well. A faller on his debut in an Irish point, he won by twelve lengths next time and looks an interesting prospect.

KALANISI GLEN (IRE) 4 br g Kalanisi (IRE) – Glen Ten (IRE)
A half-brother to Clondaw Draft, he ran in two Irish points for Colin Bowe. Fourth on his debut, he then finished second before we bought him at the Goffs Punchestown Sale in early May. He is another who will run in a bumper before going hurdling.

KATACHENKO (IRE) 5 b g Kutub (IRE) – Karalee (IRE)
Bought at the Cheltenham November Sale, he won twice over hurdles at Musselburgh and Perth. Even though he has won on soft, I think he appreciates nicer ground. His future lies over fences and he will be going novice chasing this season. We will start him off over two miles but he stays further.

KINGS BANDIT (IRE) 6 b g King's Theatre (IRE) – Gentle Lady (IRE)
He has developed into a useful horse winning all three of his starts over hurdles and carrying penalties to victory. He has a tendency to hang a bit, which we are hoping is due to immaturity. We haven't made any plans but there must be every chance he will be going chasing soon.

KONIG DAX (GER) 4 b g Saddex – Konigin Shuttle (GER)
A winner on the Flat and over hurdles in France, we bought him at the Arqana Sale in July. A very attractive horse, he was an impressive five lengths winner at Saint Malo in May and is an exciting prospect for novice hurdles.

KRUZHLININ (GER) 7 ch g Sholokhov (IRE) – Karuma (GER)
He enjoyed a good season winning twice at Kelso, including the Champion Chase in December. I thought he ran well in the Grand National because I wasn't sure he would stay the trip. He got behind after Becher's second time around but then stayed on to finish tenth. Still a young horse, there is every chance he will run in the Becher Chase and I am sure he will run again at Kelso at some stage because his owners live locally.

LOUGH DERG WALK (IRE) 5 b g Turtle Island (IRE) – Whispers In Moscow (IRE)
Previously trained by Denis Murphy, he looks a solid, hard knocking Irish pointer. A winner on his final start in April, we bought him less than a fortnight later at the Brightwells Sale at Cheltenham. He could run in a bumper before going hurdling.

MAHLER AND ME (IRE) 4 ch g Mahler – Tisindabreedin (IRE)
We also bought him at the Cheltenham April Sale. A twelve lengths winner of his only Irish point-to-point for Joseph Ryan, he looks an interesting prospect.

MAHLER LAD (IRE) 4 b g Mahler – Sister Merenda (IRE)
A smashing big horse, he is one of two ex-pointers by Mahler we bought during the spring. He won his only race for Colin Bowe on soft/heavy ground and looks a lovely horse.

MASTER DEE (IRE) 5 b g King's Theatre (IRE) – Miss Lauren Dee (IRE)
A nice horse who did nothing wrong last season winning a bumper at Sedgefield and being placed twice over hurdles. He is the type to keep on improving and I will be disappointed if he doesn't win races over hurdles. He will stay further than two miles as well.

MONBEG DOLLY (IRE) 4 ch f Flemensfirth (USA) – Laughing Lesa (IRE)
Placed in two of her three point-to-points for Sean Doyle, we purchased her relatively cheaply at the Doncaster May Sales. Sean couldn't believe she hadn't won and she looks a nice filly.

OFF THE CUFF 3 b g Zamindar (USA) – Trellis Bay
A well bred three year old we bought at the Newmarket July Sales. A half-brother to Bellamy Cay, he is from a good family and is ex-Juddmonte. We have gelded him and I think he is one for junior bumpers in the Autumn.

OPERATING (IRE) 7 b g Milan – Seymourswift
A lovely horse we bought out of Jessica Harrington's yard at the Doncaster May Sale. Twice a winner over fences, including at the Punchestown Festival in the spring, it won't be easy trying to improve him but he is a very nice horse to train. Two and a half miles suits him but I don't see why he won't stay further. He could even be an Aintree horse one day.

OUR ROBIN (IRE) 4 b g Robin Des Champs (FR) – Palm Lake (IRE)
A four lengths winner of his only Irish point, we bought him at the Punchestown Festival Sale in early May. He looks a smashing horse and we will start him off in a bumper before going hurdling.

PALERMO DON 4 b g Beat Hollow – Kristal Bridge
A grand horse and a half-brother to Overturn. Much more relaxed than his brother, he was still very green last season and it wasn't ideal making the running on him at Haydock last time. However, he still won in good style and we will try and win another bumper before going hurdling. He isn't short of speed and will stick to two miles.

PLAN AGAIN (IRE) 7 b g Gamut (IRE) – Niamh's Leader (IRE)
Twice a winner over hurdles at Kelso and Cartmel, he is a bit delicate but is a likeable horse. A strong traveller, he enjoys top of the ground and he could go novice chasing in September.

SALTO CHISCO (IRE) 6 b g Presenting – Dato Fairy (IRE)
His season was curtailed, due to a fractured pelvis, but I hope that has been sorted out. Not short of ability, he finished second at Sedgefield in November and has plenty of speed. We will keep him to two miles for the time being because he is inclined to race keenly.

SEALOUS SCOUT (IRE) 6 b g Old Vic – Hirayna
He turned the corner during the spring, winning twice at Kelso and Hexham. He stays and jumps well and the plan is to send him novice chasing.

SILVER GENT (IRE) 6 gr g Milan – All's Rosey (IRE)
A winning Irish pointer, I think he will make a good northern novice chaser. He has a likeable attitude and he won twice over hurdles during the spring at Perth and Kelso. He has a sensible mark and I think he will improve again over fences.

SIR MANGAN (IRE) 6 b g Darsi (FR) – Lady Pep (IRE)
He won over hurdles at Sedgefield in January but had some tough races either side of that. We have given him a good summer break and he ought to have benefited from it. He will be going novice chasing over three miles plus.

STARCHITECT (IRE) 3 b g Sea The Stars (IRE) – Humilis (IRE)
By the sire of the moment, he is an exciting prospect for juvenile hurdles. Trained on the Flat by Eddie Lynam, we bought him at the Newmarket July Sales. He has only raced four times and finished second behind Table Rock (won three times since including at Listed level and is rated 110) in a ten furlongs maiden at the Curragh in May. A big, rangy, raw horse, he handles soft ground and is not a typical Flat horse. Still immature, we have schooled him over hurdles and he jumps very well.

STONEBROOK (IRE) 6 b g Flemensfirth (USA) – Boberelle (IRE)
He is a grand horse who won two bumpers and twice over hurdles last season. He was in the process of running well at Aintree when being badly hampered at the second last. The race was still to develop but A.P.(McCoy) was happy with him at the time. He has had a good break since and we will see what J.P. (McManus) wants to do. I would imagine he will stay over hurdles for the time being. I don't think he will have any trouble staying two and a half miles.

SUBTLE GREY (IRE) 5 gr g Subtle Power (IRE) – Milltown Rose (IRE)
A fine big horse, he finished a close second behind the aforementioned Lough Derg Walk before winning his final Irish point. Purchased at the Doncaster Spring Sale, he has plenty of experience and has a nice way of going.

SUPREME ASSET (IRE) 6 b g Beneficial – Hollygrove Supreme (IRE)
Very consistent, he is a funny horse because he doesn't find a lot off the bridle. I am hoping it is due to immaturity. If he strengthens up and matures, he could be a nice horse. Quite a nervy sort, we have kept him largely to two miles but he stays further.

SYDNEY PAGET (IRE) 7 b g Flemensfirth (USA) – Shuil Aoibhinn (IRE)
He won on his reappearance at Haydock but never reproduced the same form in his subsequent runs. The handicapper raised him thirteen pounds and it made it much tougher. He had a setback towards the end of the season and therefore won't be running early. However, he wants soft ground and we will be aiming him at the decent staying handicap chases.

TAKE THE CASH (IRE) 5 b g Cloudings (IRE) – Taking My Time (IRE)
Runner-up in his only Irish point, we bought him at the Cheltenham November Sale. He won over hurdles at Sedgefield in March but wasn't suited by the conditions next time at Bangor. A horse with a good attitude, he will jump fences and could be one for a novices' handicap chase over two and a half miles.

THE LAST SAMURI (IRE) 6 ch g Flemensfirth (USA) – Howaboutthis (IRE)
He is a nice horse who won three times over hurdles last season. Very nervous early on, he grew up as the season progressed. We purposely didn't over race him but let him take his chance at Aintree in the Grade 1 Sefton Novices' Hurdle. However, things didn't happen for him after we decided to ride him quietly. He stays well and I think he will make a lovely staying novice chaser this winter.

THEATRICAL STYLE (IRE) 5 b g Alhaarth (IRE) – Little Theatre (IRE)

He is not over big and a bit delicate but he has won both his bumpers since joining us. Despite not enjoying the run of the race, he still won at Perth in July. Still green, he will go hurdling and isn't short of speed.

TONVADOSA 6 b m Flemensfirth (USA) – Sleepless Eye

A useful mare who is very effective on soft/heavy ground. Twice a winner over hurdles, she ran well on her final start at Perth finishing third in the Future Champions Novices' Hurdle over three miles. I am keen to send her chasing and I am expecting her to do well in mares' only novice chases over two and a half miles plus.

VITAL EVIDENCE (USA) 4 b g Empire Maker (USA) – Promising Lead

A nice horse we purchased out of Sir Michael Stoute's yard at the Newmarket July Sale. Rated 89 on the Flat, he won twice over ten furlongs, including a heavy ground success at Windsor last year. Sir Michael recommended him and he has the build of a jumper. He has settled in well and has been schooling nicely. He will go novice hurdling in October.

VOLCANIC (FR) 5 b g Al Namix (FR) – Queen of Rock (FR)

He is a grand horse who has won three out of four for us since arriving from France. His only defeat came at Hexham and A.P. (McCoy) said he was never travelling. However, he has won twice since at Bangor and Cartmel and will be going novice chasing this season.

WESTEND STAR (IRE) 5 b g Old Vic – Camlin Rose (IRE)

A lovely horse we bought at the Cheltenham Festival Sale in March. He raced twice in Irish points winning impressively on the second occasion. I think he is a very nice horse who will run in a bumper.

WHATDOESTHEFOXSAY (IRE) 5 ch m Vinnie Roe (IRE) – She's The One (IRE)

Bought cheaply at the Newbury March Sale, she has run well in a couple of bumpers. A winner at Bangor, she finished second next time at Market Rasen. Only small, she is a smashing mare who has schooled well over hurdles. There are plenty of opportunities for her in mares' novice hurdles.

WHITSUNDAYS (IRE) 5 b g Kutub (IRE) – Urdite's Vic (IRE)

He ran twice in Irish points and, having finished third on his debut, he won next time by fifteen lengths. The form looks strong with the runner-up Vayland subsequently winning a bumper at Hexham by twenty six lengths for Stuart Crawford (later sold to David Pipe for €65,000).

WILCOS MO CHARA (IRE) 6 b g Oscar (IRE) – She's A Venture (IRE)

He won his final point-to-point before we bought him and he was an eleven lengths winner of a bumper at Musselburgh in November. Forced to miss the rest of the season due to a fracture, he is fine now and may have another run in a bumper before going hurdling. He isn't over big but I hope he will make a nice novice hurdler over two and two and a half miles.

TRAINER'S HORSE TO FOLLOW: WESTEND STAR

Paul NICHOLLS

Stables: Manor Farm Stables, Ditcheat, Somerset.
2013/2014: 118 Winners / 587 Runners 20% Prize-Money £2,469,892
www.paulnichollsracing.com

ABIDJAN (FR) 4 b g Alberto Giacometti (IRE) – Kundera (FR)
A big backward horse, he raced twice in France winning a bumper in August last year. He will be going novice hurdling.

AL FEROF (FR) 9 gr g Dom Alco (FR) – Maralta (FR)
He won the Grade 2 Amlin Chase at Ascot before finishing third in the King George at Kempton. He wasn't right during the spring and has had a good break since. His owner John Hales is keen to have another crack at the King George. He didn't get home over three miles in the Aon Chase at Newbury but it was desperate ground and we are hoping he will stay on better ground. Races like the Amlin Chase at Ascot (22nd November), once again, or the Peterborough Chase at Huntingdon (7th December) are possible starting points.

ALBAHAR (FR) 3 gr g Dark Angel (IRE) – Downland (USA)
Twice a winner on the Flat in France, including at Deauville in July. Fourth in Listed company at Toulouse on his previous start, he is a nice prospect for juvenile hurdles.

ALCALA (FR) 4 gr g Turgeon (USA) – Pail Mel (FR)
A bumper winner in France when trained by Guillaume Macaire, he also finished second at Auteuil prior to joining us in the Autumn. He ran well in the Adonis Hurdle at Kempton on his only start for us and we purposely put him away after that. A big scopey horse, he has done well during the summer and I like him. He will continue in novice hurdles.

ALDOPICGROS (FR) 4 b g Tirwanako (FR) – In'Challha (FR)
He came good during the spring winning three times over hurdles Wincanton (twice) and Newbury. Previously owned by Million-in-Million, he went through the sales ring at Doncaster in May and J.P.McManus bought him and kindly sent him back to us. A progressive horse, he will be going over fences and I hope he will make a nice novice chaser.

ALL SET TO GO (IRE) 3 gr g Verglas (IRE) – Firecrest (IRE)
A nice horse who had some good form on the Flat for Andy Oliver in Ireland. He finished third in the Group 3 Ballysax Stakes at Navan on his final run before we bought him. We gelded him and have given him plenty of time. He has schooled well and is hopefully a nice prospect for novice hurdles.

ALL YOURS (FR) 3 ch g Halling (USA) – Fontaine Riant (FR)
A half-brother to Lac Fontana, he only raced once on the Flat in France finishing fourth at Chantilly in April over a mile and a half. We have gelded him and he has been schooled and is ready to go novice hurdling.

AMANTO (GER) 4 b g Medicean – Amore (GER)
He won on the Flat at Cologne last year and was placed at Baden Baden in May before joining us. My daughter Megan rode him in the Ladies Derby at Newbury in August and he was only beaten a neck. He will go novice hurdling.

ANATOL (FR) 4 b g Apsis – Teresa Moriniere
He is a very nice horse, who had a good level of form in France, winning twice over hurdles for Guillaume Macaire. He beat Geluroni at Toulouse, who won his subsequent four starts. A lovely big strapping horse, he may have another run over hurdles before going chasing.

ANNALULU (IRE) 3 b f Hurricane Run (IRE) – Louve De Saron (FR)
She won two of her six races on the Flat for Jean-Claude Rouget, including over an extended one mile five at Deauville in July. We bought her soon afterwards at the Arqana Sale in France and we will be looking towards mares' juvenile hurdles for her.

ANTARTICA DE THAIX (FR) 4 gr f Dom Alco (FR) – Nouca De Thaix (FR)
Runner-up in her only start at Vichy in July, she looks a nice filly who could run in a mares' bumper before going novice hurdling.

ARENICE ET PICTONS (FR) 4 b g Honolulu (IRE) – Quenice Des Pictons (FR)
Third on his only run over hurdles at Auteuil for Yannick Fouin in April, the race was won by the aforementioned Geluroni. Very much a chaser in the making, he will spend this season in novice hurdles.

ARPEGE D'ALENE (FR) 4 gr g Dom Alco (FR) – Joliette D'Alene (FR)
A big backward gelding, he is a half-brother to the Hennessy Gold Cup winner Triolo D'Alene. Third in a bumper at Deauville in December for Marcel Rolland, he will be going straight over hurdles.

ART MAURESQUE (FR) 4 b g Policy Maker (IRE) – Modeva (FR)
A three times winner over hurdles in France, I was slightly disappointed with him last season. Well held at Cheltenham in November, he ran OK at Ascot next time but he was in need of a break. We have given him a good summer holiday and he will be aimed at handicap hurdles this season.

AS DE MEE (FR) 4 b or br g Kapgarde (FR) – Koeur De Mee (FR)
He won a bumper in France before we bought him at the Arqana Sale in November. Quite keen and buzzy when he first arrived, he finished fourth in a 'jumpers bumper' at Kempton in February. We have given him plenty of time since and I think he will be a really nice novice hurdler this season.

BALLYCOE 5 b g Norse Dancer (IRE) – Lizzy Lamb
A big scopey individual, he won an Irish point-to-point on his second start and he will be going novice hurdling. I think he will want a trip.

BE DARLING (FR) 3 gr g Dom Alco (FR) – Quinine (FR)
A lovely, unraced gelding owned by John Hales, he is only a three year old but we will be looking towards a bumper before going hurdling.

BENVOLIO (IRE) 7 b g Beneficial – Coumeenoole Lady
A dual winner over fences last season at Newbury and Haydock, his first target is the Badger Ales Chase at Wincanton (8th November). He will run there first time out.

BLACK RIVER (FR) 5 b g Secret Singer (FR) – Love River (FR)
He beat Vautour over hurdles at Auteuil when trained by Guy Cherel but took a bit of time to acclimatise when he joined us last season. A chaser in the making, he will be going back over fences at some stage but may have another run over hurdles beforehand.

BLACK THUNDER (FR) 7 bl g Malinas (GER) – Blackmika (FR)
He had a good season over fences winning three times, including a Grade 2 novice chase at Lingfield before Christmas. He was still travelling OK when falling in the RSA Chase. Best fresh, he could go to Down Royal for the James Nicholson Champion Chase (1st November).

BROTHER DU BERLAIS (FR) 5 b or br g Saint Des Saints (FR) – King's Daughter (FR)
A winner over hurdles at Auteuil for Robert Collet, I was very pleased with him last year. He finished second at Wincanton and we were preparing him for the EBF Final at Sandown but he sustained a cut and was forced to miss the race. However, he returned at Ayr's Scottish National meeting and won in good style. Rated 139, he could have another run over hurdles before going chasing. I am hoping he will make a very nice chaser.

BURY PARADE (IRE) 8 br g Overbury (IRE) – Alexandra Parade (IRE)
He is not without his quirks but he has plenty of ability and won twice last season at Kempton and Ascot. Runner-up in the Betbright Chase, I think he is suited by trips short of three miles and we will be looking towards Graduation Chases.

CAID DU BERLAIS (FR) 5 b g Westerner – Kenza Du Berlais (FR)
Seventh in the Galway Plate during the summer, he didn't stay and is at his best over two and a half miles. He won over fences at Exeter last season and also ran very well in the Martin Pipe Conditional Jockeys' Hurdle at the Festival, plus he finished a neck second at Aintree in another valuable handicap hurdle. There is a newly formed Intermediate Chase at Newton Abbot (10th October), which is a possible target and we will have a look at the Graduation chases for him, too.

CALIPTO (FR) 4 b g Califet (FR) – Peutiot (FR)
A horse I like a lot, he finished second on his only start over hurdles for Guy Cherel before we bought him. He won twice at Newbury before finishing an unlucky fourth in the Triumph Hurdle when the leather strap broke. We probably should have made more use of him at Aintree but he still ran well in third. He has done well for a summer break and he will continue over hurdles for the time being. It is possible he could go to Auteuil for the Grade 1 four year old hurdle over two and a half miles in November, which we won last year with Ptit Zig. Otherwise races like the Elite Hurdle at Wincanton (8th November) or the Greatwood Hurdle at Cheltenham (16th November) are options. He will have no trouble staying two and a half miles but he isn't short of speed.

CEASAR MILAN (IRE) 6 br g Milan – Standfast (IRE)
Twice a winner over hurdles at Taunton, he will be going novice chasing. He likes soft ground and will be running over two and a half miles plus.

CHARTBREAKER (FR) 3 b g Shirocco (GER) – Caucasienne (FR)
Previously trained in Germany by Andreas Wohler, he won two of his four races on the Flat and had some very good form. A winner at Strasbourg on his only start as a juvenile, he won a conditions event at Compiegne in July. Prior to that, he finished fourth in a Group 2 at Cologne behind Sea The Moon, who has subsequently won the German Derby by eleven lengths. He stays well and handles soft/heavy ground and is an interesting prospect for juvenile hurdles. We have gelded him since arriving.

DO WE LIKE HIM (IRE) 4 b g Beneficial – Pattern Queen (IRE)
Still very green and backward when finishing fourth in his only bumper at Wincanton in April, he may have another run in a bumper before going hurdling.

DODGING BULLETS 6 b g Dubawi (IRE) – Nova Cyngi (USA)
He had a very good season over fences winning three times, including Grade 2 novice chases at Cheltenham and Kempton. Narrowly beaten in the Game Spirit Chase at Newbury, he finished fourth in the Arkle but was over the top by the time he ran at Aintree. Two and two and a half miles is ideal and he could start off in the Haldon Gold Cup at Exeter (4th November).

DORMELLO MO (FR) 4 b g Conillon (GER) – Neogel (USA)
A winner over hurdles in France, he won in good style at Sandown in March but was over the top next time at Newbury. He could run in the four year old hurdle at Chepstow (11th October) and then we will take it from there. Two miles suits him.

EARTHMOVES (FR) 4 b g Antarctique (IRE) – Red Rym (FR)
A half-brother to Ptit Zig, he ran in two bumpers last season winning on his debut at Wincanton before finishing third under a penalty at Taunton. He will improve enormously for those runs and ought to make a nice staying novice hurdler.

EASTER DAY (FR) 6 b g Malinas (GER) – Sainte Lea (FR)
A dual winner over fences, including at Ascot in December when beating the subsequent RSA Chase winner O'Faolains Boy, his form is very good. Unfortunately, he sustained an injury shortly afterwards, which required surgery and he hasn't run since. Back in work, he could be aimed at a Graduation Chase and we will give him an entry in the Hennessy at Newbury.

EMERGING TALENT (IRE) 5 b g Golan (IRE) – Elviria (IRE)
An exciting horse who won his only bumper at Naas in March for T.J.Nagle. Paul Barber bought him and he is a lovely, big scopey horse. He will make an awesome chaser one day but will spend this season in novice hurdles. We aren't going to rush him and anything he achieves over hurdles will be a bonus.

FAR WEST (FR) 5 b g Poliglote – Far Away Girl (FR)
I thought he would have a good season over hurdles last year but things didn't go his way. Runner-up in the Elite Hurdle, he was staying on in the *Betfair* Hurdle at Newbury when falling at the last. Disappointing in the Coral Cup, we have schooled him over fences and the plan is to go chasing. However, he could have another run over hurdles beforehand.

FULL BLAST (FR) 3 b g Khalkevi (IRE) – La Troussardiere (FR)
Third on his only run over hurdles at Enghien in March, he is a lovely horse and is likely to be one of our first runners in juvenile hurdles this season. It is possible he will run at Market Rasen (27th September) or Chepstow (11th October). A nice big horse, he has schooled well and will make a chaser.

GREAT TRY (IRE) 5 b g Scorpion (IRE) – Cherry Pie (FR)
A nice young horse who won by nine lengths on his debut in a bumper at Southwell. He will be going straight over hurdles and, having shown plenty of speed at Southwell, he will start off over two miles.

HAWKES POINT 9 b g Kayf Tara – Mandys Native (IRE)

His main target last season was the Welsh National and he ran a great race to finish second and was only beaten a head. The plan is to try and go one better and he will have one run beforehand.

HINTERLAND (FR) 6 b g Poliglote – Queen Place (FR)

He won twice over fences, including the Grade 1 Henry VIII Novices' Chase at Sandown. He was still travelling well when badly hampered and losing his rider at the fourth last in the Queen Mother Champion Chase. He bled on his final run at Aintree. We may start him off in the Tingle Creek Chase (6th December) because he likes Sandown and he goes well fresh. Otherwise, we could look at the Haldon Gold Cup and the Desert Orchid Chase at Kempton over Christmas is another option later on.

HOWLONGISAFOOT (IRE) 5 b g Beneficial – Miss Vic (IRE)

A winner over hurdles at Newton Abbot in April, he remains a novice until the end of October. Therefore we will probably run him in another hurdle before going novice chasing.

IBIS DU RHEU (FR) 3 b g Blue Bresil (FR) – Dona Du Rheu (FR)

A half-brother to Saphir Du Rheu, he is a very nice horse who was trained in France by Guillaume Macaire. Runner-up on his debut, he won next time over hurdles at Enghien. Only 16.3hh, he is a big scopey horse and very much a future chaser. We are going to mind him this season because he isn't a Triumph Hurdle horse. He is a similar model to his brother and I think he is a proper horse.

IRISH SAINT (FR) 5 b or br g Saint Des Saints (FR) – Minirose (FR)

He had a good year winning a Grade 2 handicap hurdle at Ascot by eleven lengths before finishing third in the *Betfair Hurdle* at Newbury. The plan is to send him chasing and he could start off at Chepstow (11th October) in the same novice chase Silviniaco Conti ran in a few years ago over two mile three and a half furlongs. Then, all being well, he could be one for the Rising Stars Novices' Chase at Wincanton (8th November).

IRVING 6 b g Singspiel (IRE) – Indigo Girl (GER)

He had a very good season until disappointing in the Supreme Novices' Hurdle at Cheltenham. Prior to that, he won his first four races, including Grade 2 events at Ascot and Kempton. Found to be coughing after Cheltenham, we purposely gave him a long break and he will be aimed at the good two mile hurdles. Races like the Elite Hurdle at Wincanton or Greatwood Hurdle at Cheltenham are possibilities.

IT'S A CLOSE CALL (IRE) 5 br g Scorpion (IRE) – Sherin (GER)

An expensive buy at the Derby Sales in Ireland a couple of years ago, he was an impressive winner of his only point-to-point for Richard Barber last season. Owned by Graham Roach, he is very much a chaser in the making but I hope he will develop into a nice novice hurdler in the meantime.

JUST A PAR (IRE) 7 b g Island House (IRE) – Thebrownhen (IRE)

A Grade 2 winner over fences at Newbury's Hennessy meeting, he disappointed thereafter but I think he wants a trip. With hindsight, we should have aimed him at the four miler at the Festival rather than the RSA Chase. He could be one for the Badger Ales Chase at Wincanton (8th November) and we may aim him at the Welsh National, although he might not want it too soft. It wouldn't surprise me if we gave him a Grand National entry, too.

KATGARY (FR) 4 b g Ballingarry (IRE) – Kotkira (FR)
A dual winner over hurdles in France when trained by Guillaume Macaire, he is a very nice horse who travels strongly in his races. Beaten less than a length in the Fred Winter Juvenile Hurdle at Cheltenham, he was badly hampered at the second last when Clarcam fell in front of him. Over the top when he ran at Aintree, he has plenty of speed and could start off in the four year old hurdle at Chepstow (11th October) or a week later in a similar event at Cheltenham.

KELTUS (FR) 4 gr g Keltos (FR) – Regina D'Orthe (FR)
He won over hurdles at Chepstow in the Autumn and he, too, ran well in the Fred Winter at Cheltenham finishing fourth. Ideally suited by good ground, he will go novice chasing and may reappear at Newton Abbot (29th September). He has schooled well and should make a nice chaser.

LAC FONTANA (FR) 5 b g Shirocco (GER) – Fontaine Riant (FR)
He had a fantastic second half of the season, winning the County Hurdle and a Grade 1 novice hurdle over two and a half miles at Aintree. We discovered he was suffering with ulcers but, once they were treated, he was a different horse and never looked back. I would be inclined to forget his final run at Punchestown because he had had enough by that stage. The Ascot Hurdle over two and a half miles (22nd November) could be an ideal starting point and he may stay three miles later in the year.

LAC LEMAN (GER) 3 b or br g Doyen (IRE) – Learned Lady (JPN)
Previously trained in Germany, he is another who will be going juvenile hurdling. He won a couple of times on the Flat. We have gelded him since arriving and he looks a nice prospect.

LE MERCUREY (FR) 4 b g Nickname (FR) – Feroe (FR)
A very exciting recruit from France who is officially rated 149. Very much a future chaser, he won two of his three races over hurdles at Auteuil and we may take him back there in November for the Grade 1 two and a half mile hurdle we won last year with Ptit Zig. Depending on how he fares, we could send him chasing later in the season.

LIFEBOAT MONA 4 b f Kayf Tara – Astar Love (FR)
She won her only Irish point-to-point at Fairyhouse in May when trained by Ashleigh Murphy. It is possible she will run in a bumper, otherwise she will be aimed at mares' novice hurdles.

MARRACUDJA (FR) 3 b g Martaline – Memorial (FR)
Runner-up on his debut over hurdles at Auteuil for Guy Cherel, he suffered with ulcers and disappointed on his next couple of outings. We gave him six weeks off when he first arrived and he has benefited from a break. He will go juvenile hurdling and is a fine big horse.

MORE BUCK'S (IRE) 4 ch g Presenting – Buck's Blue (FR)
Related to Big Buck's, he won a bumper on his debut at Exeter in the spring. He will improve enormously for the run and we may give him another run in a bumper before going jumping. I am expecting him to stay well over hurdles.

MR DINOSAUR (IRE) 4 ch g Robin Des Champs (FR) – Miss Generosity
A ten lengths winner of his only point-to-point at Woodford for Tom Lacey, he is a huge horse and his future lies over fences. Owned by Graham Wylie, he will spend this season over hurdles and anything he achieves will be a bonus. This time next year, he will be going chasing.

MR MOLE (IRE) 6 br g Great Pretender (IRE) – Emmylou Du Berlais (FR)

Twice a winner over fences at Warwick and Newton Abbot, I think he is crying out for a step up in trip. He could go to Newton Abbot for the new Intermediate chase (10th October). Otherwise, we will have a look at the Graduation chases and I suspect he will get an entry in the Paddy Power Gold Cup at Cheltenham in November.

OLD GUARD 3 b g Notnowcato – Dolma (FR)

A half-brother to the Group 1 winning mare Thistle Bird, he was a progressive horse on the Flat for Roger Charlton. Rated 81, he has only raced three times winning a ten furlongs maiden at Lingfield on his most recent start. We bought him in August and I am very pleased with him. He will go juvenile hurdling.

ON BLUEBERRY HILL 5 b g Flemensfirth (USA) – Mrs Malt (IRE)

A big horse, he won a bumper for Timmy Hyde, prior to us buying him in April 2013. Unfortunately, he picked up an injury and was forced to miss the whole of last season. Back in work, he will be going novice hurdling over two and a half miles plus.

ONWITHTHEPARTY 5 b g Sir Harry Lewis (USA) – Kentford Fern

A bumper winner for Charlie Swan in Ireland, we bought him at the Doncaster November Sales but he has yet to run for us. He is another who will be going novice hurdling over two and a half miles.

PEARL SWAN (FR) 6 b g Gentlewave (IRE) – Swanson (USA)

A high-class juvenile hurdler a couple of seasons ago, he missed the whole of last year. However, he is back in work and could be one for the Greatwood Hurdle at Cheltenham (16th November) and all those good two mile handicap hurdles.

PORT MELON (IRE) 6 br g Presenting – Omyn Supreme (IRE)

We aimed high with him last year and he finished third in a Grade 2 novice hurdle at Cheltenham's Paddy Power meeting. It is well documented what happened at the Festival when he ran into the rails and injured Daryl (Jacob). Only tenth at Aintree last time, I am keen to win a novice hurdle with him before going chasing. We will have a look for a suitable race at somewhere like Exeter and Wincanton.

PRESENT MAN (IRE) 4 b g Presenting – Glen's Gale (IRE)

A half-brother to Caim Hill, he is a very nice horse who finished second in his only Irish point-to-point for Eoin Doyle. Owned by Paul Barber, he is a lovely big scopey horse who will go novice hurdling.

PRESSIES GIRL (IRE) 6 b m Presenting – Leader's Hall (IRE)

A winning Irish pointer, she won a couple of races over hurdles at Chepstow and Wincanton in the spring. She is therefore a novice until the end of October. We will try and win another before aiming her at a handicap hurdle or go chasing.

PTIT ZIG (FR) 5 b g Great Pretender (IRE) – Red Rym (FR)

A Grade 1 winner at Auteuil in November, he ran a great race under top weight in the Ladbroke Hurdle at Ascot finishing second. Sixth in the Champion Hurdle and fourth in the Aintree Hurdle, he will go over fences this season. He ought to be an exciting chaser and we will be looking to start him off over two miles.

RAINY CITY (IRE) 4 b g Kalanisi (IRE) – Erintante (IRE)
A half-brother to Theatre Guide, we bought him as a three year old at Doncaster Sales and he finished fifth in a couple of bumpers at Kempton and Newbury, including in the DBS Sales event at the latter venue. He is one to look out for in novice hurdles this season.

ROB ROBIN 4 b g Robin Des Champs (FR) – Ashwell Lady (IRE)
Bought at the Newbury Hennessy Sale in November, he is a very nice unraced horse who will start off in a bumper.

ROCK ON OSCAR (IRE) 4 b g Oscar (IRE) – Brogeen Lady (IRE)
A very nice former English pointer, who bolted up on his only start at Littlewindsor for Jack Barber. I don't know what he beat but he couldn't have won any easier. He is a big, scopey horse who will go novice hurdling.

ROCKY CREEK (IRE) 8 b g Dr Massini (IRE) – Kissantell (IRE)
He ran three very good races last season in the Hennessy, Argento and Grand National. However, on all three occasions, he didn't quite finish off his races. We have therefore operated on his breathing and I hope that will make a difference. If it does, then we will be in business. The Grand National is his main target and he will start off in the Hennessy, once again.

ROLLING ACES (IRE) 8 b g Whitmore's Conn (USA) – Pay Roll (IRE)
He won the Grade 2 chase at Down Royal in November and returned to form towards the end of the season at Aintree with an excellent run in the Grade 1 Melling Chase finishing second. Ideally suited by a flat track, he doesn't really handle soft ground so we are hoping conditions will be in his favour in the Old Roan Chase (25th Aintree).

ROTHMAN (FR) 4 b g Michel Georges – Bravecentadj (FR)
A winner over hurdles at Pau in France, he was very disappointing on his only run for us at Newton Abbot in April. However, he was extremely light when he came over and I would be inclined to put a line through the run. We have given him a long break and we will probably run him in a handicap hurdle before thinking about going chasing.

SALUBRIOUS (IRE) 7 b g Beneficial – Who Tells Jan
The plan last season was to send him chasing but his schooling didn't go as we hoped so we kept him over hurdles. Despite not winning, he ran some very good races, including when second in the Relkeel and Long Walk Hurdles at Cheltenham and Ascot respectively. He stays three miles but I think two mile six is ideal for him. The intention is to go novice chasing this time.

SAM WINNER (FR) 7 b g Okawango (USA) – Noche (IRE)
A horse I have always liked, we should have run him in the National Hunt Chase at the Festival even though he ran creditably in fifth in the RSA Chase. The old track at Cheltenham is too sharp for him. Over the top when contesting the Scottish National, he is rated 147 and we may have a look at one of the Graduation chases for him. Better going left-handed, it is possible we will give him an entry in the Hennessy, too.

SAN BENEDETO (FR) 3 ch g Layman (USA) – Cinco Baidy (FR)
He is a nice juvenile hurdle prospect who was placed a couple of times on the Flat in France. He also finished second on his only run over hurdles at Auteuil in late April. We have schooled him and he is a very good jumper.

SAPHIR DU RHEU (FR) 5 gr g Al Namix (FR) – Dona Du Rheu (FR)

A very exciting prospect, who we have minded so far during his career. He needed his first run last season at Sandown but he didn't look back thereafter winning at Sandown before following up in the Lanzarote Hurdle at Kempton and the Welsh Champion Hurdle at Ffos Las. He beat the subsequent Coral Cup and Grade 1 winner Whisper, conceding six pounds, on the latter occasion. He was ready for a break when only fourth in the National Spirit Hurdle at Fontwell on his final start. A huge horse, he has done very well during the summer and looks like Denman now – he is a tank. The original plan was to go straight over fences but we may have a look at the Long Distance Hurdle at Newbury's Hennessy meeting (29th November), He is only five and I am conscious of that. However, I am not ruling out chasing this season. I need to sit down with Andy (Stewart) and discuss it. I don't think he will have any trouble staying three miles.

SHE'S DA ONE (IRE) 5 b m Presenting – Leader's Hall (IRE)

A full-sister to Pressies Girl, she won her only Irish point for Daniel Murphy before we bought her at the Goffs Punchestown Sale in May. In all likelihood, she will run in a mares' bumper before going hurdling.

SILSOL (GER) 5 b g Soldier Hollow – Silveria (GER)

Very consistent, he did well last season winning twice at Ayr and Newton Abbot and remains a novice until the end of October. Rated 144, the Persian War Novices' Hurdle at Chepstow (25th October) is a possible target. We then have the option of running in handicap hurdles or going chasing. Two and a half is his trip.

SILVINIACO CONTI (FR) 8 ch g Dom Alco (FR) – Gazelle Lulu (FR)

He had a fantastic season winning the King George at Kempton and Betfred Bowl at Aintree. Despite running very well in the Gold Cup and winning at Aintree, I don't think he was at his best on either occasion. I thought he would win the Gold Cup jumping the last but he didn't gallop all the way to the line. I have been pleased with him during the summer and the plan is to start him off in the Charlie Hall Chase at Wetherby (1st November), which he won a couple of years ago. Last year, he wasn't fit enough in the *Betfair* Chase, so we will give him a run beforehand this time. Therefore his programme will be Charlie Hall, *Betfair* Chase, King George and Gold Cup.

SIMON SQUIRREL (IRE) 4 b g Robin Des Champs (FR) – Misty Heather (IRE)

Another new arrival, he looks a nice horse who won a bumper at Chepstow for Charlie Brooks in the spring. From the family of Rock On Ruby, he is a big, scopey horse who will be running in novice hurdles this season.

SOLAR IMPULSE (FR) 4 b g Westerner – Moon Glow (FR)

Ex-French he won over hurdles at Auteuil, prior to joining us, and he ran well in the Adonis Hurdle at Kempton finishing third before winning at Chepstow on his final start. He has been schooled over fences, he jumps well and will be running in a novice chase early on.

SOUTHFIELD THEATRE (IRE) 6 b g King's Theatre (IRE) – Chamoss Royale (FR)

A hugely exciting horse, I love him and I think he will develop into an awesome chaser. Only beaten a nose in the Pertemps Final at the Cheltenham Festival, he was given a very good ride by Sam (Twiston-Davies) to win a Listed hurdle at Sandown on the final day of the season. We will probably start him off over two and a half or two miles six but he stays three and we will be aiming him at the RSA Chase.

TAGRITA (IRE) 6 b m King's Theatre (IRE) – Double Dream (IRE)

She had a good season winning three times, including a Listed hurdle at Wincanton in February. Her first target is the Listed handicap hurdle at the same track (8th November) and then we will consider the Graded mares' hurdles. Already a winning pointer, we also have the option of going chasing later on.

TARA POINT 5 gr m Kayf Tara – Poppet

Another winning pointer, she looks very well. She had a few minor problems early on but bolted up in a mares' bumper at Taunton in April. We are going to aim her at the Listed mares' bumper at Cheltenham's Paddy Power meeting (15th November) before going hurdling.

THE BROCK AGAIN 4 ch g Muhtathir – Half Past Twelve (USA)

He could be an interesting one. A dual winner on the Flat in France, he was placed in his three races over hurdles before we bought him at the Arqana Sales in February. Rated 127, he could be fairly treated, although he is still a novice. We have plenty of options with him.

THE EAGLEHASLANDED (IRE) 4 b g Milan – Vallee Doree (FR)

A half-brother to Pepe Simo, he is a nice horse who won his only English point-to-point. I would imagine he will run in a bumper before going novice hurdling.

THE OUTLAW (IRE) 4 b g Presenting – Bonnie Parker (IRE)

I like him a lot, although he proved very difficult to break initially. We were keen to get a run into him and he behaved himself at Taunton and ran well in second. His first target is the Listed bumper at Cheltenham's Paddy Power meeting (16th November).

UNIONISTE (FR) 6 gr g Dom Alco (FR) – Gleep Will (FR)

I think he has Grand National written all over him. He won a Listed chase at Aintree and finished third in the Skybet Chase at Doncaster last season. However, I was disappointed with him in the spring but it was a similar story the previous season. Good fresh, he will be aimed at the decent staying chases.

URUBU D'IRLANDE (FR) 6 b g Sleeping Car (FR) – Noceane (FR)

A winning pointer and bumper horse, he missed the whole of 2013, having suffered with colic. However, I thought he ran well under a penalty on his reappearance at Taunton in May finishing second. He will go straight over hurdles in the Autumn and is a nice horse.

V NECK (IRE) 5 b g Sir Harry Lewis (USA) – Swift Settlement

Despite winning a point-to-point, he was still very green last year. Runner-up over hurdles at Plumpton and Exeter, he is still a novice but he looks on a fair mark, if we decided to run him in a handicap.

VAGO COLLONGES (FR) 5 b g Voix Du Nord (FR) – Kapucine Collonges (FR)

I like him and he is back in work having missed the whole of last season. Runner-up in a Listed bumper at Newbury, he also finished second in the Grade 2 event at Aintree on Grand National day. He will go novice hurdling and he could be a very interesting horse over two and a half miles.

VIBRATO VALTAT (FR) 5 gr g Voix Du Nord (FR) – La Tosca Valtat (FR)
Twice a winner over hurdles, he had a good season winning twice at Exeter in a Listed race and Ayr. He was also placed in the Imperial Cup and Swinton Hurdle. Rated 138, he will go chasing and I am hoping he will come back a stronger horse this season. It is possible he will have one more run over hurdles beforehand.

VICENTE (FR) 5 b g Dom Alco (FR) – Ireland (FR)
A good winner at Wincanton, he was disappointing next time at Ayr's Scottish National meeting but came back with a fibrillating heart. We have given him plenty of time since and he may have another run over hurdles before going chasing.

VIRAK (FR) 5 b g Bernebeau (FR) – Nosika D'Airy (FR)
He won a couple of times over hurdles at Taunton before finishing sixth in the Martin Pipe Conditional Jockeys' Hurdle at the Festival. He then stayed on well on his final run at Cheltenham in April and we will step him up in trip this season. The plan is for him to go chasing.

VIVALDI COLLONGES (FR) 5 b g Dom Alco (FR) – Diane Collonges (FR)
A half-brother to Cheltenham Festival winner Nenuphar Collonges, he is a nice horse who has only raced four times. An eight lengths winner over three miles at Ayr in the spring, he is another possible for the Persian War Novices' Hurdle at Chepstow because he is a novice until the end of October. Otherwise, he is likely to go novice chasing.

WONDERFUL CHARM (FR) 6 b g Poliglote – Victoria Royale (FR)
He had a good season over fences winning three times, including a couple of Grade 2 novice chases at Wincanton and Newbury. He had a minor foot injury halfway through the season and it was a struggle to get him ready for the spring. Fifth at Cheltenham in the Jewson, he ran better at Aintree finishing third over three miles. We may aim him in the Grade 2 chase at Down Royal (1st November) over two and a half miles, which we have won a few times in recent years.

ZARKANDAR (IRE) 7 b g Azamour (IRE) – Zarkasha (IRE)
He ran some very good races in defeat last year, being placed in the likes of the Ascot, International and Kingwell Hurdles. Fourth in the World Hurdle, he also finished third in a Grade 1 hurdle at Auteuil during the summer. There is every chance he will go to Wetherby for the West Yorkshire Hurdle (1st November) and we will consider taking him back to Auteuil.

> ## TRAINER'S HORSE TO FOLLOW: SAPHIR DU RHEU

David PIPE

Stables: Pond House, Nicholashayne, Wellington, Somerset.
2013/2014: 90 Winners / 591 Runners 15% Prize-Money £1,433,118
www.davidpipe.com

ALL FORCE MAJEURE (FR) 4 gr g Dom Alco (FR) – Naiade Du Moulin (FR)

I think he is one of the most backward horses I have ever run in a bumper but it didn't prevent him from winning on his debut at Worcester in May. He was on and off the bridle throughout but Tom (Scudamore) gave him a very good ride and he led close home. The penny dropped in the home straight and he rallied well to win by a neck. There should be a lot more to come from him. We have given him a break during the summer and he ought to return stronger and much more streetwise. It is possible he will have another run in a bumper before going novice hurdling. I would imagine he will require two and a half miles over jumps.

ALTERNATIF (FR) 4 b g Shaanmer (IRE) – Katerinette (FR)

An exciting new recruit we bought at the Arqana Sale in France during the summer. He won on the Flat and over hurdles but, due to the fact he won on the 27th April, he remains a novice over here this season. Third at Auteuil last time, he has some decent form and was one of the nicest horses at the sales. We had marked him down as a horse to look at, after going through the catalogue, and he is a lovely looking horse. A strong individual with plenty of scope, he has been bought by Professor Caroline Tisdall.

BALGARRY (FR) 7 ch g Ballingarry (IRE) – Marie de Motreff (FR)

Absent since finishing seventh in the Coral Cup at Cheltenham in 2012, he has only raced four times during his career but is a horse with a lot of ability. We planned to run him last season but he fractured his jaw at home and it kept him off for the whole year. An impressive winner at Newbury, prior to being sent off favourite for the Coral Cup, he didn't get home at Cheltenham. He remains an exciting prospect for both handicap hurdles and fences over two miles.

BALLYNAGOUR (IRE) 8 b g Shantou (USA) – Simply Deep (IRE)

He enjoyed a fantastic season winning the Byrne Group Plate at the Cheltenham Festival and being placed in two Grade 1 chases at Aintree and Punchestown. His bleeding problems have been well documented but he was very consistent during the spring, which is encouraging for the future. Following his run in the Paddy Power Gold Cup at Cheltenham, his owner was very patient and said it was OK to wait until the Festival before his next run. He bolted up and the manner of his success was impressive. He arguably produced even better performances at Aintree and Punchestown and it was pleasing to see him so effective over two miles at the latter track. It gives us plenty of options and I would like to try him over three miles at some stage, too. We haven't made any definite plans but we are still training him the same and won't overdo him at home.

BALTIMORE ROCK (IRE) 5 b g Tiger Hill (IRE) – La Vita E Bella (IRE)

We will see what his owner Roger Brookhouse wants to do but I would think he will have another run over hurdles before deciding whether to go chasing or not. He improved at a rapid rate of knots last season, culminating in victory in the Imperial Cup at Sandown and finishing fourth in a Grade 1 novice hurdle at Aintree. He was very good in the Imperial Cup but I think it was an improved effort at Aintree. Still growing, there should be further improvement to come and he has the size for jumping fences.

BATAVIR (FR) 5 ch g Muhtathir – Elsie (GER)

We also bought him at the Arqana Sale in France in July and he has a similar profile to Alternatif. A winner over hurdles in May, he was second at Auteuil in a handicap the following month with his best form being around two and a half miles. He is a chaser in the making but we will keep him over hurdles for the time being and see how far he can progress.

BIG OCCASION (IRE) 7 b g Sadler's Wells (USA) – Asnieres (USA)

He missed the whole of last season due to a tendon injury but, all being well, he will be back in action during the second half of the campaign. Prior to his injury, he had some very good form winning the Midlands National and finishing second in the Scottish version. While it is never good to suffer an injury, the time off won't not have done him any harm. He has put weight on and we are hoping he can resume where he left off. There is a possibility he will be given an entry in the Grand National.

BROADWAY BUFFALO (IRE) 6 ch g Broadway Flyer (USA) – Benbradagh Vard (IRE)

He ran some good races in defeat, including in the Pertemps Final at the Festival, prior to winning a decent staying handicap hurdle at Haydock in May. I thought it was a good performance because he battled all the way to the line. We then sent him chasing and he finished second at Wetherby. It wasn't an ideal race with a small field and he was probably feeling the effects of a long season, too. He will continue over fences when reappearing in the Autumn with two and a half miles plus being his trip.

CENTASIA 7 b m Presenting – Cent Prime

A big strapping mare, I still don't think we have seen the best of her. She won over hurdles at Uttoxeter in November before finishing second at Exeter. Fourth last time at Doncaster, I would imagine her owner Roger Brookhouse will be keen to send her chasing because she has the size and scope for fences.

CHIC THEATRE (IRE) 4 gr g King's Theatre (IRE) – La Reine Chic (FR)

Well bred, he is a lovely, unraced gelding we bought as a three year old at the Arqana Summer sale last year. He was close to running last season but sustained a small injury. We therefore gave him time off but he will be running later this year. We have been pleased with everything he has done at home and he has shown us plenty of ability. He will run in a bumper before going hurdling.

CLOUGHERNAGH BOY (IRE) 6 ch g Flemensfirth (IRE) – Windy Bee (IRE)

A half-brother to Wind Instrument, he won an Irish point before joining us during the spring. An out and out stayer, we were keen to get a run into him before turning him out for the summer and he won a bumper at Towcester. I think he will improve when encountering softer ground and he will be running over two and a half miles plus over hurdles this season.

DAVY DOUBT (IRE) 5 b g Kalanisi (IRE) – Trompe L'Oeil (IRE)

Another winning Irish pointer, he isn't over big but shows a good attitude. Runner-up on his first start for us in a bumper at Wincanton in January, he was disappointing next time at Taunton and never ran his race. We have given him a long break since and the plan is to run him in two mile novice hurdles to begin with. He has shown ability both on the track and at home.

DELL' ARCA (IRE) 5 b g Sholokhov (IRE) – Daisy Belle (GER)

He was a superstar last season and is a real battler. He never ran a bad race and delighted us when winning the Greatwood Hurdle at Cheltenham in November on his British debut. Runner-up in the *Betfair* Hurdle at Newbury, he also ran well in the Coral Cup at the Festival and rounded off his season with a very good third in a Grade 1 novice hurdle at Aintree on Grand National day. The manner in which he finished at Aintree suggested two and a half miles may be on the short side for him. He hit a flat spot and then ran on. Tom (Scudamore) said afterwards he is worth a try over three miles at some stage. He has summered well and, while he isn't the biggest of horses, I think he will jump fences. In all likelihood, he will have another run over hurdles and then we will decide what to do for the rest of the season.

DOCTOR HARPER (IRE) 6 b g Presenting – Supreme Dreamer (IRE)
Developed into a really decent hurdler last season, although he has always shown a lot of ability. A four times winner last term, he appreciated the step up to three miles at Aintree in the spring and won a good handicap hurdle. Even though he is not the most natural jumper of hurdles and, we haven't schooled him over fences, I think he will respect them more. I am hoping he will make a smashing staying novice chaser this season, although we may give him one more run over hurdles first.

DYNASTE (FR) 8 gr g Martaline – Bellissima De Mai (FR)
He is a very good horse and, once again, proved it last season winning the Ryanair Chase at the Festival and finishing second in the *Betfair* Chase at Haydock and at Aintree on his final start. He has raced nine times over fences and the only time he has disappointed was in the King George last season when he returned home sore. It is possible he didn't quite get home over three mile one at Aintree. Alternatively, he may have been feeling the effects of a long season. He is likely to follow a similar programme this time, although he may drop in trip at some stage. The *Betfair* Chase is certainly a possible starting point, although the outer track at Haydock puts more emphasis on stamina, which isn't ideal.

EASTER METEOR 8 b g Midnight Legend – Easter Comet
He had some very good form for Emma Lavelle and I am delighted to be training him. He is a nice horse to have in the yard and we will be aiming him at the decent two and a half mile handicap chases. Still in front when falling at the second last in the Paddy Power Gold Cup last season, there is every chance we will give him an entry in this year's race. It is, however, possible he prefers flatter tracks.

EDMUND KEAN (IRE) 7 b g Old Vic – Baliya (IRE)
Somewhat in and out last season, he won twice over fences at Leicester and Ludlow. Pulled up in the Scottish National, he didn't have the best of luck because he made a mistake and then nearly got brought down. He likes soft ground and we will be aiming him at the decent long distance handicap chases.

GEVREY CHAMBERTIN (FR) 6 gr g Dom Alco (FR) – Fee Magic (FR)
He produced a very good performance to win the Grade 3 fixed brush handicap hurdle at Haydock in November. We then decided to send him chasing and he made his fencing bow in the Reynoldstown Novices' Chase at Ascot. He stopped very quickly though having gone hard from Swinley Bottom. We felt we had nothing to lose by running him in the RSA Chase at Cheltenham and decided to change the tactics. He was running OK until making a mistake and then he was hampered by a faller and nearly got brought down. His two races over fences weren't a true reflection of his ability because he is a good jumper and I hope he will make a nice staying novice chaser this season. Two and a half to three miles is his trip.

HEATH HUNTER (IRE) 7 b g Shantou (USA) – Deep Supreme (IRE)
A dual winner at Sedgefield, he also ran well at Ascot and Haydock in his two subsequent starts. Indeed, he may have finished even closer at the former had we held on to him a bit longer. He has had one or two issues but he is tough and possesses a good attitude. Not over big, he is likely to continue over hurdles because I feel he is on a fair mark.

KATKEAU (FR) 7 b g Kotky Bleu (FR) – Levine (FR)
He deserves a change of luck having missed the whole of last season due to injury. He has only raced three times for us and was still going well at Haydock in the fixed brush hurdle race a couple of seasons ago when making a mistake three out. Narrowly beaten at Kempton during the same season, he has a good engine but hasn't enjoyed the best of fortunes since joining us. He loves soft ground.

KINGS PALACE (IRE) 6 b g King's Theatre (IRE) – Sarahs Quay (IRE)

Produced some very good performances last year winning his first three races over hurdles, including a Grade 2 event at Cheltenham in December. We then saved him for the Albert Bartlett Hurdle at the Festival but he took a heavy fall at the last when beaten. Thankfully, he was OK afterwards but it took him a while to get over it. We were hoping for a good run but he never ran his race and we know he is much better than he showed that day. The plan is to send him over fences and he should be an exciting novice chaser.

KNIGHT OF NOIR (IRE) 5 b g Winged Love (IRE) – At Dawn (IRE)

Twice a winner at Exeter and Wincanton, he is a strong traveller but doesn't want to hit the front too soon. His form looked good prior to running in the EBF Final at Sandown but he wasn't at his best there. I think there is room for further improvement and, while we have always thought he was a three miler in the making, we will keep him to shorter trips for the time being. Chasing is on the agenda following one or two more races over hurdles.

LADY OF LONGSTONE (IRE) 4 ch f Beneficial – Christdalo (IRE)

We bought her at the Derby Sales in Ireland last year and she is out of a mare my dad trained and is therefore from the family of Broadway Buffalo. She made a winning start to her career in a bumper at Worcester during the summer. It wasn't the strongest of races but she won well and is open to improvement both mentally and physically. We may give her another run in a bumper before looking towards mares' only novice hurdles. I think she will want a trip over jumps.

LEGACY GOLD (IRE) 6 b m Gold Well – Durgams Delight (IRE)

She is a decent mare who remains unexposed. Third in a Listed bumper at Cheltenham's Paddy Power meeting in November, she switched to hurdles and won three out of four. Fourth at Kempton last time, she found the ground too quick and was taken off her feet. However, she still acquitted herself well and has strengthened up during the summer. We will be looking at two and two and a half mile mares' hurdles.

MARTABOT (FR) 3 gr g Martaline – Reine De Sabot (FR)

By a good sire, we acquired him at the Arqana Sale in France in July. Runner-up over hurdles on his final start of three, he looked quite light when first arriving so we have given him a break. Still a maiden, he will be running in juvenile hurdles during the Autumn.

MINELLA SCAMP (IRE) 5 b g King's Theatre (IRE) – Forgotten Star (IRE)

A winning Irish pointer, he ran well in a decent bumper at Chepstow, despite racing keenly. Third next time at Taunton in November, he hasn't run since but I will be disappointed if there isn't more to come from him. He isn't over big but he goes nicely at home and has strengthened up since last season.

MOLO 4 b f Kalanisi (IRE) – Belle Magello (FR)

We bought her at the Derby Sale in Ireland as a three year old and she is a half-sister to Banjaxed Girl. Still very backward last season, she surprised us when making a winning debut at Uttoxeter in a bumper in March. Tom (Scudamore) gave her a reminder and she responded well and won in good style. She can only improve and we may give her another run in a bumper.

MOON RACER (IRE) 5 b g Saffron Walden (FR) – Angel's Folly

He was a big price when winning a bumper at Fairyhouse's Easter Festival for Michael Ronayne. However, he won well and we purchased him on behalf of Bryan Drew and Professor Caroline Tisdall at the Cheltenham April Sales a few days after his victory. We have given him a holiday since arriving and he is an exciting prospect. There is every chance he will run in another bumper before going hurdling.

MOUNT HAVEN (IRE) 4 b g Mountain High (IRE) – Castlehaven (IRE)
We also bought him at the Cheltenham April Sale, having finished second in his only Irish point. We were keen to get a run into him before his summer break and he won a bumper at Fontwell in June by sixteen lengths. It wasn't the greatest of races but he couldn't have won any easier. His victory didn't surprise us because he had been going nicely at home. He is another who will be going novice hurdling but we may try and find another bumper for him beforehand.

NO DICE (IRE) 5 ch g Presenting – Roxbury
I thought he ran very well in a decent bumper at Ascot in February on his only start last season. He was ready to run again during the spring but the ground dried out so we put him away and have given him a good break. He has come back in looking stronger and is capable of winning a bumper before going novice hurdling.

OUR FATHER (IRE) 8 gr g Shantou (USA) – Rosepan (IRE)
Once again, he will be aimed at the good staying handicap chases but he is becoming increasingly cute. He ran well for a long way in the Kim Muir at the Festival and the blinkers definitely helped. He has the ability and has dropped to a fair mark but he isn't the easiest to catch right.

PLEASANT COMPANY (IRE) 6 b g Presenting – Katie Flame (IRE)
A winning Irish pointer, he is a big horse whose future lies over fences. He won a bumper at Ascot in great style and then ran OK over hurdles at the same track. Only fourth at Exeter last time, he didn't run his race that day and is much better than that. He may have another run or two over hurdles but fences are very much the plan.

PRIDEOFTHECASTLE (IRE) 7 b g Waky Nao – Park's Pet (IRE)
An old fashioned chasing type, his future also lies over fences. He had a good season over hurdles last term winning at Exeter and Huntingdon. He ran with credit on his final start at Kempton but found the ground too quick. An ex-pointer, he loves the mud and will be going novice chasing this season.

RED SHERLOCK 5 ch g Shirocco (GER) – Lady Cricket (FR)
He had a very good season winning four times, including a Listed bumper at the Paddy Power meeting and a Grade 2 novice hurdle at Cheltenham in January. A horse with a good engine, he produced some really good performances. He didn't finish off his race in the Neptune Novices' Hurdle at the Festival. It was the fastest ground he had encountered against top horses and he didn't come up the hill. We have given him a break since and I hope there is a lot more to come from him. In all likelihood, he will start off in a handicap hurdle and then we will make a decision whether to continue over hurdles or go chasing.

SAIL BY THE SEA (IRE) 6 b g Heron Island (IRE) – Trajectus
He is a nice horse but the handicapper has allocated him a ridiculously high rating (141) for winning easily at Newton Abbot in April. He won a point-to-point in Ireland and his future lies over fences but we will probably give him a run over hurdles first. He didn't appear to stay two mile six at Wincanton before winning well over two mile one last time.

SEVEN NATION ARMY (IRE) 5 gr g Rock of Gibraltar (IRE) – Crepe Ginger (IRE)
A bit quirky, he has ability though and won a Listed bumper at Ascot in December. Well held at Newbury next time, he ran OK in the Grade 1 championship bumper at the Punchestown Festival. He has come back a stronger horse this time and will go novice hurdling.

SHOTAVODKA (IRE) 8 ch g Alderbrook – Another Vodka (IRE)
He is only small but he possesses a big heart. His best run came last time when winning a decent handicap chase at Haydock. Life is going to be difficult off his new mark and he was well held at Newton Abbot in a valuable handicap in August but he has been a very good horse for his owners and I am sure he will continue to pay his way. I think he is at his best over trips short of three miles.

SMILES FOR MILES (IRE) 6 b g Oscar (IRE) – Native Kin (IRE)
Placed over hurdles a few times last season, he has promised to win races but has yet to deliver. He likes cut in the ground and we are hoping a switch to fences will help. Rated 111 over hurdles, we will be looking towards a novices' handicap chase to begin with.

STANDING OVATION (IRE) 7 b g Presenting – Glittering Star (IRE)
He enjoyed a great first half of the season, winning four times and I thought he ran very well at the Cheltenham Festival finishing sixth. He has obviously climbed the weights but he ran well off 131 at the Festival and is now 129, so hopefully he will continue to be competitive off such a mark. Effective over trips ranging from two and a half to three miles, we also have the option of going back over hurdles because he is still a novice.

SUSIE SHEEP 4 ch f Robin Des Champs (FR) – Haudello (FR)
A nice big filly we bought at the Cheltenham April Sale. She won her only English point-to-point for Tom Lacey and is an interesting prospect. She is likely to start off in a bumper.

SWING BOWLER 7 b m Galileo (IRE) – Lady Cricket (FR)
Unfortunately, she is in the grip of the handicapper having run well in a number of big handicap hurdles last season. Raised three pounds for finishing fifth in the *Betfair* Hurdle at Newbury, she was then put up another six pounds for finishing fourth in the Scottish Champion Hurdle. It was frustrating and then she had had enough for the season by the time she contested the Swinton Hurdle at Haydock. She will continue in handicap and mares' hurdles.

TAJ BADALANDABAD (IRE) 4 ch g Shantou (USA) – Last Chance Lady (IRE)
He is a character but he has plenty of ability, too. Runner-up in his only point-to-point in Ireland, Gerry Hogan bought him for us and he has won both his starts in bumpers at Ffos Las since. A tough, feisty horse, he stays well and, while he isn't over big, he will hopefully win more races in novice hurdles over two and a half miles plus.

THE LIQUIDATOR 6 b g Overbury (IRE) – Alikat (IRE)
He was an impressive winner of his first two starts over hurdles, including a Grade 2 event at Cheltenham's Paddy Power meeting. However, he never recaptured the same form thereafter. I thought he ran well though in the Supreme Novices' Hurdle at the Festival, considering his preparation, and then he was far from disgraced at Punchestown. Two miles on drying ground proved too sharp for him. Indeed, he needs soft ground over the minimum trip but will be OK on good ground over two and a half miles. I think there is still improvement to come and he appears to be on a workable mark.

THE PACKAGE 11 br g Kayf Tara – Ardent Bride
Placed for the third time in the same handicap chase at the Cheltenham Festival, he ran well for a long way in the Grand National but didn't quite stay. Once again, the three mile handicap chases will be on his agenda and we are hoping for a full season with him.

TOP GAMBLE (IRE) 6 ch g Presenting – Zeferina (IRE)
He didn't have the best of luck last season. A faller at Exeter when finding the trip too far, he looked like winning at Haydock next time until coming down at the third last. Despite that, he is a decent jumper and we think he will respect fences more. We have given him a long holiday and he has the potential to develop into a lovely chaser.

UN TEMPS POUR TOUT (IRE) 5 b g Robin Des Champs (FR) – Rougedespoir (FR)
Bought at the sales in November having shown good form in France, he ran well over an inadequate trip in a Grade 2 novices' hurdle at Haydock in January on his first start for us. He then produced a very good performance to beat Cole Harden by sixteen lengths over two and a half miles at Ascot. His final run of the season was also a cracking one when finishing third off 11st 10lb in a competitive handicap at the Punchestown Festival. He is a horse with a high level of ability and hopefully he will have another exciting season. I would expect him to start off in another handicap hurdle and I think he will improve again when tackling three miles for the first time.

VAYLAND 5 ch g Generous (IRE) – Dotandadash (IRE)
Runner-up in an Irish point, he won a bumper at Hexham by twenty six lengths in June for Stuart Crawford. We bought him later that month at the sales in Ireland and he looks a nice individual. Richard Johnson rode him at Hexham and liked him. It is early days to be making plans but he could run in another bumper before going hurdling.

VAZARO DELAFAYETTE (FR) 5 bl g Robin Des Champs (FR) – Etoile Du Merze (FR)
A winning English pointer who we purchased during the spring of last year, he ran very well in a competitive bumper at Cheltenham's October meeting. Unfortunately, it was a rough race though and he got barged about. As a result, he didn't want to know in his subsequent races, including twice over hurdles. He needs to start enjoying it again, if he is going to win races.

VIEUX LION ROUGE (FR) 5 ch g Sabiango (GER) – Indecise (FR)
He won three times over hurdles at Wincanton (twice) and Sedgefield before disappointing in my father's race at the Festival. He ended his campaign with a good run though at Cheltenham in April finishing third. A decent horse over two and a half miles, he finished off well at Cheltenham and may stay further. We will probably give him another run or two over hurdles but it won't be long before he goes chasing.

VIRTUEL D'OUDON (FR) 5 b g Network (GER) – La Belle Illusion (FR)
We acquired him at the Cheltenham January Sales having won one of his four Irish points. He has done well since arriving winning a bumper at Plumpton and two of his three races over hurdles. A good jumper who stays well, he will have one run in a handicap hurdle before going novice chasing. He likes soft but also handles better ground and I think he will make a nice long distance chaser.

VOLT FACE (FR) 5 ch g Kapgarde (FR) – Jourenuit (FR)
Another who is very high in the handicap for winning a small novice hurdle at Newton Abbot in the spring. He was doing too much in his races, hence we fitted him with a hood, and it has definitely helped. Two and a half miles is probably his trip and he has the potential to improve again.

TRAINER'S HORSE TO FOLLOW: ALL FORCE MAJEURE

John QUINN

Stables: Bellwood Cottage Stables, Settrington, Malton, North Yorkshire.
2013/2014: 18 Winners / 85 Runners 21% Prize-Money £177,644
www.johnquinnracing.co.uk

ARTHURS SECRET 4 ch g Sakhee's Secret – Angry Bark (USA)
He was never right last year hence we didn't send him jumping. However, he has been in much better form on the Flat this season and the plan is to send him novice hurdling. A winner at Doncaster in March, he has schooled well and has plenty of pace for two miles over jumps.

AURORE D'ESTRUVAL (FR) 4 ch f Nickname (FR) – Option D'Estruval (FR)
She is a good mare and I was delighted with her last season. Previously trained in France by Guillaume Macaire, she only made her debut in December last year and has achieved a lot in a short space of time. An easy winner at Wetherby on her first start for us, she was narrowly beaten in the Victor Ludorum at Haydock and then we were aiming her at the Triumph Hurdle. Unfortunately, she suffered a minor niggle beforehand, which prevented her from running at the Cheltenham Festival. However, she ran a blinder at Aintree finishing fifth in the Grade 1 four year old hurdle. Despite that, the handicapper actually dropped her four pounds but she has risen another two pounds since. I think she is on a fair mark though and she will appreciate a step up to two and a half miles plus this season. Her ultimate target is the David Nicholson Mares' Hurdle at Cheltenham in March, which has been elevated to Grade 1 status. She is a very good jumper and I like her a lot. I have been pleased with her during the summer because she has done well physically. She handled good ground at Aintree but wouldn't want it quick.

BOLD CAPTAIN (IRE) 3 b g Captain Rio – Indianaca (IRE)
A lovely horse who is very genuine and I think he will make a very nice juvenile hurdler this winter. Placed a couple of times on the Flat last year, he won on his reappearance over a mile at Ripon in July before disappointing at the same track next time. We haven't schooled him yet but his dam won over hurdles so he is bred to be a jumper. He is a gritty sort who likes a bit of cut in the ground. I don't think he will have any trouble staying two miles over jumps.

CALCULATED RISK 5 ch g Motivator – Glen Rosie (IRE)
A decent horse who benefited from a step up to two and a half miles last season and won at Sedgefield on Boxing Day. He was placed on the Flat at Pontefract during the spring and, while we may give him another run or two over hurdles, I am keen to try him over fences at some stage this season. I think he will make quite a nice novice chaser.

CHIEFTAIN'S CHOICE (IRE) 5 b g King's Theatre (IRE) – Fairy Native (IRE)
He is a grand horse who I like a lot. Fourth on his debut in a bumper at Musselburgh, he won well next time at Stratford in March. He is better than he showed at Ayr on his final start and we have given him a good break since. We will keep him in the north during the first half of the season and try and win a few novice hurdles. However, I think he will come into his own during the spring. A very good jumper, he will start off over two miles because he isn't slow but he will stay further, in due course. He wouldn't want heavy ground though.

COCKNEY SPARROW 5 b m Cockney Rebel (IRE) – Compose
She is a cracking mare who enjoyed a very good season winning the Scottish Champion Hurdle and finishing second in the Fighting Fifth Hurdle at Newcastle. She will follow a similar programme, starting off with the Listed mares' hurdle at Wetherby (1st November), a race she won last season, followed by the Fighting Fifth Hurdle again. We will then give her a break because she doesn't want soft ground and bring her back for the Grade 2 mares' hurdle at Doncaster in late January. She fell in the race last year. We will skip Cheltenham this time because I don't think she handled the undulations of the track in March. Indeed, she is at her best on flat tracks or when she is meeting rising ground. We will therefore consider Aintree and Ayr in the spring.

EL BEAU (IRE) 3 ch g Camacho – River Beau (IRE)
A winning juvenile on the Flat last year, he was placed on his first three starts as a three year old, including twice at Pontefract. The ground on both occasions was quick enough for him because he wouldn't let himself down on it in the closing stages. We have schooled him and I think he will make a nice juvenile hurdler with some ease in the ground.

FORCED FAMILY FUN 4 b g Refuse To Bend (IRE) – Juniper Girl (IRE)
He is a grand horse we bought at the Newmarket Horses In Training Sale in October. Twice a winner over hurdles at Hexham and Doncaster, he also won on the Flat at Newcastle in April. We are going to give him another couple of runs on the Flat, including at Ayr's Western meeting in September, before going back over hurdles. I think he will win a nice handicap hurdle this winter with two miles being his trip. He may get further in time but he isn't slow.

L'AIGLE ROYAL (GER) 3 b g Sholokhov (IRE) – Laren (GER)
An exciting new arrival from France, he was trained by Guillaume Macaire and has shown a good level of ability. He has raced four times, winning at Nancy in May. Last time out, he finished fourth in a conditions hurdle at Clairefontaine. James Reveley rode him twice and he is a fantastic jumper. Bought by Anthony Bromley on behalf of Terry Warner, we are looking forward to running him in juvenile hurdles.

MR GALLIVANTER (IRE) 3 ch g Heliostatic (IRE) – Purepleasureseeker (IRE)
A consistent performer on the Flat, he won at Hamilton last season and has been placed four times this year. I thought he was unlucky not to win at Doncaster in July when his rider dropped his whip and then he wasn't suited by making the running at Haydock next time. He had schooled nicely prior to making a winning debut over jumps at Stratford in late August and Dougie (Costello) was impressed. There is plenty of improvement to come and he is a nice prospect for juvenile hurdles.

PEARL CASTLE (IRE) 4 b g Montjeu (IRE) – Ghurra (USA)
Bought at the Newmarket Horses In Training Sales in October, he has been a good buy winning twice over hurdles at Doncaster before running creditably at Cheltenham and Punchestown. He then won the Queen Mother's Cup at York during the summer before finishing sixth in the Galway Hurdle. Fourth in a competitive twelve furlongs handicap at York's Ebor Festival, he may have another run on the Flat before going back over hurdles. We will be aiming him at a decent handicap hurdle in the Autumn before giving him a winter break. He likes good ground and is at his best on flat tracks. We will be looking towards Aintree and Ayr during the spring. I think the Scottish Champion Hurdle could be tailormade for him because he is a horse with a bit of class and plenty of speed.

POETIC VERSE 4 gr f Byron – Nina Fontenail (FR)
She is only a small filly but she has done well this summer winning on the Flat at Doncaster and a mares' handicap hurdle at Cartmel. Fourth at Pontefract in August since, she has plenty of speed and we will aim her at two mile handicaps and mares races. She likes good ground.

RACING PULSE (IRE) 5 b g Garuda (IRE) – Jacks Sister (IRE)
A lovely horse we bought off Michael Winters in Ireland, having won a point-to-point and a bumper. He was an impressive winner on his first run for us at Newcastle before finishing third at Cheltenham on New Year's Day. I don't think he was at his best thereafter and we have given him a good holiday during the summer. In fact, I think he has really benefited from a break because he had been on the go for a long time last season. Still only five, we are going to take our time with him and I feel we will see the best of him during the second half of the season. We haven't decided whether to stay over hurdles or go chasing this season but I would be inclined to keep him over hurdles for the time being. He is a very good jumper and he will make a smashing chaser when the time comes. He has always worked like a very good horse. Indeed, prior to his run at Newcastle, his work was unbelievable. I have no doubts he is much better than he showed in his final two runs at Musselburgh and Aintree. He is a very nice horse.

RUTHERGLEN 4 b g Tiger Hill (IRE) – Hanella (IRE)
Another we purchased at the Horses In Training Sale at Newmarket last Autumn, he is an admirable horse. A three times winner over hurdles last season, his only defeat came in the Triumph Hurdle when finishing fifth. Considering his level of form, I don't think he is too badly treated off 136. He hasn't been over raced and I hope he will improve again, especially when stepped up to two and a half miles.

SWNYMOR (IRE) 5 b g Dylan Thomas (IRE) – Propaganda (IRE)
He only joined us in the spring and was an impressive winner at Chester in late May. His work had been good beforehand and I thought he would run well. He then ran a blinder at Galway in late July finishing fifth from a poor draw. There are a lot of good staying prizes on the Flat to aim him at but we are tempted to go back over hurdles with him this winter. There is no doubt he is potentially well handicapped off 129. He has enough speed for two miles and, despite views to the contrary, he doesn't want heavy ground.

TAHIRA (GER) 4 ch f Doyen (IRE) – Tennessee Queen (GER)
A three times winner on the Flat in Germany, she has been running well for us this summer, finishing second at Chester before finding the ground too quick in the John Smith's Cup and Listed Lyric Stakes at York. We have schooled her over hurdles and she jumps very nicely so we have decided to go down that route with her. I think she could be very good indeed over jumps. She is a very nice filly with plenty of speed, although she doesn't want heavy ground. If everything went to plan, she could be smart in the spring.

TARTAN TIGER (IRE) 8 ch g Flemensfirth (USA) – River Clyde (IRE)
He came back from nearly two years off this spring/summer and ran well at Hexham in June. Chasing was always going to be his job though and he will be going over fences this season. Despite two wins, hurdling was never going to bring out the best in him.

THINGS CHANGE (IRE) 6 b g Old Vic – Northwood May
I think he will make a grand novice chaser this season. Given time off last season, he has really strengthened up and he will be a different proposition jumping fences and stepping up in trip this time. I really like him and he has a very good pedigree. Bred to stay, he did well to achieve what he did over hurdles because it was always going to be a bonus. Very honest, he jumps well and it is possible he could end up in something like the four miler at the Cheltenham Festival in the spring.

VILLORESI (IRE) 5 b g Clodovil (IRE) – Villafranca (IRE)
Bought out of James Fanshawe's yard in October, he ran two good races over hurdles, including behind Splash of Ginge at Aintree in December when the ground was too soft for him. Runner-up at Wetherby in the spring, he picked up an injury soon afterwards. He looks well treated over hurdles off 119 and, if we can keep him right, he will win plenty of races both on the Flat and over jumps.

WORLD RECORD (IRE) 4 b g Choisir (AUS) – Dancing Debut
A winner on the Flat at Beverley in July, we made a mistake running him a week later at Hamilton because the race came too soon. Runner-up at Carlisle next time, he has schooled over hurdles but unfortunately fell on his jumping debut at Bangor in late August. I will be disappointed if he doesn't win races over hurdles.

ZERMATT (IRE) 5 ch g Strategic Prince – Await (IRE)
He is a smashing horse who won a bumper at Hexham on his debut. Third over hurdles behind Oscar Rock at Wetherby on his reappearance last season, he knocked himself soon afterwards, which meant he was off for a couple of months. By the time he was ready again, the season was nearly over and there was no point losing his novice status. He is a grand horse and we will be targeting National Hunt novice hurdles over two and two and a half miles.

TRAINER'S HORSE TO FOLLOW: AURORE D'ESTRUVAL

Lucinda RUSSELL

Stables: Arlary House Stables, Milnathort, Kinross, Tayside
2013/2014: 66 Winners / 521 Runners 13% Prize-Money £503,244
www.lucindarussell.com

BACK TO BRACKA (IRE) 7 b g Rudimentary (USA) – Martha's Glimpse (IRE)

A new arrival, we bought him at the Tattersalls (Ireland) August Sale. Derek Fox, who works for us, recommended him having ridden him over hurdles at Limerick in April. Previously trained by Noel Kelly, he won a bumper at Galway last season and over hurdles at Sligo in May. A strong traveller, he enjoys soft ground and, while he will continue over hurdles for the time being, he has the scope for fences and may go chasing later in the season.

BALLYBEN (IRE) 6 ch g Beneficial – I'm Maggy (NZ)

A winner over hurdles at Hexham in October, he has had four runs over fences and, while he hasn't won yet, he is on a fair mark compared to his hurdles rating. He has come in from his summer break a much stronger horse and we will aim him at novice handicap chases over three miles.

BALLYBILL (IRE) 4 ch g Presenting – Corrieann (IRE)

A lovely unraced gelding, his owners bought him at the Goffs Land Rover Sale last year. He was in training last season and we were keen to run him but he, unfortunately, threw a splint. He is fine now and going nicely at home. All being well, he will be running in a bumper in September/October.

BALLYCOOL (IRE) 7 b g Helissio (FR) – Carnoustie (USA)

An impressive winner over fences at Kelso around Christmas, we could never get him right thereafter and found he was suffering with ulcers. The plan is to run him at Uttoxeter (21st September) and take it from there. We will keep him to two miles for the time being but will be stepping him up in trip later in the season.

BOLD SIR BRIAN (IRE) 8 b g Brian Boru – Black Queen (IRE)

He missed the whole of last season having suffered a broken vertebrae. He was back in training after Christmas but we decided to give him plenty of time. Rated 152 over fences, he is a very good chaser who won the Colin Parker Memorial Chase at Carlisle and a Listed Intermediate Chase at Sandown by sixteen lengths the previous season. We haven't made any definite plans but he will be aimed at the good three mile chases. All being well, he will be back in action around November time.

CLONDAW KNIGHT (IRE) 6 b g Heron Island (IRE) – Sarah Supreme (IRE)

He jumped very well when making a winning start to his chasing career at Kelso in November. Unfortunately, the handicapper raised him twelve pounds, which made life much tougher for him. Third in his subsequent three starts, he has summered well and strengthened up. Still only six, I hope he will improve again and he seems versatile in terms of trip.

DUN BAY CREEK 3 b g Dubai Destination (USA) – Over It

A nice, unraced horse we bought at the Doncaster Sales in May. I am a big fan of junior bumpers and we will be aiming him at one in the Autumn. He gives the impression he will stay well and appreciate soft ground.

FIFTEEN KINGS (IRE) 4 b g King's Theatre (IRE) – Mistletoeandwine (IRE)

Bought at the Tattersalls Derby Sale, he is by a sire I like and achieved a good level of form in Irish points. A winner on his third start, the runner-up has won since. He doesn't look short of speed and could be one for bumpers. Only four, we aren't in a rush with him because he has the scope to make a nice chaser in time.

FIGHT AWAY BOYS (IRE) 6 ch g Vertical Speed (FR) – Say Ya Love Me (IRE)

A winning Irish pointer for Denis Murphy, we bought him at the Cheltenham December Sale. Well held in a bumper, he ran OK in a couple of novice hurdles at Kelso and we will be looking to use his rating of 104 and aim him at a novices' handicap hurdle. A tough sort, his work at home has been good.

FINAL ASSAULT (IRE) 5 b or br g Beneficial – Last Campaign (IRE)

A very consistent horse, I was delighted with him last season winning at Ayr and being placed on three other occasions. Another former Irish pointer, he will be going over fences and ought to improve as a chaser. Effective over two miles, we will be looking to step him up in trip again at some stage this winter.

GREEN FLAG (IRE) 7 b g Milan – Erin Go Brea (IRE)

We were very pleased with his first season over fences. Successful on his first three starts, he then finished second in the Grade 1 Feltham Novices' Chase at Kempton on Boxing Day. I was delighted with his run at the Cheltenham Festival finishing fourth in the Grade 3 handicap chase. We then allowed him to take his chance in the Scottish National and, while he ran well in sixth, I think it came a year too soon. He stayed the trip but it came at the end of a long season, which began in early November. The Scottish National is his long-term aim, once again, but we may consider running him in the Becher Chase at Aintree (6th December). He is a very good horse who handles decent ground but I think he prefers some cut. He appears to have improved again during the summer because he has come back in looking a different horse.

IMJOEKING (IRE) 7 b g Amilynx (FR) – Go Franky (IRE)

We operated on his wind during the spring and it has made a huge difference. Twice a winner over fences in the summer at Hexham and Perth, he was suited by the step up to two and a half miles at the latter and was very impressive. He has always been a good jumper and that will stand him in good stead if we take him to the likes of Aintree and Cheltenham in the Autumn. He handles most types of ground.

ISLAND CONFUSION (IRE) 6 b g Heron Island (IRE) – Anshan Gail (IRE)

Absent last season, due to a leg injury, he will be back in action around late November/December. A point-to-point and bumper winner, he has only raced once over hurdles but his long-term future lies over fences. He is a nice type and the time off won't have done him any harm.

ISLAND HEIGHTS (IRE) 5 b g Heron Island (IRE) – La Reina (IRE)

A winner of his only Irish point for Donnchadh Doyle, we purchased him at the Cheltenham December Sale. He is tough and honest and just the sort we like to train. An easy winner over hurdles at Ayr in March, he finished second a couple of times, too. Two and a half miles suit him and we may send him straight over fences. I think he will make an even better chaser.

IT'S HIGH TIME (IRE) 6 b g Kalanisi (IRE) – Windsor Dancer (IRE)
Previously trained by Charlie Swan, I like him a lot. Still quite backward, we and his owners have purposely taken our time with him. Only beaten half a length on his first start for us in a bumper at Musselburgh in November, he went one better next time at the same track. Eighth in the Grade 2 championship bumper at Aintree in April, he ought to make a lovely novice hurdler this season. We will probably start him off over two miles but he will have no trouble staying further in due course. Long-term, he is a chaser in the making.

ITSTIMEFORAPINT (IRE) 6 b g Portrait Gallery (IRE) – Executive Pearl (IRE)
Bought relatively cheaply at the Doncaster November Sale, he was runner-up in an Irish point for Paul Walsh. A good jumper, he was placed twice over hurdles last season but I view him as a long distance chaser in the making. He may have another run or two over hurdles but it won't be long before he is contesting novices' handicap chases.

JUST FOR PLEASURE (IRE) 4 b f Kayf Tara – Heltornic (IRE)
She is from a very good family, being out of Heltornic. She didn't totally surprise us when making a winning debut in a bumper at Newcastle in January because we thought she would stay well. Still immature and backward last year, she went quite light afterwards so we purposely gave her time off to strengthen and develop. A tough genuine filly, she has improved over the summer and is one to look forward to in mares' only novice hurdles.

KILBREE CHIEF (IRE) 6 b g Dr Massini (IRE) – Lame Excuse (IRE)
Consistent over hurdles last winter, he won at Hexham and was placed at the likes of Wetherby and Ayr. Three miles is his trip and I think he will improve again when tackling fences.

KINGSWELL THEATRE 5 b g King's Theatre (IRE) – Cresswell Native (IRE)
Bought as a three year old at the Doncaster May Sales, he is well bred and showed promise on his only start in a bumper at Ayr in the spring. Unfortunately, he fell to bits, physically, afterwards so we have given him a good break. There is no doubt he has ability and we will probably send him straight over hurdles. He has schooled well and I think he will be suited by two and a half miles.

KUMBESHWAR 7 b g Doyen (IRE) – Camp Fire (IRE)
I am delighted to be training him and I think he could be well handicapped. He is a lovely horse who has had a lot of racing but he is still only seven. I was keen to buy him at the Doncaster Sales in May and bought him on spec. However, five of our existing owners joined together to form a syndicate, which is great. Very tough, he ran well in the Haldon Gold Cup at Exeter last season off a mark of 152 but has dropped to 135 over fences since. Kelso stage a twilight fixture on the 17th September and the plan is to start him off there in either the handicap hurdle or handicap chase. They are both 0-140 which is ideal. He seems effective over two and two and a half miles.

LADY OF VERONA (IRE) 7 b m Old Vic – Innovate (IRE)
She has really got her act together over fences winning twice at Hexham and Kelso in the spring. Like her mother, she is tough and stays well. Even though her two victories came on soft ground, I think she will be even better on decent ground.

LIE FORRIT (IRE) 10 b g Subtle Power (IRE) – Ben Roseler (IRE)

He is in great form at home and we were very pleased with him last season. We exploited his favourable mark over hurdles winning at Wetherby and Kelso and finishing third in the fixed brush handicap hurdle at Haydock in November. I also thought he ran OK for a long way in the Scottish National. Only rated 128 over fences (compared with 144 over hurdles), we will try and make use of such a mark and possibly aim him at some of the veteran chases. He certainly hasn't lost his enthusiasm.

MAKE IT HAPPEN (IRE) 5 b g Saffron Walden (FR) – Kelpie (IRE)

A nice type we bought at the Doncaster May Sales this year. He raced in three Irish points for James Cregan finishing second on his most recent outing. There is every chance he will run in a bumper before being aimed at staying novice hurdles. I think three miles will be his trip eventually.

NO DEAL (IRE) 8 b g Revoque (IRE) – Noble Choice

Unbeaten in two races since joining us from Ireland, he hasn't run since January 2013 due to a stress fracture. He came back into the yard in September and, all being well, he will be running in November/December. A huge horse, his future lies over fences and I hope he will make a nice staying chaser.

NUTS N BOLTS 8 b g Marju (IRE) – Anniversary

A six lengths winner on his reappearance at Haydock in November, he will be aimed at the same race again. He is very genuine but he doesn't take a lot of racing and is best fresh. Fourth in the Grand National Trial at the same track in February, he will follow a similar programme with the Scottish National his ultimate target. He likes soft ground.

ONE FOR ARTHUR (IRE) 5 b g Milan – Nonnetia (FR)

A lovely horse who won and was placed in two Irish points for Liam Kenny. We acquired him at the Cheltenham December Sale and he finished second in a bumper at Newcastle and a novice hurdle at Kelso. I was pleased with both runs and it turned out to be a blessing in disguise that he didn't win on his latest start because he is still a novice for this season. We also found he was suffering from ulcers, which have been cleared up and he has benefited from a summer break. I think he will stay three miles in time.

PRESENT FLIGHT (IRE) 5 ch g Presenting – Grangeclare Flight (IRE)

Placed in two Irish points for Paul Cashman, his form looks strong with Free Expression subsequently winning the point-to-point bumper at the Fairyhouse Easter Festival. Runner-up in a bumper at Hexham on his first run for us in late March, he looks capable of winning a bumper before going hurdling. We are expecting him to stay well over jumps.

REVOCATION 6 b g Revoque (IRE) – Fenella

Absent since finishing fifth at Haydock in November, he sustained a leg injury and won't be running until after Christmas. Prior to that, I had been pleased with him winning over hurdles at Hexham and finishing third at Aintree. He handles soft ground and we will keep him to handicap hurdles for the time being.

RHYMERS STONE 6 b g Desideratum – Salu

He is not over big, but he had a good season winning twice over hurdles at Newcastle. He loves soft ground and is only a couple of pounds higher than his last win. We will continue to run him in two mile handicap hurdles at the likes of Newcastle and Kelso and I hope he will improve again.

SETTLEOUTOFCOURT (IRE) 8 b g Court Cave (IRE) – Ardagh Princess

Joined us last summer, he had a fantastic season winning four times over fences. He is obviously higher in the ratings now, which will make it tougher but he ran well at Bangor in August finishing second and I think he remains open to further improvement. In terms of trip and ground, he is versatile having won over two and a half and three miles and on good and heavy ground.

SEVENBALLS OF FIRE (IRE) 5 b g Milan – Leadamurraydance (IRE)

Another who ran in Irish points for Denis Murphy, he was placed twice before we bought him at the Cheltenham May Sale, having been recommended to us. I am a big fan of his sire but we haven't done a great deal with him yet. There is a possibility he will run in a bumper before going hurdling.

SPIRIT OSCAR (IRE) 6 b m Oscar (IRE) – Grange Classic (IRE)

A lovely mare who won twice over hurdles for Oliver Sherwood last season and runner-up a couple of times over fences. Bought at the Doncaster Spring Sale, she is a good jumper and we are looking forward to running her in mares' only novice chases. Trips around two and a half miles appear to suit her.

STAR DATE (IRE) 5 b g Galileo (IRE) – Play Misty For Me (IRE)

Runner-up three times over hurdles for Oliver Sherwood, he had his first run for us at Perth in July finishing fifth. We felt he was in need of a break so we will be aiming to bring him back in October/November. He has some decent form over hurdles and looks capable of winning races.

STYLISH CHAP (IRE) 4 b g New South Wales – Curragh Bawn Lass (IRE)

A nice horse we bought out of John Quinn's yard at the Doncaster Sales in May. Third on his only run in a bumper at Wetherby, I know John liked him and we may try and win a bumper before going hurdling.

TANTAMOUNT 5 b g Observatory – Cantanta

A dual winner over hurdles at Perth and Aintree, he missed the second half of the season, due to a stress fracture. However, he is OK now and we are looking forward to seeing him running again. The time off won't have done him any harm and he will continue in staying handicap hurdles. Still lightly raced, I hope there is more improvement to come.

TAP NIGHT (USA) 7 ch g Pleasant Tap (USA) – Day Mate (USA)

Runner-up in the Colin Parker Memorial Chase at Carlisle, he also ran well at Cheltenham's Trials meeting in January. It was tough for him competing in those competitive handicaps and the plan is to step him up in trip this season. We will see where J.P. (McManus) and Frank Berry want him to run and go from there. I think he will have benefited from a good summer break.

THE COBBLER SWAYNE (IRE) 5 b g Milan – Turtle Lamp (IRE)
A very nice horse who won an Irish point for Sam Curling by fifteen lengths in March. We bought him three weeks later at the Newbury Sale and he has done well during the summer. One to look forward to, he will probably run in a bumper before going novice hurdling.

THE FRIARY (IRE) 7 b g Kris Kin (USA) – Native Design (IRE)
He is not the quickest but he stays well and loves soft ground. Twice a winner at Hexham and Ayr, he will follow a similar programme. He ought to be ideal for those three and a quarter mile chases at Carlisle.

THE WAY IT WORKS (IRE) 4 b f Kalanisi (IRE) – Hamari Gold (IRE)
She is a very nice filly who I like a lot. We thought she would run well on her debut in a bumper at Perth and she kept on well to finish third. She is capable of winning a similar event and is one to look out for in mares' only novice hurdles later on.

THIS THYNE JUDE 6 gr m Silver Patriarch (IRE) – This Thyne
Homebred from the family of Dalkey Sound, she has shown ability finishing second in a bumper at Perth. However, like a lot of Silver Patriarch's she has taken a long time to come to herself and keeps running up light. We have therefore given her plenty of time and I hope she will make her mark over hurdles. She will appreciate stepping up in trip in due course.

THORPE (IRE) 4 b g Danehill Dancer (IRE) – Minkova (IRE)
Bought out of Ralph Beckett's stable at the Newmarket Horses In Training Sale last October, he was placed in all three starts over hurdles, including the Listed Scottish Triumph Hurdle at Musselburgh. We were preparing him for the Fred Winter Juvenile Hurdle at the Cheltenham Festival when he incurred a cut on his fetlock, which was frustrating. Back in training, he is still a maiden over hurdles, which is a bonus, and I will be disappointed if he can't win races.

THROTHETHATCH (IRE) 5 b g Beneficial – Castletownroche (IRE)
A lovely type, he won an Irish point for Pat Doyle before we purchased him at the Cheltenham November Sale. Still immature, he is much better than he showed in a bumper at Ayr in early January. He wasn't right afterwards, hence we gave him the rest of the season off. It is possible we will run him in another bumper before concentrating on novice hurdles.

ULTRA DU CHATELET (FR) 6 b g Network (GER) – Grandeur Royale (FR)
A winner over fences at Hexham in May, he jumps well and stays three miles thoroughly. He also enjoys soft ground and will continue to run in staying handicap chases.

VOYAGE A NEW YORK (FR) 5 b g Kapgarde (FR) – Pennsylvanie (FR)
He is a winning pointer who joined us from Tim Vaughan towards the end of last year. He won over hurdles at Carlisle and finished second a couple of times, too. A horse I like, he still has some maturing to do so we will keep him over hurdles for now. I think two and a half miles will be his trip.

TRAINER'S HORSE TO FOLLOW: FINAL ASSAULT

BROMLEY'S BEST BUYS

The *Highflyer Bloodstock* buying team, which comprises of Anthony Bromley, David Minton and Tessie Greatrex, had another great National Hunt season purchasing the winners of 50 Graded/Listed races during the 2013/2014 campaign. The pinnacle of the season was no doubt their 10 winner haul at Aintree's Grand National meeting – led by Grade 1 winners The New One, Silviniaco Conti and Whisper, plus Graded novice winners Balder Succes, Josses Hill, Lac Fontana and Uxizandre. Silviniaco Conti also won the King George VI Chase at Kempton and My Tent Or Yours landed a brace of Grade 1 hurdles, whilst former Cheltenham Gold Cup winner Bobs Worth took the Lexus Chase in Ireland at Christmas.

Bromley's Best Buys produced 31 winners in last year's *One Jump Ahead* at a strike-rate of 23%. The feature highlighted **ALDOPICGROS** (3 wins), **JOSSES HILL** (3 wins), **KILCOOLEY** (3 wins), **URBAN HYMN** (3 wins) and **VOLNAY DE THAIX** (3 wins). For the fifteenth consecutive year, Anthony Bromley has kindly put together a list of names he has bought in France and Ireland, who are set to make an impact in their new surroundings in the UK this winter.

ABRICOT DE L'OASIS (FR) 4 b g Al Namix (FR) – La Normandie (FR)
Trainer: D.McCAIN. Cholmondeley, Cheshire.
A scopey four year old APQS bred, he comes from the same source as Volcanic, who has won three races from four starts for Donald (McCain). Interestingly, they are both by Al Namix and the pair won their last start in France at the provincial course of Cluny. This fellow actually won a four year old chase on the 18th May and is therefore a novice under all codes for this season.

A DOLL IN MILAN (IRE) 4 b f Milan – Tawny Owl (IRE)
Trainer: N.A.TWISTON-DAVIES. Naunton, Gloucestershire.
A very attractive filly who ran really well in her only four year old point-to-point in Ireland in mid May. She finished a close second, despite showing signs of greenness after the final fence, becoming a bit unbalanced on the uphill run-in. Her dam is a half-sister to two smart Nigel Twiston-Davies trained horses in Frantic Tan and Irish Raptor. She may have enough speed to run in a mares' bumper in the Autumn.

ALL YOURS (FR) 3 ch g Halling (USA) – Fontaine Riant (FR)
Trainer: P.F.NICHOLLS. Ditcheat, Somerset.
This tall half-brother to the Grade 1 winning hurdler Lac Fontana was purchased soon after he had made his racecourse debut at Chantilly at the end of April. It was a maiden for debutants over twelve furlongs on soft ground and he ran with plenty of promise to finish fourth. Beaten around four lengths, the horse just behind him in fifth, Balmat, has won his maiden since and finished third in a Listed race. We hope he can develop into a useful juvenile hurdler for his owners Potensis Ltd, who are also responsible for Lac Fontana.

ANATOL (FR) 4 b g Apsis – Teresa Moriniere
Trainer: P.F.NICHOLLS. Ditcheat, Somerset.
A good looking former Guillaume Macaire trained gelding, he was massively impressive when winning his second hurdle race (his fifth start) at Toulouse in March. He easily beat into third a stablemate called Geluroni, who was making his debut that day. Subsequently, Geluroni has won his next four starts at Auteuil, including a Grade 3 and Listed four year old chase. Anatol has yet to run over fences, although the way he attacks French hurdles suggests that should not be a problem. Purchased for John De Le La Hey, who also owns Irish Saint, he should prove above average and appears more of a two miler than further.

ARENICE ET PICTONS (FR) 4 b g Honolulu (IRE) – Quenice Des Pictons (FR)
Trainer: P.F.NICHOLLS. Ditcheat, Somerset.

A rangy APQS bred, he showed plenty of promise when finishing third of fourteen in a strong four year old hurdle at Auteuil on the 9th April on his jumps debut behind the aforementioned Geluroni. The latter subsequently won three chases at Auteuil, including a Grade 3 on his latest outing and is clearly a smart four year old. This youngster had not been with trainer Yannick Fouin long before he ran and is therefore open to plenty of improvement.

ATLANTIC GOLD (IRE) 4 b or br g Robin Des Pres (FR) – Marys Isle (IRE)
Trainer: C.LONGSDON. Chipping Norton, Oxon.

There is usually quite a sizeable premium placed on winning four year old pointers from Ireland these days. However, Tessie Greatrex managed to buy four of them at the two Brightwells Spring Sales for what appeared to be really 'sensible' figures. One of them, namely Atlantic Gold, was initially led out unsold but was bought privately outside the ring to join Charlie Longsdon. He needed his first run when seven lengths fourth to Birch Hill, before stepping up on that effort to readily win his maiden point in Northern Ireland on good ground on the 10th May, quickening up well in the process. He gives the impression he may be sharp enough to win a bumper before going hurdling.

AYALOR (FR) 4 b g Khalkevi (IRE) – Physicienne
Trainer: H.FRY. Seaborough, Dorset.

Ayalor is a big jumps bred four year old who has won his only career start, a minor hurdle in the Provinces on the 6th April. He still looked green on that occasion and appears to have plenty of improvement in him. The third has won since but, due to the date of his win, he is only a novice hurdler until the 1st November, so expect him to be out running under a penalty during October.

BIRCH HILL (IRE) 4 b g Kalanisi (IRE) – Miss Compliance (IRE)
Trainer: N.J.HENDERSON. Lambourn, Berkshire.

David Minton bought this athletic son of Kalanisi at the Punchestown Festival Sale on behalf of Ronnie Bartlett to join Nicky Henderson. The Simonsig connection was strong as the Northern Irish trainer Ian Ferguson had also handled him to win his point-to-point before changing hands. Birch Hill appeared to be going well when exiting at the third last in his first point but soon made amends by easily winning at Loughbrickland on the 26th April. As discussed, the fourth Atlantic Gold won nicely next time and has joined Charlie Longsdon. Birch Hill looks like a classy addition to the Seven Barrows team for this winter.

BLACKTHORN PRINCE 4 b g Black Sam Bellamy (IRE) – Quark Top (FR)
Trainer: J.J.O'NEILL. Temple Guiting, Gloucestershire.

Purchased at the Cheltenham Festival Sale in March by David Minton on behalf of J.P.McManus, the athletic four year old posted a great debut effort in a strong looking four year old point on the 9th March. Both he and the Gigginstown House Stud owned winner Victory Mill looked high-class prospects in the manner in which they quickened up impressively over the last few fences, putting daylight between themselves and the rest of the field. He joined Jonjo O'Neill immediately after the sale but he was never likely to run during the spring/summer. I would think he will have the speed for a bumper before going hurdling.

BLAMEITALLONMYROOTS (IRE) 4 b f Turtle Island (IRE) – Makingyourmindup (IRE)
Trainer: O.M.C.SHERWOOD. Upper Lambourn, Berkshire.

She looked a good value purchase by Tessie Greatrex on behalf of Tim Syder and Oliver Sherwood early on in the Cheltenham April Sale. She cost £30,000 after winning her four year old fillies' maiden point-to-point in really gutsy style at the end of March by five lengths from a subsequent winner. Both her races came on soft/heavy ground, but her action suggests she ought to cope with better ground, too.

CANUWEST (IRE) 5 b g Westerner – High Court Action (IRE)
Trainer: N.J.HENDERSON. Lambourn, Berkshire.

David Minton bought this good looking five year old Irish point winner for Dai Walters at the Cheltenham April Sale. From the same female family as Large Action, he was vastly improved this spring on better ground, winning really well on his final outing at Inch on good ground in mid April, beating a horse called Ballycoe seven lengths into third. The latter won his next start and is now trained by Paul Nicholls so the form looks interesting and, being a five year old, he should be up to having a busier season than these other four year old ex-Irish pointers.

CHARLIE BREEKIE (IRE) 5 b g Alkaadhem – Highland Breeze (IRE)
Trainer: B.PAULING. Bourton-on-the-Water, Gloucestershire.

Tessie Greatrex found some inexpensive nuggets for Ben Pauling in his first season last year, including three times scorer Raven's Tower for £2,000 and Cadeau George for £12,000. She made a number of shrewd looking buys again for him this spring at the form horse and store sales but one I want to pick out is this fellow. He ran a cracking race to be a close second to the gambled on Simple Assignment in a Sedgefield bumper in May with the winner being bought privately to join J.P.McManus' string. I don't think this chap was expensive at £22,000 at Brightwells in late May. He was rather lean at the sales but, following a good summer's grass, I think he could be a horse to follow in National Hunt novice hurdles this winter.

CHOSEN WELL (IRE) 5 b g Well Chosen – Killmaleary Cross (IRE)
Trainer: A.KING. Wroughton, Wiltshire.

A good looking five year old with plenty of size and scope, who showed progressive form in his point-to-points this spring on both good and heavy ground. A bold jumping battler, he clocked a fast time when taking his last Irish point in early April. He should be placed to good effect by his canny trainer.

DIFFERENT GRAVEY (IRE) 4 b g High Chaparral (IRE) – Newtown Dancer (IRE)
Trainer: N.J.HENDERSON. Lambourn, Berkshire.

Exquisitely bred, this youngster was the second most expensive pointer bought by the company this year. David Minton signed for him on behalf of Richard Kelvin-Hughes and Nicky Henderson. His dam was a useful hurdler/chaser and his sire is currently proving very hot as a dual purpose stallion, including amongst others Hadrian's Approach (who won the Bet365 Gold Cup the very next day after this sale had taken place). A tall four year old, he won his only point-to-point in decisive fashion in late April on good ground and came from the same owner/ trainer that sold us the promising Clondaw Banker last November. It is possible he is a horse who will appreciate another season on his back but he is a nice prospect for hurdling this time around, nevertheless.

FULL BLAST (FR) 3 b g Khalkevi (IRE) – La Troussardiere (FR)
Trainer: P.F.NICHOLLS. Ditcheat, Somerset.

This bouncy young French juvenile hurdler showed a lot of promise in his only start – the first three year old hurdle run in Paris on the 3rd March at Enghien. He finished a close third of fourteen. The runner-up, The Saint James, then won his next two starts in Paris, including the Prix Go Ahead at Auteuil and, in doing so, placing himself very near the top of the pecking order in the French three year old hurdle division. We secured this athletic gelding shortly after his debut and he has been bought for the same Broughton Partnership for whom I purchased Taquin Du Seuil a couple of years ago.

GLADSTONE (FR) 3 br c Mizzen Mast (USA) – Bahia Gold (USA)
Trainer: W.GREATREX. Upper Lambourn, Berkshire.
A tall, good moving three year old, he was purchased at the Arqana July Sale from Jean-Claude Rouget, having won a claimer at Maisons-Laffitte (1m 7f) by an impressive four lengths towards the end of June. He had some good form prior to that in a couple of conditions events, having won his maiden over ten furlongs on the all-weather at Cagnes-sur-mer in February. He has form on various types of ground and had an official rating of 84 in France. In addition, the fact his best run was over an extended trip suggests the National Hunt game should prove lucrative for him this winter.

HARGAM (FR) 3 gr g Sinndar (IRE) – Horasana (FR)
Trainer: To be Confirmed
This is the smartest Flat three year old I have purchased so far for next year's Triumph Hurdle and he was bought for J.P.McManus. He went straight from the Aga Khan's in Chantilly to J.P.'s Martinstown Stud in Ireland, where I believe he is going to be gelded. I am not sure who will train him yet, although I expect him to be prominent in the Triumph Hurdle betting during the coming winter. Officially rated 97 on the Flat in France, he has only raced three times and has strong form with a number of subsequent Group performers. Indeed, he was only beaten half a length on his debut at Longchamp in April by Teletext (who has since finished a close third in the Group 1 Grand Prix de Paris) before narrowly beating Guardini (won the Group 3 Prix du Lys since) at the same track over twelve furlongs. Inexplicably, his trainer Alain de Royer-Dupre dropped him back three furlongs in trip for his first and only foray into black type company, finishing a never nearer fourth beaten under three lengths in a nine furlongs Listed race. He was acquired soon afterwards and I have high hopes for him.

HERITAGE WAY 5 b g Tamayuz (CAN) – Morning Caller (IRE)
Trainer: N.J.HENDERSON. Lambourn, Berkshire.
The unbeaten Heritage Way is the most expensive Million In Mind recruit for this season. He was an impressive winner of a slowly run bumper at Ayr in February beating some good yardsticks in the process, including The Unsub (won and finished second (Scottish National meeting bumper at Ayr) in two subsequent starts) and Uppertown Cave. The trainer's brother Stephen Crawford rode him with the utmost confidence that day and was gutted when an eleventh hour cut meant he had to miss the Aintree championship bumper. He was soon back in strong work and I bought him just before he was due to run again. He should do well in National Hunt novice hurdles this winter for Nicky Henderson.

HORSEHILL (IRE) 5 b g Flemensfirth (USA) – Maid For Adventure (IRE)
Trainer: O.M.C.SHERWOOD. Upper Lambourn, Berkshire.
This progressive winning five year old Irish pointer is a half-brother to the top-class Menorah. He has shown plenty of ability on heavy and good ground and looks a hardy customer who should be able to take a full winter's campaign this season.

KILCREA VALE (IRE) 4 b g Beneficial – Inflation (FR)
Trainer: N.J.HENDERSON. Lambourn, Berkshire.
The Brightwell Sales complex has been quite lucky for owner Alan Spence as I have purchased three horses from there for him and all three have won, namely Josses Hill, Big Hands Harry and Clondaw Banker. His sole 2014 purchase is this big son of Beneficial, who won his only four year old point-to-point for Co.Tipperary trainer Pat Doyle in May. Pat has sold me the likes of Tataniano and Royal Boy previously and we are hopeful this horse develops into a decent chaser over the next season or two.

L'AIGLE ROYAL (GER) 3 b g Sholokhov (IRE) – Laren (GER)
Trainer: J.J.QUINN. Settrington, Malton, North Yorkshire.
I bought a nice prospect for John Quinn last December from Guillaume Macaire called Aurore D'Estruval and I returned to the same source for him this summer. This good looking three year old caught my eye when finishing fourth in a decent juvenile hurdle at Clairefontaine when I was over for the Arqana July Sale. Given too much to do that day, he had won impressively the time before at Nancy (beating Mercoeur by thirteen lengths), and looks above average.

MERCOEUR (FR) 3 gr g Archange D'Or (IRE) – Erivia (FR)
Trainer: W.GREATREX. Upper Lambourn, Berkshire.
An interesting French juvenile hurdler whom we bought for €35,000 at the Arqana July Sale. He never raced on the Flat but had contested four competitive juvenile hurdles in France, prior to the sale. He had shown promise in two events at Auteuil, initially, before two decent placed efforts outside of Paris at Nancy and Lyon (behind Wells De Lune). His shrewd handler should be able to place this maiden three year old to good effect.

MISSED APPROACH (IRE) 4 b g Golan (IRE) – Polly's Dream (IRE)
Trainer: W.GREATREX. Upper Lambourn, Berkshire.
Another one of Tessie's good value winning four year old point-to-pointers from Brightwells Sales. He made much of the running to win his only start on soft ground in early May. He cost £27,000 and has been bought for a new client of David Minton's called Alan Turner. We are now all hoping that the first horse Alan owns can be a winner.

PAIN AU CHOCOLAT (FR) 3 b g Enrique – Clair Chene (FR)
Trainer: A.KING. Wroughton, Wiltshire.
One of the new Million In Mind Partnership horses, the scopey three year old has been placed once from two Flat starts in the Provinces before finishing a close second over hurdles on his only jumps start in April at Le Teste. By the same sire as Binocular and Blood Cotil, he is nicely conditioned for the UK, being a three year old maiden with jumps experience already under his belt.

PEGGY DO (IRE) 6 b m Pierre – So Marvellous (IRE)
Trainer: N.J.HENDERSON. Lambourn, Berkshire.
A great big, masculine type of mare who was one of the highest rated point-to-point mares in Ireland last season. She improved rapidly during the spring winning her maiden easily by ten lengths on the 12th April, before spread-eagling a strong field of winning mares at the end of season Fairyhouse meeting in May in a fast time. The Irish Point-to-Point Form book has given her an official rating which leaves her the second top-rated mare to run in points/hunter chases in Ireland, who started last season as a maiden. Therefore, despite the fact she wasn't cheap at the sales, I am rather hoping she will do well for the Seven Barrows team.

SAN BENEDETO (FR) 3 ch g Layman (USA) – Cinco Baidy (FR)
Trainer: P.F.NICHOLLS. Ditcheat, Somerset.
The Listed Wild Monarch Hurdle at Auteuil for debutant three year old hurdlers each spring always produces some smart future prospects. I recall Le Duc finishing second to the Gallorini trained Nickname a few years ago as well as Long Run running a close second in the same event to another Gallorini runner. This year's renewal saw San Benedeto finish a good second to a Gallorini trained juvenile (who was incidentally a son of Nickname) with the front two pulling a long way clear of the rest of the field. A rangy three year old, he also boasted some good form on the Flat being placed over a mile and nine furlongs as a two year old and had an official rating of 86. An extremely exciting recruit for hurdling, he is certainly one to follow this winter.

SIMPLY THE WEST (IRE) 5 b g Westerner – Back To Stay (IRE)
Trainer: C.LONGSDON. Chipping Norton, Oxon.
This decent looking five year old made all to win his point-to-point easily at the second time of asking in May – he was found to be sick after pulling up on his debut in December. The form has been franked subsequently with Padawan, who was already being ridden along in second place when falling at the penultimate fence, winning easily himself since (and later sold at the same Cheltenham Sale for £50,000). He looks a tough sort who should be up to winning over hurdles this season.

SON DU BERLAIS (FR) 4 ch g Muhtathir – King's Daughter (FR)
Trainer: N.J.HENDERSON. Lambourn, Berkshire.
I am hopeful that this highly impressive four year old Auteuil hurdle winner will become a well known name over the next few seasons. However, the fact he won on the 29th March on only his second career start, means his trainer is going to find him a bit tricky to place this winter whilst he gains more racing experience. I am sure Nicky (Henderson) will want to wait a year before going chasing so he will therefore have to go handicap hurdling this winter so he can learn the ropes.

STONEY SILENCE 6 b g Generous (IRE) – Stoney Path
Trainer: W.GREATREX. Upper Lambourn, Berkshire.
This was one of my 'googly' selections of the spring and I was pleased both Tessie and Warren ran with my suggestion and bought him at the Doncaster May Sales. His Rules form for Charlie Mann went downhill after a promising bumper debut fourth at Huntingdon behind Lemony Bay in March 2013. However, Marcus Foley conjured two cosy victories in English point-to-points on good to soft ground this spring from him and this 16.2hh individual cost £22,000 at the DBS. Following one more maiden hurdle race, he ought to be qualified for novice handicaps and could be worth following.

TANIOKEY (IRE) 4 b f Scorpion (IRE) – Creation (IRE)
Trainer: O.M.C.SHERWOOD. Upper Lambourn, Berkshire.
A tough medium sized filly, she is another from the Crawford academy in Northern Ireland. She dead heated in her only start, a mares' bumper at Carlisle on soft ground in early May, with a point-to-point winning mare of Michael Scudamore's called Grace Tara. I think both mares may prove above average and this mare's grandam was the smart Irish hurdler/chaser Palette, who won 9 races and was placed in the Royal Bond Hurdle and the Thyestes Chase amongst others. She has joined a good trainer of fillies/mares, so she should be placed to win over hurdles this season.

THEINVAL (FR) 4 b g Smadoun (FR) – Kinevees (FR)
Trainer: N.J.HENDERSON. Lambourn, Berkshire.
A four year old maiden who was busily campaigned in France, he managed seven places from ten starts. He appeared to have improved in his three races during the spring and, in fact, his second over fences on his latest start saw his handicap mark rise by eleven pounds. I expect him to be rated around 130 over fences in the UK. He should prove a fun sort for his enthusiastic owners Sandy and Caroline Orr, who are also responsible for Hennessy Gold Cup winner Triolo D'Alene.

VAYLAND 5 b g Generous (IRE) – Dotandadash (IRE)
Trainer: D.PIPE. Nicholashayne, Somerset.
A tall son of Generous, he absolutely bolted up in a summer bumper at Hexham for the Crawford's and I bought him subsequently at the Fairyhouse Derby Sales in their very small form horses section. He cost €65,000 which, for a horse who won his bumper by twenty six lengths, did not look bad value. He had shown promise in the spring when second in a point-to-point and he looks a horse worth following this winter because it was soft ground when he won at Hexham.

VOIX D'EAU (FR) 4 b g Voix Du Nord (FR) – Eau De Chesne (FR)
Trainer: H.FRY. Seaborough, Dorset.
He is an attractive four year old who was purchased at the Arqana July Sale for the Masterson family to join Harry Fry. The same owners have the very promising Punchestown Festival bumper winner Fletchers Flyer already with Harry and I have previously purchased Balder Succes for them. This youngster showed massive improvement for a change of stables to win a hurdle in the Provinces on the 1st June from a couple of fairly useful four year olds trained by Guillaume Macaire. Plus, given the fact he has the look of a chaser, I envisage him winning plenty of races in the UK in the seasons to come.

WELLS DE LUNE (FR) 3 b g Irish Wells (FR) – Pepite De Lune
Trainer: C.LONGSDON. Chipping Norton, Oxon.
The former Guillaume Macaire trained three year old won on his debut over hurdles on the 26th April at La Teste (second, third and fourth have all won subsequently) before finishing a close second at Lyon under a penalty in early June (Mercoeur behind in third). As with all graduates from the Macaire Academy, he is a very accurate jumper and I think Charlie (Longsdon) should do well with him as a juvenile hurdler. It almost goes without saying, too, he will make a nice chaser in time.

WESTSTREET (IRE) 4 b g Westerner – Klipperstreet (IRE)
Trainer: O.M.C.SHERWOOD. Upper Lambourn, Berkshire.
A really bonny horse Tessie purchased for Oliver (Sherwood) for £22,000 at the Doncaster May Sale. He looks an excellent value for money buy. Beaten a length in his only four year old point-to-point on soft ground in early May by the aforementioned Missed Approach, he went down fighting after surviving a mistake at the last. He should do well in novice hurdles this winter as he looks the type to come to hand fairly early.

In other news
Last year's novice chase division proved to be a really successful one for *Highflyer Bloodstock* with 13 Graded/Listed wins by our purchases. This season the same division looks equally exciting with possible Festival contenders like **DEPUTY DAN, GITANE DU BERLAIS, GRUMETI, IRISH SAINT, PTIT ZIG, SAPHIR DU RHEU** and **WHISPER** all raring to go over the larger obstacles. The Champion Hurdle was denied us last season but **MY TENT OR YOURS** and **THE NEW ONE** both remain over timber this time and either one could easily rectify that situation next March. I feel **SILVINIACO CONTI** was the best staying chaser around last season and, with some headgear applied this winter, I can see him proving the point conclusively.

HIGHFLYER BLOODSTOCK'S HORSE TO FOLLOW: HARGAM

For all the latest news and how to get involved in the
Million In Mind partnership, please visit

www.millioninmind.co.uk

HANDY HINTS

As discussed, **Jonjo O'Neill** was responsible for a personal best 134 winners last winter, his win and place prize-money crept past the £1.5m barrier and Jackdaws Castle housed three Cheltenham Festival winners in March. Jonjo's runners are worth looking out for at the majority of National Hunt tracks throughout Britain but he did particularly well with his runners at **CATTERICK** last season. The Irishman trained 4 winners from only 12 runners, with his hurdlers excelling (3 winners from 5 runners). Indeed, during the last five seasons, Jonjo O'Neill runners at the North Yorkshire track have yielded 6 winners from 20 runners (30%). It is interesting to note high-class staying novice chaser Holywell had two of his seven starts over the larger obstacles at Catterick, winning once and finishing second on the other occasion. Promising novice hurdler Capote also won at the track on his Rules debut in February. When it comes to educating and handicapping his horses, Jonjo has few peers and I would expect him to continue to use Catterick as a stepping stone to bigger and better targets in the spring.

Talking of **CATTERICK**, make a note of the **KEITH REVELEY** trained runners at their meeting on **Tuesday 16th December**. The Cleveland based handler drew a blank at the corresponding meeting last year but he registered 3 winners in 2011 (Sambelucky (8/1), Karingreason (9/2), Special Catch (3/1)) and 2 winners in 2012 (Flora's Pride (9/2) & Special Catch (13/8)). The fixture invariably pays for the Reveley's Christmas.

Philip Hobbs had a strong team of novice hurdlers last season and the Minehead trainer did extremely well with those he raced in handicaps, making the most of lenient marks. Examples included Champagne West (won at Wincanton on Boxing Day off 123 (now rated 143)), Sausalito Sunrise (won at Haydock off 129 (now rated 145)) and The Skyfarmer (won at Cheltenham in December off 123 (now rated 137)). It is possible this season's crop aren't as good as last term's but keep an eye on them running in handicap hurdles, nevertheless.

Paul Nicholls has been the man to follow when it comes to the **novices' limited handicap chase at Newbury's Hennessy meeting** (27th November). A 0-135 event run over two mile six, the champion trainer has won it in recent years with Opera Mundi (2006), Rolling Aces (2012) and Easter Day (2013), plus Fistral Beach finished second in 2009. Keep an eye out for his 2014 respresentative. Unfortunately, the race has been downgraded from a 0-140 but Ayr winner Vivaldi Collonges is a possible with a mark of 135.

Sixteen year old **Sean Bowen** has already been tipped for the top and his career is set to take another significant step forward when joining **Paul Nicholls** as a conditional jockey. Following a successful career in pony and point-to-point racing, he rode Kozmina Bay to victory at Uttoxeter on the 20th December on his first ever ride under Rules. An amateur at the time, he has already ridden seven winners this season as a conditional. His allowance is expected to prove a huge advantage this winter. Therefore look out for the Nicholls/Bowen combination. It looks sure to be a profitable one.

The **'Fixed Brush' Handicap Hurdle** at Haydock Park has been dominated in recent seasons by Pond House Stables. **David Pipe** has collected the three mile event with Grands Crus (rated 132) in 2010, Dynaste (141) in 2011 and Gevrey Chambertin (143) last year. Look out for his runner in the 2014 renewal on Saturday 22nd November. The Greatwood Hurdle winner **DELL'ARCA** is rated 145 and Tom Scudamore recommended trying him over three miles following his excellent run at Aintree in Grade 1 company. The ex-French trained gelding could be the one.

Wind operations have become commonplace, especially amongst National Hunt horses, in recent seasons. Paul Nicholls has been a huge advocate with many of his horses over the years undergoing surgery on their breathing. One trend which developed last season and, worth bearing in mind for this year, too, is the fact **a number of horses showed the true benefit from a wind operation on their second run back after the operation**. Boston Bob (Melling Chase) and Shutthefrontdoor (Irish National) were two high profile examples in the spring and, to a lesser extent, Blenheim Brook when he won at Haydock in mid April.

IRISH POINTERS

Once again, Irish point expert **Declan Phelan** has compiled his list of those horses which caught his eye 'between the flags' last winter and feels will make a major impact racing under Rules this season and beyond. Last year's article produced **34 winners at a strike rate of 22%** and a £10 level stake **PROFIT** of **£142.50**. They featured **CONCORDIN (9/1), DESOTO COUNTY (3 wins), FESTIVE AFFAIR (10/1), IS LOVE ALIVE (20/1), MINELLA FORU (8/1), MOSSPARK (3 wins)** and **WESTERN WARHORSE (33/1)**.

ADAM DU BRETEAU (FR) 4 ch g Network (GER) – Odelie De Fric
Trainer: Jonjo O'NEILL   **Form Figures: FU1**
White faced chestnut son of Network: exited late when in contention in first two races: atoned with a polished display at Dromahane (Soft) in March when Nina Carberry turned up to partner him for a rare pointing ride. Jonjo O'Neill paid £280,000 to secure him at the Brightwells Cheltenham Sale in April. To date, he has shown signs of nervousness pre race: he tends to travel smoothly in his races, and that cruising speed can translate into track victories in hurdle and chase races. When he comes out of his comfort zone and forced to battle, the chinks in his armour may surface. Likely to function on good ground as well as in soft/heavy conditions and that versatility may be an asset.

ALPHA DES OBEAUX (FR) 4 b g Saddler Maker (IRE) – Omega Des Obeaux (FR)
Trainer: Mouse MORRIS   **Form Figures: 1**
Ploughed through the near waterlogged track at Tinahely (Heavy) to record a debut win: his main danger, Adam Du Breteau, fell three out easing his task: a son of a little known French sire called Saddler Maker, he seemed to demonstrate a knee action, indicating that deep winter conditions favour him. He ran right to the line and tests of stamina may be right up his street. This gelding would be interesting in the near term, if contesting a bumper at Naas or Navan (although Mouse does not like bumpers), and he should pick up a staying novice hurdle or more this winter. Down the line he could develop into a fair staying handicap chaser.

AQUA DUDE (IRE) 4 br g Flemensfirth (USA) – Miss Cozzene (FR)
Trainer: Evan WILLIAMS   **Form Figures: 1**
A hobdayed son of Flemensfirth: he made light work of the task in hand when quickening from the final fence to seal a pleasing debut win at the new track in Fermoy (Soft). It was a professional performance, as he was positioned close to the pace and, once the button was pushed to go, he delivered for Corky Carroll. The Doyle brothers from Wexford had a big squad of four year old pointers and they rated this fellow as good as any and they cashed him in for €150,000 at the Punchestown Festival Sale: expect him to be competitive at Graded level, if he develops at his new posting.

ARCTIC SKIPPER (IRE) 5 b g Flemensfirth (USA) – Coco Opera (IRE)
Trainer: Vincent HALLEY   **Form Figures: 12**
A giant of a horse with a bit of character: he trounced a useful field when clocking a fast time on his sole point run at Glenbane (Yielding) in October. The son of Flemensfirth was then given a few months to help the maturity process and reappeared in a Limerick bumper in April (Soft/Heavy). He dumped his rider on the way to the start: when reunited, the partnership then ran a cracker when just foiled by half a length. He is a highly exciting prospect, but keeping a horse of his structure in one piece does, however, require a large degree of luck and patience.

ATTRIBUTION 4 ch g Alhaarth (IRE) – Competa
Trainer: Gordon ELLIOTT   **Form Figures: 13**

An expensive store, which is not surprising given that this son of Alhaarth is a sibling of former Champion Hurdle winner Punjabi. A flashy chestnut, he was firmly a stable second string on his only point run at Durrow (Soft/Heavy) and looked to be receiving a quiet spin out the back door, when the race fell apart three from the finish, and he came bombing home to collect readily: his jumping was slick. He then appeared in a Punchestown Festival bumper and ran an honest third, doing his best work at the end. On pedigree he is bred to be sharp, in National Hunt terms, but, judged on performance, he is a proper honest stayer: I like horses who put in their best work at the finish of races and this fellow should acquit himself at a fair level this winter in the staying novice hurdle category.

BALLY BEAUFORT (IRE) 6 b g Old Vic – Miss Compliance (IRE)
Trainer: Nigel TWISTON-DAVIES   **Form Figures: 6 wins from 13 starts**

The only six year old I am including in the compilation: as a four year old, he won a Lisronagh maiden for Wilson Dennison in March 2012...five months later he got injured in another point and that necessitated a period of fifteen months on the sidelines before he returned last November with two tame efforts. He suddenly recaptured his mo-jo at the start of 2014...he gave the unbeaten Venitien De Mai a real test at Tinahely in January, and from that day went from strength to strength...winning no less than 5 points, including 3 open wins (commendable for a young horse). He is an old style stayer and, importantly, does possess a gear or two. With bags of experience under his belt, I expect him to hit the ground running for his new yard, nailed on to win staying novice hurdles and, if he remains sound (the big question mark) could be another Twiston Davies horse for marathon staying chases. Very effective with cut in the ground, but also has wins to his name on good and yielding, hinting at versatility.

BALLYKNOCK LAD (IRE) 5 b g Bach (IRE) – Ballyknock Lass (IRE)
Trainer: Kim BAILEY   **Form Figures: 41**

A fair fourth in a fast run race at Lingstown, he delivered second time out when impressing me at Curraheen in May (Soft). Held up, Colman Sweeney moved this white faced son of Bach to lead at the fourth last and, from that point, he upped the tempo and jumped fast and bravely when the chips were down over the last couple of fences. His dam won a bumper for John Kiely and this gelding, who was bought privately for a price in the £70,000 region, seems to have a very good attitude to the game. I think could be one of the surprise packets to emerge for the past pointing season.

BELLSHILL (IRE) 4 b g King's Theatre (IRE) – Fairy Native (IRE)
Trainer: Willie MULLINS   **Form Figures: 2**

A big gelding by King's Theatre, who placed a close second on his one run for the Dennison team at Maralin in March (Heavy). A blunder two out did not help his cause and he did appear rather one paced in the taxing conditions. A big galloping circuit may bring the best out of him and I am sure when he fully develops and strengthens he will become a more accomplished performer. He did not sing out "star material" based on the Maralin run, this gelding could be in the long term staying handicap chaser mould rather than an instant Graded hurdling model.

BIRCH HILL (IRE) 4 b g Kalanisi (IRE) – Miss Compliance (IRE)
Trainer: Nicky HENDERSON   **Form Figures: F1**

This Kalanisi half brother to multiple point winner Bally Beaufort looked above average on his second run at Loughbrickland (Good) in April: always in contention, he jumped to the lead at the penultimate fence and readily kicked clear, asserting for a pleasing win. The style of the victory hinted that he definitely had a touch of class and may be capable of operating at a relatively high level on the track proper. Subsequently changed hands for £160,000 at the Punchestown Sales, he has joined Nicky Henderson. He may prefer flat tracks.

BLACKTHORN PRINCE 4 b g Black Sam Bellamy (IRE) – Quark Top (FR)
Trainer: Jonjo O'NEILL   **Form Figures: 2**

Once raced progeny of Black Sam Bellamy: engaged in one of the most exciting head to heads of the 2014 point season at Lingstown (Soft) in March. Together with the eventual winner Victory Mill, the pair went at it hell for leather over the last three fences, neither wilting and both showing courage and honesty in jumping and effort respectively: he only gave best close to the finish. He has a decent frame to fill out over the course of time and one could readily imagine him being good enough to progress into a "Saturday chaser" for some quality events over time, assuming full health in the interim. Coped with the testing conditions and could prove versatile on the ground preference front.

BORDINI (FR) 4 b g Martaline – Didinas (FR)
Trainer: Willie MULLINS   **Form Figures: 3**

A son of Martaline, interestingly, Willie Mullins bought him out of France as a store and then farmed him out to Aiden Fitzgerald for a pointing run. He ran a promising third at Maralin (Soft/Heavy) in a hot maiden won by Mahler Lad: ridden just off the pace, he made a few minor jumping errors, and was challenging at the final fence when a bad blunder sealed his fate (probably would have been second otherwise). Seemed to enjoy the heavy sod that day and, whilst the run reeked of greenness, in time Mullins will have plenty of raw material at his disposal to possibly mould him into a half decent jumper.

BORIS DE BLAE (IRE) 4 ch g Mahler – Almost Trumps
Trainer: Alan FLEMING   **Form Figures: 1**

Found generously from the second last to snatch a narrow win in a six runner maiden at Dromahane (Good) in April. In the context of the rest of the day's racing, the time was decent: an angular chestnut son of Mahler, he subsequently changed hands for €110,000. Given his rather light pedigree, the winning effort was critical in transforming a £4,000 foal into a six figure four year old. One of the trickier pointers to assess, he is likely to be a 115-135 staying chaser and I could see him operating effectively around tracks like Fairyhouse. Will sport the silks of Barry Connell, who has helped the repatriating Alan Fleming set up as a trainer back in Ireland.

CAPTAIN VON TRAPPE (IRE) 5 b g Germany (USA) – Culmore Native (IRE)
Trainer: Gordon ELLIOTT   **Form Figures: 31**

Gordon Elliott paid £115,000 for this twice raced pointer by Germany: he debuted in a hot maiden at Dromahane (Good), ridden to the fore, he lost many lengths by jumping to his right throughout and eventually did well to place third, in the circumstances. Switched to the right handed track at Dawstown (Yielding) next time out, he dominated the race from the start and showed tactical speed at times as he coasted to a bloodless two lengths victory, jumping accurately. Tony O'Brien, his point trainer, produced Beneficient in the past, and there is a very good chance that this fellow could replicate the Graded track success of that ex-inmate. The Captain has class and may prove money well spent, the issue of being one dimensional on track preference (ie possibly only a right handed track performer) may resurface in time or the horse may be corrected along the way.

CHAMPAGNE PRESENT (IRE) 4 br g Presenting – My Name's Not Bin (IRE)

Trainer: Jonjo O'NEILL **Form Figures: 41**

Gained a deal of confidence and experience from a debut fourth to new stablemate Adam Du Breteau at Dromahane, and then comprehensively outclassed inferior opposition when posting a polished win a fortnight later at Kilmallock (Soft), taking the lead after a mile and thereafter jumping slickly and keeping on strongly to the line. Looks to have plenty to offer for the future and, as a son of Presenting, he might be just as effective on good ground. He is capable of winning a middle of the road bumper to start with. For figures sake...he can make a 120-130 hurdler at his leisure.

CHILDRENS LIST (IRE) 4 b g Presenting – Snipe Hunt (IRE)

Trainer: Willie MULLINS **Form Figures: 1**

Bay gelding, a Presenting half-brother to former quality chaser Schindlers Hunt: changed hands a few times as a store and failed to command a big price, so there may be a lack of physical perfection given the pedigree. Sent off favourite for an early season 2m 4f point at Belharbour (Soft) and gradually overhauled the experienced Capbreton approaching the final fence to eventually shoot clear for a five lengths winning margin. The actual form has not been significantly franked by those behind. His more famous sibling never won beyond 2m 5f and therein may be a clue to the future of this new recruit of Rich Ricci's. Many of the star point graduates had what I would term "a striking presence" when racing between the flags...in my judgement this lad lacked that component and he is another that may qualify for the "good but not great" category.... in time, the 2m to 2m 4f conditions chases likely to be the route that will see him earn his keep, at Grade 2 or 3 level.

CLASSIC PLACE (IRE) 4 b g Beneficial – Your Place Or Mine (IRE)

Trainer: Willie MULLINS **Form Figures: 1**

Made his move at the second last and displayed courage to squeeze through a tight gap to take the lead at the final fence before finding plenty on the climb to the line at Largy (Good) in May. This, his only point run, spoke volumes for his character and will to win. A son of Beneficial he will probably operate just as well on softer ground, so may be a versatile track recruit. I would rate this four year old maiden as one of the top 3 from the Northern/Ulster circuit in 2014 and it has a tradition of unearthing decent horses. I can envisage this youngster developing into a highly competitive 130-140 handicap chaser, perhaps a level or two below the top rank.

CORNER CREEK (IRE) 4 b g Presenting – No Moore Bills

Trainer: Michael SCUDAMORE **Form Figures: 1**

He produced a commendable debut success at Toomebridge (Heavy) in April. He quickened to lead at the second last before stretching clear for an emphatic win under a hand ride from Jamie Codd. The opposition may have been modest, the track rather tight, nonetheless the authority of the victory hinted at a bright future. Set to race in the silks sported successfully last term by Next Sensation, connections have been prepared to be patient with their Irish point imports, that patience leading to exploitable handicap ratings. When Corner Creek matures and acclimatises, he can be just as successful as Next Sensation....the path travelled with this project could be entertaining!

CRACKED REAR VIEW (IRE) 4 gr g Portrait Gallery (IRE) – Trip To Knock
Trainer: Donald McCAIN   Form Figures: F21

A powerfully made grey son of Portrait Gallery: he fell on his point debut at Dromahane inside the first mile. His jumping stood the test the following week at Laurencetown (Good), where he ran a solid race. Ridden to the fore, he failed to counter the kick of Pylonthepressure, yet kept on to be a game second. He added value to his stock by easily landing a modest Sligo bumper a fortnight later...in fairness, the rivals he encountered in that bumper were vastly inferior to his pointing opposition. Donald McCain paid £130,000 for him at Brightwells in May - there are upsides and downsides - given that he ran three times in the space of a month and was progressive and competitive augurs well. The pedigree is rather light and Flat based on the dam line, which may lead to limitations, and I think the best of him will be seen on good ground.... hence he may be a horse to oppose on Soft/Heavy terrain and don't be fooled by the Sligo success (from a ground perspective): may be at his peak in spring time on a sound surface.

DALLAS COWBOY (IRE) 4 b g Beneficial – Watson River (IRE)
Trainer: Gordon ELLIOTT   Form Figures: 2

The trainer and owners (The Howleys) have had some great sport out of the likes of Chicago Grey in the past and it is possible this once raced pointer with an appealing name could be capable of making headlines himself. Point to point rider Damien Murphy bred this son of Beneficial and an honest second on his debut at Largy (Good) behind Classic Place augered well for the future. When he fills his fine frame, he will strengthen into a competitive staying chaser, his big ears often a characteristic of a genuine jumper hint he is one to follow. Might be touch and go whether he wins a bumper, should have no trouble securing a staying novice/ maiden hurdle....chasing will be his true vocation.

DEFINITLY RED (IRE) 5 ch g Definite Article – The Red Wench (IRE)
Trainer: Steve GOLLINGS   Form Figures: 2P - 1117

Commenced the 2013/14 point-to-point season as one of the best four year old maidens from the spring campaign. It did not take him long to lose his maiden tag, as he bolted up at Loughanmore (Soft) in October. Bought for £110,000 at the Cheltenham Brightwells Sale in November, he found a new home at the Gollings yard and this chestnut gelding quickly made his mark, relishing the heavy ground to win bumpers at Uttoxeter and Newbury (Listed), before placing a commendable seventh in the Cheltenham Festival bumper on ground that was too fast. I think he could become the Ballyalton of the 2014/15 novice hurdle season...the horse from the small yard that mixes it with the big boys...he is top class in bottomless ground and can win from two to three miles....he does function on good ground (proved in Easter 2013 when pointing), but is not as potent. If astutely campaigned, he may win a Grade 1 or 2 novice hurdle.

DETROIT BLUES 4 ch g Tobougg (IRE) – Blue Missy (USA)
Trainer: Jamie SNOWDEN   Form Figures: 1

A son of Tobougg, he is certainly not bred with pointing or jump racing in mind, with most of the family being dirt racers in the United States. When winning at Dromahane in March (Good/ Soft), he showcased sound jumping, stamina and steely determination amongst his qualities.... attributes one would more associate with stoutly bred jumps stock. Always to the fore, he was challenged from the second last by Adam Du Breteau and Native Tribe: with all three close together at the last, Detroit Blues put in a monster leap, in the process, forcing Adam Du Breteau into a race ending blunder and the incident also put Native Tribe out of the equation...in the end, Detroit was left with a twelve lengths winning margin. Jamie Snowden previously shelled out a six figure sum to purchase Present View and, after a couple of below par seasons, that gelding rewarded connections with a Festival win in 2014. Detroit Blues became Snowden's second big expensive point purchase at exactly £100,000 through the sales ring: he would not necessarily convince as one that will make inroads as a hurdler: hence a slow preparation aimed at handicap chasing within two or three years could be the game plan. This horse represents one of those odd National Hunt conundrums: pedigree says he is not intended for the game, as an individual he may be a freak and be capable of defying his breeding.

DIFFERENT GRAVEY (IRE) 4 b g High Chaparral (IRE) – Newtown Dancer (IRE)
Trainer: Nicky HENDERSON   **Form Figures: 1**
This tall gelding proved a rare point winner for sire High Chapparal when landing a debut win at Loughanamore (Good) on Easter Monday. Well touted pre-race and supported in the betting ring, he travelled within his comfort zone for most of the contest, then was produced on the home bend and a big jump took him to the front at the final fence and he looked set for an easy win. Inside the last 100 yards with his rivals rallying, he curled up a little under pressure and just obliged. He subsequently cost £140,000 at the sales. His dam Newtown Dancer was a slight mare, who won 4 times mixing Flat and hurdles for Tom Hogan, and 2m 2f was her optimum trip. Different Gravey is one I would have my fears about, in that he could be all style and no substance. I think he may be a smooth traveller who may do it all on the bridle and could be found wanting when pressurised. Ideally, he is the type to arrive with one late run off a strong pace.

FACT FILE (IRE) 4 b g Catcher In The Rye (IRE) – Mini Minor (IRE)
Trainer: Charles BYRNES   **Form Figures: 1**
Made virtually all the running when landing an early season 2m 4f maiden at Bennettsbridge (Yielding/Soft) in February. I liked the manner he quickened when challenged heading to the final fence. White faced bay gelding, a son of Catcher In The Rye, he jumps efficiently and could be borderline Graded novice hurdle material this coming season.

FREE EXPRESSION (IRE) 5 b g Germany (USA) – Create A Storm (IRE)
Trainer: Gordon ELLIOTT   **Form Figures: 11**
Emerged on top having engaged in a full blooded battle with Present Flight in a high class maiden at Dromahane (Soft) in December: he was asked plenty of questions and came up with the answers. J.P. McManus stepped in to buy him privately and his next engagement was the point-to-point bumper at Fairyhouse on Easter Monday and this son of Germany made relentless progress under Nina Carberry to lead inside the distance to earn a valuable prize. The key to this strapping gelding is that he likes to come off a strong gallop.... A slowly run race would do him no favours....he should be competing at Graded level with the best of the staying novice hurdlers this winter and will be an exciting novice chaser further down the line.

FULHAM ROAD (IRE) 4 b g Shantou (USA) – Bobomy (IRE)
Trainer: Willie MULLINS   **Form Figures: F**
Turned up for the 2m 4f maiden at Punchestown in February (Heavy) with a bit of a reputation: alas, all did not go to plan, as he fell two from home when starting to flag. He looked rather unfurnished and a few hairy awkward jumps suggested he might require some refinement in the jumping department. One attribute he has in spades is a big frame to fill: he could go forward in one of two ways....always be a big lazy brute or, alternatively, Willie Mullins may be able to sculpt a racehorse out of the basic raw model at hand....if he can transform this son of Shantou into a 2014/15 Festival candidate it will be a real water into wine training performance. He is still only a shell of a horse to my eyes and therefore it is tricky forecasting his long term prospects.

GO CONQUER (IRE) 5 b g Arcadio (GER) – Ballinamona Wish (IRE)
Trainer: Donald McCAIN **Form Figures: FU1**

Failed to get round twice in point races. He fell three out when cantering at Maralin (Soft), then attempted to make all at Dromahane (Soft/Heavy), and looked likely to achieve that task, only to thump the final fence and lose his jockey Barry O'Neill...plenty of winners emerged from that race. He excited many, despite coming a cropper, and Donald McCain was in the fan club paying £140,000 for him at Brightwells Sale in January. He bagged his first success on his sole UK outing, winning a weak Carlisle bumper (Good/Soft), making all and winning in workmanlike fashion. I suspect the horse may have been below his best and, with a summer under his belt, he may now return a powerful customer to contend with in novice hurdles. He could be good enough to deserve a crack at the heavy artillery down south. His jumping technique needs some attention before he goes novice chasing.

GOLD MAN (IRE) 5 b g Presenting – Mama Jaffa (IRE)
Trainer: Kim BAILEY **Form Figures: 1**

A chestnut son of Presenting, he gave some positive indicators when collecting on his debut at Ballydarragh (Yielding) in February. In a tight race, with the field well grouped four out, he quickened to the front at the second last and, whilst running green when in front, he held on for victory. The winning margin of half a length does not do justice to his superiority. He changed hands for £60,000: his dam won three races for Charlie Swan and I think the best of this five year old may be witnessed on good ground. A raw product, he lacks experience but has a touch of quality.

JEWELOFTHEOCEAN (IRE) 4 b g Flemensfirth (USA) – Coole Assembly (IRE)
Trainer: Alan FLEMING **Form Figures: 1**

Clocked the fastest time on the six race card at Monksgrange (Heavy) in March when winning a competitive maiden on his debut for Denis Murphy. Covered up in midfield by Jamie Codd, he was five lengths down at the third last but this athletic son of Flemensfirth gradually reeled in Potters Point, to claim a narrow win in the final strides. He jumped accurately and was not found wanting when asked a few serious questions. Looks a real three mile staying type but not necessarily all about stamina, as he may have tactical speed and that combination may result in this gelding becoming potent at a high level as a novice/handicap chaser in a couple of seasons time. Even though this win illustrated his effectiveness on heavy terrain, given his size and shape, I wouldn't think good ground would cause him trouble. Another addition to owner Barry Connell's squad, he has realistic prospects of gaining Graded success during his career.

LIFT THE LATCH (IRE) 4 b g Beneficial – Queen Astrid (IRE)
Owner: J.P.McMANUS **Form Figures: 1**

Won the traditionally strong four year old maiden at Lemonfield in March (Soft/Heavy). Jumping accurately, as one has come to expect from Enda Bolger trained pointers, he was headed two out, and Derek O'Connor had to give him a few smacks approaching the final fence before he asserted on the run in, for a workmanlike as opposed to polished win in the presence of his owner J.P. McManus. My read is that he will become another 120-140 McManus handicapper given a clean run health wise. A son of Beneficial, his dam is the four times winning ex-Dermot Weld trained Queen Astrid: this Listed winner on the Flat, required plenty of give underfoot to perform and was never really effective on a sound surface: this characteristic may feature with Lift The Latch as his knee pounding action relates that he, too, may be a mudlark.

LIMOS (GER) 4 br g Sholokhov (IRE) – La Prima (GER)
Trainer: James EWART   Form Figures: 1

A racy German bred son of Sholokov: looked primed for the day when buckling down to the task to land a quality maiden at Inch (Good), accounting for The Last Euro and Double Shuffle after a good set-to over the last three fences in the home straight. Not a natural three miler in my way of thinking, he could be more forward than most, and may prefer flat, speed biased tracks. Musselburgh ought to be bountiful hunting ground given his new Scottish base.

LIVELOVELAUGH (IRE) 4 b g Beneficial – Another Evening (IRE)
Trainer: Willie MULLINS   Form Figures: 1

Had plenty of use made of him as he proceeded to make all the running to win the hard way on his one outing at the stiff Oldcastle track (Yielding) in April. Given that he was never headed, the impressive time he posted indicated a touch of class: save for a blunder at the second last, it was the near perfect debut. Purchased privately for a six figure sum to join Willie Mullins/Rich Ricci, winning a bumper looks a given, and the fact that he climbed the stiff hill to the finish with vigour, hints that the likes of Navan or Naas may be ideal starting points for a bumper. Is he Cheltenham bumper standard for this spring? Possibly, if he demonstrates that he can deliver back to back performances....his dam was a modest race-mare, so his sire Beneficial has obviously made a key contribution to the genetic structure of this bay gelding.

LOUGH DERG WALK (IRE) 5 b g Turtle Island (IRE) – Whispers In Moscow (IRE)
Trainer: Donald McCAIN   Form Figures: 3F1

Raced three times in the space of four weeks in the spring: arguably the hottest race he contested was at Dromahane (Yielding) in March when he ran a cracker without being punished to place third behind Pulled Mussel: a couple of weeks later, he was set for victory at Monksgrange (Heavy), only to land steeply at the last and unseat Jamie Codd. I think he may not have been at his peak when he won third time at Oldcastle (Yielding), as he made very hard work of winning a weak maiden. A son of Turtle Island, suited to testing terrain, he has a willing attitude and will be a fair performer in staying novice hurdles on the northern circuit.

MASTER OF VERSE (IRE) 5 b g Milan – Bacchonthebottle (IRE)
Trainer: Willie MULLINS   Form Figures: 1

Jamie Codd enjoyed an armchair ride aboard this son of Milan at Dromahane (Yielding/Soft) in December as this gelding travelled in a lovely relaxed manner throughout and needed little encouragement to put the race to bed from the second last. Subsequent events would highlight that he beat nothing of merit in this maiden but one cannot deny the ease of victory. Another six figure Willie Mullins buy (£150,000), judged on this one performance, we are perhaps entertaining a minimum Grade 3 jumper and therefore a debut bumper win is a likely outcome to his racetrack career.

MINELLA BERRY (IRE) 4 b g King's Theatre (IRE) – Grape Love (FR)
Owner: J.P.McMANUS   Form Figures: 1

A grand model son of Kings Theatre, he collected at the first time of asking for John Nallen, when pleasing favourite backers in the maiden at Kilworth (Good) in March. He has a lovely relaxed manner of running and I chalked him down as a 125+ horse, who could be equally competitive in 2m 4f hurdles and chases. He is the sort to perhaps feature as a player in a Coral Cup inside two seasons before heading down the chase route. His sibling won a bumper on his sole start in December 2013, and he could follow suit.

MINELLA ROCCO (IRE) 4 b g Shirocco (GER) – Petralona (USA)
Trainer: Jonjo O'NEILL   **Form Figures: 1**

During the early stages of his win at Horse And Jockey, this gelding raced in a laboured manner and was far from foot perfect. He had to be hard ridden but responded to pressure to eventually get firmly on top in the closing couple of furlongs as his reserves of stamina kicked in on the taxing soft ground. Visually this performance conveyed mixed messages in that it appeared easy to get him off the bridle and that he had bags of stamina. With the runner up Taj Badalandabad subsequently advertising the form in UK bumpers, the value of this point win has been enhanced. The McManus team paid £260,000 to add him to their squad via the Cheltenham Festival sale in March. He may struggle to win a bumper, if he repeats his pointing display: his sire Shirocco, a recent addition to the Irish stallion roster, is becoming popular thanks to the likes of Annie Power. There are races to be won with Minella Rocco on soft/heavy ground, and McCoy might be made for him. However, I doubt if he will reach the summit of the jumps game.

MURPHYS WAY (IRE) 4 b g Oscar (IRE) – Festival Leader (IRE)
Trainer: Rebecca CURTIS   **Form Figures: 1**

Ran green for most of the journey at Ballynoe (Good), it was therefore commendable the way this son of Oscar woke up when brought to a challenging position at the final fence and won going away by three lengths. One of those cases of a young horse winning without really knowing what was happening, proving natural ability. He may require another season to get him fully tuned in. When that point is reached, this will be a very nice staying prospect. His dam actually placed fourth in the Graded bumper at Aintree against the geldings, so I could make a case for him featuring in a bumper as well. An exciting prospect bound to win races on his local circuit and capable of progressing to the big Festivals.

NICKNAME EXIT (FR) 4 b g Nickname (FR) – Exit To Fire (FR)
Trainer: Willie MULLINS   **Form Figures: 2**

A son of the ex-two mile chaser Nickname, a horse who enjoyed a profitable career in Ireland before embarking on stud duties. This fellow was tucked in close to the pace at Kirkistown (Soft) and looked set to win when produced to lead at the final fence. The gluey terrain may have impacted upon him as he tied up in the final twenty yards and lost out on the nod. Lost nothing in defeat and taking pedigree into account, he may be a more lethal player over trips from two miles to two and a half miles. A horse you will hear plenty about when he goes chasing....and one that can win a bumper, too.

PRESENT MAN (IRE) 4 b g Presenting – Glen's Gale (IRE)
Trainer: Paul NICHOLLS   **Form Figures: 2**

Tested the aforementioned Lift The Latch from the third last fence before finally surrendering on the run in at Lemonfield (Soft): appeared to travel the smoother of the two during the race and the fact that they pulled clear of the remainder is a positive indicator. The Ditcheat trainer has not really found a top pointer from Ireland since Denman: this son of Presenting will definitely collect on the track and may excel on a sounder surface but may have to settle for a Grade below the premier class. He has the speed to be competitive from 2m 4f and upwards.

PYLONTHEPRESSURE (IRE) 4 b g Darsi (FR) – Minnie O'Grady (IRE)
Trainer: Willie MULLINS   **Form Figures: 1**

Whilst nothing special in terms of looks, this son of Darsi commanded a fair Laurencetown maiden (Yielding) in May: leading from the start and going through the gears to quicken from the second last fence, he easily resisted the subsequent bumper winner Cracked Rear View. Mullins and Rich Ricci stumped up £110,000 for him at Brightwells Sale in May, which pocketed the Doyle brothers from Wexford a profit of £100,000 from their investment eleven months previously. This horse has a light pedigree, the positive aspect of his character is that he possesses a winning attitude: I can see him racking up a couple of bumpers this winter, if that is the planned route: perhaps a maiden bumper and a winners' bumper at the Fairyhouse or Punchestown Festivals. Sure to win loads of prize money, if he can take his racing.

OUR ROBIN (IRE) 4 b g Robin Des Champs (FR) – Palm Lake (IRE)
Trainer: Donald McCAIN   **Form Figures: 1**

Demonstrated a telling blend of smart jumping and tactical speed when picking up the Quakerstown four year old maiden on Easter Sunday (Good), a race won in the past by Champagne Fever. Might be ideally suited to middle distance hurdles and chases and could prove a money spinner: delving into the family, he ought to also act on softer ground and, if so, he may be a versatile performer. He could be one of those hidden gems who may sparkle at some point.

RATHNURE REBEL (IRE) 4 b g Beneficial – Euro Magic (IRE)
Trainer: Noel MEADE   **Form Figures: 1**

The chief enigma amongst the four year old crop: he ran once at Dromahane in April (Good) and made all to win by ten lengths: he did pack plenty of content into the 5m 52 seconds that he raced. A son of Beneficial from the family of prolific winner Sweet Kiln, the display in reality was of the white knuckle ride variety. He started off like a raging bull, bolting off in front on the way to the first fence: he crashed through the fence and jockey Rob James defied gravity to maintain the partnership: he then charged down the hill to the three fences in the home straight and I guess the jockey closed his eyes coming to each fence as the horse was bossing the argument: after a mile or so, the jockey got him to settle a little. One suspected that, having basically blown a gasket in the first mile, it would only be a matter of time until he ran out of juice and came back to the pack and folded. The truth was he never came back and he stayed at least ten to fifteen lengths and more clear all the time: perhaps the other jockeys expected the "fold" and were caught out by his ability to keep going. Ultimately, freak performance or not, the display excited the attendance on the day. Gigginstown were quick off the mark to buy him privately. I have no idea if this performance was in keeping with character, or just a debutant over heating: he may be a talented nutcase or a young green horse with huge potential.

STONEHARD (IRE) 4 b g Robin Des Champs (FR) – Amber Light (IRE)
Trainer: Willie MULLINS   **Form Figures: 1**

Accounted for an experienced rival in Capbreton when claiming victory at Oldtown (Yielding) in March: in a small field of seven runners, he bided his time in second and, once squeezed, by Jamie Codd jumped to the lead at the second last and kept on to win by four lengths. It was a controlled win rather than a flashy effort. A son of Robin Des Champs, he was incidentally knocked down to Willie Mullins as a three year old store for £215,000, Gordon Elliott trained him for his point and now he returns to Mullins. He has all the physical qualities deemed necessary to succeed at a high level. He could be suited to 2m4f-3m races on stiff tracks, because I formed the view that he is one of those horses that lengthens and keeps finding steadily rather than one with automatic gears.

THE LAST EURO (IRE) 4 b g Scorpion (IRE) – Nitelite
Trainer: Emma LAVELLE   **Form Figures: 2**
An imposing unfurnished son of Scorpion: far from the finished article and it was his naked talent that almost got him home on his Inch (Good) debut. Waited with at the rear, he came powering through the field with what looked like a winning challenge to lead arriving at the final fence. He may have used too much fuel making that run, as the always prominent Limos rallied and regained the lead close to the winning post. I felt that The Last Euro emerged from the race with most credit and was one with a bright future. If given the necessary time to mature and acclimatise, I reckon new connections have a potential Graded jumps horse on their hands.

UTMOST ZEAL (IRE) 4 b g Big Bad Bob (IRE) – Dusseldorf (IRE)
Trainer: Gordon ELLIOTT   **Form Figures: F**
Not my idea of a jumpers pedigree...a son of Big Bad Bob, out of a mare who won three of her thirty starts and never stayed a yard beyond two miles.....some defy pedigree....this small gelding was about to trounce some well-regarded rivals in the 2m 4f race at Punchestown (Heavy)...six lengths ahead and drawing further clear with every stride, only to take a crunching fall at the final fence. He has not been seen since, so one would naturally hope that he has recovered from the ordeal. He has an engine, stature may dictate that he could find hurdling his premier calling.

VENITIEN DE MAI (FR) 5 b g Network (GER) – Meylba (FR)
Trainer: Jim DREAPER   **Form Figures: 1111**
Alan Potts bought this French bred son of Network for €130,000 as a store and clearly planned, given his size, to educate him through the pointing ranks with Jim Dreaper. Well, he completed his points season with a perfect 4 from 4 record, cannily placed, winning a maiden at Rockfield (Yielding), a winners of one at Tinahely (Soft), a winners of two at Oldtown (Yielding) and finishing off with a winners of three at Dromahane (Good/Yielding) in April. An excellent jumper, he stays three miles at his leisure and has some gears, plus he acts on soft or good. There are plenty of positives. I doubt if he will be wasted over hurdles, in the old days he would be a natural candidate to plan a crack at the four miler at Cheltenham with....and that may happen...Jamie Codd jelled with him....and he will in years to come be a contender for any of the Grand National races.

VICTORY MILL (IRE) 4 b or br g King's Theatre (IRE) – Full of Surprises (IRE)
Trainer: Dessie HUGHES   **Form Figures: 1**
Out of the handful of Gigginstown House Stud four year old point winners, his performance was the most enlightening: he engaged in a great battle with Blackthorn Prince at Lingstown (Soft) and, producing accurate jumping and steely determination, gained the victory. The dam, who was 0 from 3 with Willie Mullins on the track, has already bred some track winning chasers, such as Gus Macrae: this son of King's Theatre is likely to become at least a 130+ track horse and is another Gigginstown player with genuine aspirations of winning in Graded company.

WHITE ARM (FR) 5 b g Turgeon (USA) – White Consel (FR)
Trainer: Tony MARTIN   **Form Figures: 317**
This could be a decent horse, although we could be kept waiting for some time before he proves it on the track. A French bred son of Turgeon out of a four times winning dam, he enjoyed a leisurely educational when third to Paddy The Deejay on debut at Punchestown (Heavy). He then made all to win apologising at Maralin (Soft/Heavy), looking every inch a classy individual. Then the first hint of what was to come...he lined up in a hunter chase at Killarney and placed a never threatening seventh behind On The Fringe...a gentle racecourse educational, which may double up as part one of a three or four stage ploy to get a low handicap rating. Can run to 120+ when the handbrake is released....will be one of those horses that you can sit back and laugh at the way connections play their cards this winter.....jokes aside, this could be a fine chaser in time.

DECLAN PHELAN'S NATIONAL HUNT SERVICE

If you would like to join Declan's winter jumps service, please contact him on mrdeclanphelan@hotmail.com for full details.

Included in the service:

- Each weekend, clients receive a jumps preview (October to March)....I focus on the lesser races, they tend to be more punter friendly.
- Cheltenham and other Festival previews.
- unraced dark horses from Ireland and the UK
- Plus a special treat... I have scripted a very informative Irish pointers dossier, with individual essays on over 200 track bound, ex-pointers aged 4 and 5 from the 2013/14 season (not available from any other source, and prepared with punters in mind)....on a day to day basis this dossier may give you a punting edge this winter.

For Irish (only) clients, if you would like to hear Declan's nightly views on the next day's racing, they are available from 10pm on 1560 111 112.

STABLE GOSSIP

The 2013/2014 campaign couldn't have gone much better for **Dr Richard Newland**. The Worcestershire based handler sent out a career best 38 winners at a strike-rate of 23% with **PINEAU DE RE** providing the highlight with victory in the Crabbie's Grand National at Aintree. Bought out of Philip Fenton's yard, having won the Ulster version twelve months earlier, the eleven year old won the world's greatest race by five lengths. Raised eight pounds to a mark of 151, all roads will lead back to Liverpool this season, according to his trainer. **"The handicapper has put him up eight pounds, which is fair enough, and I don't think he is too badly treated. We will keep him over hurdles until the weights are published in order to protect his mark."**

Richard has made his name by getting the best out of other trainer's 'cast-offs' without paying a fortune. Ahyaknowyerself, Bobowen and Changing The Guard have won six times apiece since being acquired privately and Night Alliance only cost 10,000gns when rated 110 in Ireland. The nine year old has won on four occasions since, including the Tommy Whittle Chase at Haydock, and is now rated 131 over the larger obstacles. Royale Knight has seven races in less than two years and Smalib Monterg was bought out of a selling hurdle for 6,000gns before winning five times. More recently, Neverownup finished runner-up in a similar event at Fakenham in April for his previous connections. Less than two months later, the nine year old had won four of his next five races with his official rating over fences escalating from 89 to 128.

Ironically, Dr Newland made his most expensive 'signing' of his training career during the spring when paying £58,000 for the ex-Irish gelding **ROCK GONE** at the Cheltenham May Sale on behalf of his cousin Chris Stedman. A six year old by Winged Love, he only raced four times for his previous handler Edmond Kent and improved with each start. Fourth at Limerick in a maiden hurdle in April over 2m 3f (Heavy), he seemingly appreciated the step up to three miles at Cork last time. Beaten a length and a quarter on better ground, his new trainer explains: **"He is the most I have ever paid for a horse but he showed some form in Ireland and I liked the fact he is still a maiden. A lovely big horse with plenty of size and scope, he measures 16.3hh and certainly looks the part. I view him as a staying chaser in the making but I am hoping he will make his mark over hurdles this winter. He has a good pedigree being related to the likes of Goss and I think he is a nice prospect."**

BOONDOOMA is bred to come into his own over fences being a half-brother to Rocky Creek and the ill-fated Tell Massini. Formerly trained across the Irish Sea by Michael Griffin, the seven year old joined Newland in January, having won a point-to-point and bumper at Limerick. A dual winner at Fakenham and Newcastle in March over distances ranging from two to two and a half miles, he wasn't disgraced at Cheltenham the following month when fifth behind Brother Brian. Rated 123 over the smaller obstacles, Richard feels: **"He is a very good novice chase prospect. A strong traveller, we will probably start him off over two or two and a half miles and, even though he is bred to stay three miles plus, I am not convinced he will be an out and out stayer. Bearing in mind his mark, I would imagine we will look for a suitable novices' handicap chase in October/November. He started his pre-training in late June and, while we haven't schooled him over fences, he is a former pointer and I am not envisaging any problems, as far as jumping is concerned."**

The United House Gold Cup at Ascot (1st November) has been earmarked for **ARDKILLY WITNESS**. Twice a winner over fences at Wincanton and Market Rasen last season, the eight year old also ran some good races in defeat, including when fifth in the Betbright Chase at Kempton in February. **"He needs to go right-handed, which restricts our options somewhat, and three miles is his trip. We ran him in the Be365 Gold Cup at the end of last season but he didn't stay the trip. I hope he will continue to be competitive off his mark of 135 and hopefully he can win a good race this winter."**

My *Racing UK* colleague Jonathan Neesom, who specialises in point-to-points and hunter chases, is looking forward to seeing how dual winner **MOR BROOK** performs under Rules for **Kim Bailey** this season. Twice a winner in 'points' for Philip Rowley at Siddington in March and Chaddesley Corbett, both victories were gained over three miles. Subsequently bought by Bailey for £82,000 at the Doncaster May Sales, his new trainer said: **"I've known about him for some time – he's a horse I really like. I hope he'll develop into a very special chaser."**

Middleham trainer **Phil Kirby** had a particularly good season with his bumper horses last term. The head of Sharp Hill Farm sent out 9 winners from only 31 runners in that department. My *Racing UK* colleague Niall Hannity has a close association with the yard and he has advised me to follow the progress of **LADY BUTTONS** over hurdles this winter. Considered the stable's number one bumper performer by some distance, the Beneficial filly won two of her four starts and was unfortunate not to win the Listed mares' bumper at Aintree's Grand National meeting. Beaten a head by Avispa, she had previously won twice at Wetherby (Good/Soft and Heavy). She will take some stopping in mares' only novice hurdles, especially on the northern circuit. The other Kirby inmate to keep an eye on is **ANIKNAM**. A four year old by Nickname, his ten lengths victory at Hexham on his racecourse bow in March wasn't a surprise. Eighth next time in the Grade 1 championship bumper at the Punchestown Festival, he ran respectably but the ground had dried out too much. Connections will be disappointed if he doesn't make an impact in northern novice hurdles when the emphasis is on stamina. Two and a half miles will be ideal.

Sire De Grugy provided **Gary Moore** with his first Grade 1 successes last term and the West Sussex trainer has a couple of horses to keep an eye on who have yet to race under National Hunt rules. Chicquitta (€6m) was undoubtedly the star of the show at the Goffs November Sale last year with owner/breeder Paul Makin's Dispersal the feature of the sale. Moore paid €35,000 for the unraced Galileo colt **DRACO'S CODE**. A half-brother to useful Flat performers Chicago and Mikhail Glinka (won the Queen's Vase in 2010), he could be one for junior bumpers. He was previously in training with Jeremy Noseda. Stablemate **TALL SHIP** failed to win any of his five races on the Flat for Sir Michael Stoute before being purchased at the Newmarket July Sales for 32,000gns. The gelded son of Sea The Stars hasn't looked back since joining Gary Moore winning twice at Goodwood (1m 3f + 1m 4f). A seven lengths winner in August, he has been raised sixteen pounds to a mark of 95. Slow ground is a concern but he could be a useful juvenile hurdler on a sound surface. Ryan Moore presumably recommended the three year old to his father, having partnered him three times when trained by Sir Michael Stoute.

The unbeaten **RHYTHM STAR** is another filly to follow in mares' only novice hurdles this winter. Owned by ValueRacingClub.co.uk, the four year old won both her bumpers at Taunton and Fontwell last season. Cheltenham Festival winning trainer **Jamie Snowden** has been delighted with her during the summer reporting her much stronger than last season. Successful on good and heavy ground, she is expected to make her jumping bow in October.

Nick Williams has done well with juvenile hurdlers in recent seasons (Reve De Sivola, Le Rocher & Fox Norton) and it may pay to follow **BRISE VENDEENNE** this winter. A daughter of Dom Alco, she is a half-brother to the aforementioned Vroum Vroum Mag and she finished a promising third on her debut in an APQS bumper at Le Lion-D'Angers in August (1m 4f : Very Soft). Having been tapped for speed, she stayed on nicely in the closing stages and will appreciate the step up to two miles over hurdles.

WHAT'S THE CRAIC IN IRELAND?

Last year's selections produced **11 winners** at a strike-rate of 37%. They included high-class novices **ADRIANA DES MOTTES** (2 wins), **CLONDAW COURT** (2 wins), **FOXROCK** (3 wins) and **MOYLE PARK**.

APACHE STRONGHOLD (IRE) 6 b g Milan – First Battle (IRE)
Trainer: N.MEADE. Navan, Co.Meath.
Career Form Figures: 133 - 1142
"He was cantering the whole way and jumped great, other than the last. He's something to really look forward to," enthused Noel Meade after Apache Stronghold had easily landed the Grade 2 Monksfield Novice Hurdle at Navan (2m 4f : Good/Yielding) in November. Unfortunately, the Milan gelding wasn't seen again until Fairyhouse's Easter Festival in early April due to an injury (missed the Navan Hurdle in December, due to an abscess on his off-fore foot and then got cast in his box and banged his other leg). Fourth behind Lieutenant Colonel in Grade 2 company, he was reportedly in need of the run on that occasion and proved it with an excellent run at the Punchestown Festival. Only beaten three and a half lengths behind Vautour, Meade commented: **"I'm delighted with him, but I think he's a bit better than that. We were struggling to get him back and that has to have had an effect on him. He's been beaten fair and square on the day, but there's more to come."** Rated 149 over hurdles, Apache Stronghold is built like a chaser and promises to be even better over larger obstacles. Yet to race beyond two and a half miles, he isn't slow either and may even drop back to the minimum trip over fences. Noel Meade has two potentially very good novice chasers for this season in Apache Stronghold and Very Wood.

DON POLI (IRE) 5 b g Poliglote – Dalamine (FR)
Trainer: W.P.MULLINS. Bagenalstown, Co.Carlow.
Career Form Figures: 2 – 21112
Along with Clondaw Court and Pont Alexandre, Willie Mullins has another obvious contender for the RSA Chase in the shape of the ex-French trained Don Poli. The five year old provided Mullins and Gigginstown House Stud with their second win in the Martin Pipe Conditional Jockeys' Hurdle at the Cheltenham Festival following Sir Des Champs's win in 2011. **"He looks like he wants fences already. He has got chaser written all over him,"** remarked Mullins after his four and a half lengths victory at Prestbury Park in March. His rider Michael Fogerty added: **"He's crying out for a trip and his stamina definitely helped him. He's open to improvement over fences and could be very good."** The Poliglote gelding produced an even better effort at the Punchestown Festival when only denied by three parts of a length in the Grade 1 novice hurdle over three miles behind Beat That. A winner on good and heavy ground, he provided Bryan Cooper with his first ever winner for Willie Mullins when scoring at Thurles in January. The twenty one year old, who was appointment first jockey for Gigginstown House Stud in January, but, unfortunately, broke his right leg aboard Clarcam in the Fred Winter Hurdle at Cheltenham in March, will be itching to return to the saddle to partner this exciting gelding over fences. Willie Mullins has won the RSA Chase three times (Florida Pearl (1998), Rule Supreme (2004) and Cooldine (2009)), while Gigginstown House Stud landed the three miles prize in 2010 thanks to Weapons Amnesty. The pair have a prime candidate for the 2015 version.

FINE ARTICLE (IRE) 5 b g Definite Article – Finemar Lady (IRE)
Trainer: P.NOLAN. Enniscorthy, Co.Wexford.
Career Form Figures: 214

Joncol was a dual Grade 1 winner for Paul Nolan, capturing the John Durkan Memorial Chase at Punchestown in 2009 and followed up in the Hennessy Gold Cup at Leopardstown two months later. In total, the Bob's Return gelding won 7 times earning £310,315 in prize-money. His sibling Fine Article has some way to go to match his achievements but he is a good prospect, nevertheless. The Definite Article gelding raced three times last season, winning a bumper at Gowran Park (Heavy) in March by a length and a quarter. His trainer Paul Nolan reported: **"He's very backward, although he's been showing improvement at home. Being by Definite Article, you'd think he'd like better ground. But all of the family, including Joncol, were mudlarks. Robbie (McNamara) is adamant though that this fellow is a bit different."** A running on fourth behind Shaneshill in the Grade 1 Champion bumper at the Punchestown Festival (Good/Yielding), Fine Article will appreciate a step up to two and a half miles over timber and is held in high regard by the Nolan team.

TWENTYTWO'S TAKEN (IRE) 6 b m King's Theatre (IRE) – Persian Desert (IRE)
Trainer: S.R.B.CRAWFORD. Larne, Co.Antrim.
Career Form Figures: 11

Northern Ireland based handler Stuart Crawford had a profitable campaign on either side of the Irish Sea last term (10 winners in Ireland and 14 in the UK). The stable did particularly well with their bumper horses with the likes of Heritage Way (Nicky Henderson), Knocklayde Express (30,000gns), Taniokey (£34,000 and joined Oliver Sherwood) and Vayland (€65,000 and joined David Pipe) all winning before being subsequently sold. One inmate who remains at Newlands Farm is the unbeaten mare Twentytwo's Taken. A six year old by King's Theatre, she is a half-sister to six times winner Prince Massini and looked a smart mare last winter. A ten lengths winner on her debut in a bumper at Down Royal (Soft) on Boxing Day, her trainer said afterwards: **"She's a lovely, lovely mare but we'd never taken her away to the track before today, so I'm obviously thrilled."** She then defied a penalty to win another mares' bumper at Fairyhouse (Heavy) in early February. Displaying a sharp turn of foot, Twentytwo's Taken quickened clear to win by nearly four lengths. **"We felt she had improved a fair bit from her first run at Down Royal. We didn't know what we had going to Down Royal but we have a much better idea of what we have now,"** remarked Crawford afterwards. She was being aimed at the Listed mares' bumper at Aintree's Grand National meeting, a race the stable won in 2013 with Legacy Gold. Her trainer said a few days beforehand: **"This race has been the plan for some time and everything has gone well since Fairyhouse. We took her away to Navan for a gallop a couple of weeks ago and she went really nicely. There was a bit of strength in depth to the race she won at Fairyhouse and we think she has come on since then."** Unfortunately, Twentytwo's Taken scoped badly on the eve of the race and was unable to take her chance. She is set to go novice hurdling this winter but there is a possibility she will contest the Grade 2 bumper at Navan (14th December) beforehand. Stuart Crawford was awarded the race last year in a subsequent enquiry, which featured Royal Caviar and Fine Rightly. She is a smashing mare who ought to do very well over hurdles. She has only raced on testing ground and on right-handed tracks to date.

WESTERN BOY (IRE) 5 b g Antonius Pius (USA) – Skala (IRE)
Trainer: P.A.FAHY. Rathellen, Co.Carlow.
Career Form Figures: 24 – 211275

County Carlow trainer Pat Fahy sent out Mariah Rollins to win the Grade 1 novice chase over two miles at Leopardstown on Boxing Day in 2004 and he may have the same event in mind for Western Boy. A bumper winner at Thurles (Yielding) in November, the five year old followed up on his hurdles debut at Leopardstown (Soft) over Christmas when beating Kylestyle by three and a half lengths. Rated 143 over hurdles, his best performance came in the Grade 2 Moscow Flyer Novice Hurdle at Punchestown (Soft/Heavy) in January when forcing Vautour to pull out all the stops. Only beaten three parts of a length, the Antonius Pius gelding pulled eleven lengths clear of the third. A creditable seventh in the Supreme Novices' Hurdle at Cheltenham, Western Boy wasn't disgraced at the Punchestown Festival either behind Faugheen. Subsequently bought by J.P.McManus, he could be a smart two mile novice chaser, although he may stay further.

VELVET MAKER (FR) 5 b g Policy Maker (IRE) – Evasion De L'Orne (FR)
Trainer: A.J.MARTIN. Summerhill, Co.Meath.
Career Form Figures: 13

Previously trained in France by Guy Cherel, Velvet Maker won an APQS Flat race at Pornichet-La-Baule (1m 4f: Standard) from stablemate Vibraye (finished fourth over hurdles at Auteuil since) by two lengths in August. Bought by Barry Connell soon afterwards, the five year old made his hurdles debut in a hotly contested maiden hurdle at Navan (2m : Good/Yielding) in December and ran a cracker in third. Only beaten seven lengths by Vautour (rated 158) and Lieutenant Colonel (143), he raced keenly early on but jumped well and kept on in the latter stages. It was a most encouraging performance. His trainer Tony Martin commented in *The Irish Field* in mid January: **"He had a good run at Navan and he wouldn't be mad about this real bad ground, so we'll give him a chance and have him out in the next month or so. You'd like to think he will win his maiden hurdle but the year is getting on and we might keep him as a novice for next season."** Indeed, Velvet Maker hasn't been seen since and he remains eligible for novice hurdles this term. He could be very much one to follow this winter because his form at Navan is outstanding.

Other Notes

As discussed, dual Grade 1 winning novice hurdler **THE TULLOW TANK** has joined Dessie Hughes. Likely to be sent over fences this season, his big pay day may be in the Grade 1 Drinmore Novice Chase at Fairyhouse (30th November). The step up to two and a half miles will suit and he is arguably a better horse going right-handed (11). Finally, Willie Mullins has yet another interesting prospect for juvenile hurdles in the ex-French trained **PETITE PARISIENNE**. Formerly handled by Jean-Claude Rouget, the daughter of Montmartre raced four times on the level with form figures of 3132. A length and a half winner at Senonnes (1m 3f) in May, she subsequently finished third in a Listed contest at Bordeaux during the same month. Runner-up at Chantilly (1m 2f) last time, she was bought at the Arqana Sale in early July for €135,000.

Don't forget to check out the Diary @
www.mhpublications.co.uk

Extracts from this year........

Thursday 24th July 2014
I am hopeful the horse featured on page 30 (**MUTHMIR**) of *Ahead On The Flat* will go close on Saturday. His trainer believes he has improved from his last run and the track and trip should be ideal. **MUTHMIR wins the Skybet Dash @ 4/1 (26/7/14)**

Thursday 17th July 2014
Godolphin won the seven furlong fillies' maiden at Doncaster this evening with Adelasia. Fifth over course and distance on her debut last month, the daughter of Iffraaj was much more streetwise on this occasion and won going away under William Buick. However, I was taken by the performance of the fifth **MAHSOOBA**, who was sporting the second colours of owner Hamdan Al Maktoum. Ridden by Dane O'Neill, the Hard Spun filly kept on well in the closing stages under a hand ride and is one to note in her next couple of starts. I will be surprised if she can't win races. **MAHSOOBA won next at Newmarket @ 3/1 (2/8/14)**

Monday 12th May 2014
I strongly suggest clients add the James Fanshawe trained **SPIRIT RAISER** to their notebooks. A daughter of Invincible Spirit, she caught the eye on her reappearance at Haydock and did so again in the one mile maiden at Doncaster this afternoon. Hayley Turner didn't subject her to a hard race and that kindness is likely to be repaid once tackling fillies' handicaps. Bred to improve with age, I will be amazed if Spirit Raiser can't win races. **WON at Newmarket (27/6/14) @ 9/4**

Wednesday 16th April 2014
Elsewhere, the other performance I liked came from **BLAINE** in the five furlongs handicap at Beverley. Kevin Ryan's four year old won the Group 2 Gimcrack Stakes at York a couple of seasons ago but proved bitterly disappointing last term. Gelded since last season, he was once rated 107 but raced off 95 at the Westwood. Drawn wide in stall 10, he was running on nicely in the latter stages and will benefit from a return to six furlongs (this was his first run over the minimum trip). He is one for those competitive sprint handicaps this spring/summer. Blaine could even be one for the Ayr Gold Cup in September. **WON the Scottish Stewards' Cup at Hamilton (18/7/14) @ 6/1 & York (20/8/14) @ 12/1**

Monday 14th April 2014
It is also worth noting the performance of **KINSHASA**, who finished fourth in the same race. The well bred son of Pivotal was beaten around six lengths and never looked like winning but his finishing effort was eyecatching. Partnered by Lemos de Souza, who was having his first ride in the UK, he was green early on but the penny dropped during the latter stages. A half-brother to Kikonga and from the family of Milan, he was included in *Ahead On The Flat* on the recommendation of his trainer Luca Cumani. I will be surprised if he doesn't have a future over middle distances later in the year. **WON at Kempton (4/6/14) @ 7/2 & Salisbury (25/6/14) @ 9/4**

What The Clients Said:
"Once more, superb information at York. Thank you very much indeed. I filled my boots as it were on the Knavesmire." **S.R.**

"Just a note to say thanks for Muthmir. Outstanding service." **B.M.**

APPENDIX

As in previous years, I have attempted to highlight a number of horses (those who have not already been covered in the other sections of *OJA*), in various categories, who are expected to contest the major prizes during the 2014/2015 campaign.

Two Mile Chasers:
The star of the show in the two mile division last season was undoubtedly **SIRE DE GRUGY**, who won six of his seven races. Four of those victories were gained in Grade 1 events, including the Queen Mother Champion Chase at Cheltenham. His six lengths victory was providing Gary Moore's with his first Cheltenham Festival winner since Tikram won the Mildmay of Flete Chase in 2004. It was announced in August the eight year old underwent an operation to remove bone chips from both ankles. Either the Shloer Chase at Cheltenham (16th November) or the Tingle Creek at Sandown (6th December) is his likely starting point. He enjoyed a fantastic season last winter but he hardly won a vintage Champion Chase and I feel he could be vulnerable this time.

Arguably the biggest disappointment last season was the fact we only saw former Champion Chaser **SPRINTER SACRE** once and it resulted in him pulling up after the seventh fence in the Desert Orchid Chase at Kempton's Christmas fixture and, in doing so, losing his unbeaten record over fences. Found to be suffering with an irregular heartbeat, the eight year old missed the rest of the season. Nicky Henderson issued an upbeat report in mid August saying: **"Sprinter Sacre looks magnificent after his long summer break and everything is A1 with him. We've tweaked a couple of minor things and he's fine. I imagine he'll start off in the Tingle Creek and suspect he'll be seeing Sire De Grugy there. Then I would think it'll be a similar programme to the winter before last leading up to Cheltenham."** A nineteen lengths winner of the 2013 Queen Mother, it remains to be seen though whether he will ever return to his brilliant best.

With Arkle Trophy winner Western Warhorse sidelined and runner-up Champagne Fever due to step up in trip, it will be interesting to see which of last season's leading novices emerge as threats to the more established two milers. **BALDER SUCCES** was rated 145 over hurdles but the six year old has developed into an even better chaser winning five of his eight races. A four lengths winner of the Grade 1 Maghull Novices' Chase at Aintree, his trainer Alan King said afterwards: **"He used to be a bit soft over hurdles but fences have made a man of him and he's getting better all the time. He stays two and a half miles but is probably at his best over two."** Narrowly beaten at Punchestown last time, the Goldneyev gelding is suited by small fields with his chase wins gained in field sizes of 5, 5, 5, 6 and 7.

NEXT SENSATION won handicaps at Plumpton, Newcastle and Doncaster last season off marks of 105, 118 and 133. However, Michael Scudamore's former Irish pointer produced his best performance at the Cheltenham Festival when fourth in the Grand Annual Chase. Given an overly aggressive ride by Richard Johnson, he ran a remarkable race considering the tempo he set and was still only beaten a length and three quarters. The seven year old was almost certainly still feeling the effects when well held in the aforementioned Maghull Novices' Chase at Aintree. His Cheltenham effort suggests he still has a lot more to offer his current mark of 146. He is a spectacular jumper and his return to action is eagerly anticipated.

DEFY LOGIC claimed some notable scalps in the Grade 1 *Racing Post* Novice Chase at Leopardstown on Boxing Day. Paul Nolan's Flemensfirth gelding beat Trifolium and Champagne Fever by upwards of three and a half lengths. A leading fancy for the Arkle Trophy as a result, he burst a blood vessel in the Irish equivalent at the same track in late January trailing in a well beaten fifth and hasn't been seen since. Lightly raced, the seven year old goes well fresh and is one to watch out for on his reappearance (1st time out record is 211). However, the fact he has bled once immediately casts a doubt over his future and whether he will fulfil his undoubted potential.

Two and a half Mile Chasers:

SIMONSIG was another star from the previous season who was missing last winter. Nicky Henderson explained in mid December: **"The fracture line on the splint has gone and he's sound, but there's too much risk involved. We're going to keep him in light exercise until the spring, turn him out in the summer and bring him back ready for the King George next year."** Unbeaten in three races over fences, the eight year old is a dual Cheltenham Festival winner and is rated 162. The King George on Boxing Day is reportedly his first target with the likelihood of one race beforehand.

TAQUIN DU SEUIL is rated 159 and ended his first season over fences with a career best win in the Jewson Novices' Chase at Cheltenham. **"He is proven at this trip and hopefully he will step up to the Gold Cup trip. He won over a mile seven on the Flat in France. If he does get the trip, he's a proper horse,"** enthused Jonjo O'Neill after his three parts of a length win at Prestbury Park. The seven year old's record in Grade 1 company is 1631 and his form figures at Cheltenham are 6121. If he stays three miles, he doesn't have to improve too much to develop into a Cheltenham Gold Cup contender. A winner at Haydock, it will be interesting to see if he is given an entry in the *Betfair* Chase.

J.P.McManus paid £100,000 for **UXIZANDRE** at the Doncaster May Sales in 2013. The six year old remained in training with Alan King and the Fragrant Mix gelding rewarded his new owner with three wins over fences, including the Grade 1 Manifesto Novices' Chase at Aintree. A length and a half winner, his handler said afterwards: **"He has to go left-handed. It will limit his opportunities but you could never ride him right-handed. The Ryanair may be the race for him, but he could even come back in trip as he has plenty of pace."** He seemingly gets on very well with A.P.McCoy (1151).

It is debatable whether **MA FILLEULE** has justified an official rating of 163 but she was a spectacular eight lengths winner of the Grade 3 Topham Chase over the National fences at Aintree off a mark of 150. **"The biggest problem I had was getting Ma Filleule to go into the fences on a short stride. She wanted to go long on everything and take the fences on, but she did jump brilliantly,"** remarked Barry Geraghty afterwards. Nicky Henderson's mare has struck up a good association with the Irishman (2223P11). A winner at Kempton in December, the King George is expected to come under serious consideration with the Ryanair Chase her obvious end of season target. There is no doubt she was hugely impressive at Aintree but whether she will be able to reproduce such a performance in Grade 1 company is open to question.

The Colin Parker Memorial Chase at Carlisle (2nd November) has already been earmarked as the likely starting point for **EDUARD**. The Future Champions Novices' Chase at Ayr's Scottish National meeting was kind to the late Gordon Richards with the Greystoke trainer winning it five times between 1976 and 1996 and his son Nicky won it in 2006 with Monet's Garden. The seven year old added his name to the roll of honour following a twenty lengths victory in Ayr. A three times winner over the larger obstacle, Richards said of his stable star: **"I've had full confidence in this horse from the day he ran in a bumper and he's done what I thought he'd do. He had a bit of a problem after he sprawled on landing at Carlisle, so we've taken our time with him. He's got the most fantastic National Hunt pedigree and he's closely related to Monty's Pass and Harbour Pilot – he'd get any trip."** The Morozov gelding has only raced twice over two and a half miles and, as his pedigree suggests, he could be even better over further.

BALLYCASEY hasn't always been the easiest horse to train, hence he has only raced a dozen times (three of those races in point-to-points). He is therefore not the sort to recommend ante-post but it would be no surprise to see Willie Mullins' grey gelding develop into a leading contender for the Ryanair Chase. A four lengths winner of the Grade 1 Dr P.J.Moriarty Chase at Leopardstown in February, he didn't get home in the RSA Chase at Cheltenham finishing fourth. He was then an unlucky loser of the Grade 1 Powers Gold Cup when hitting the deck at the second last at Fairyhouse when seemingly in control. Runner-up at Punchestown on his final start, he looks ideal for races like the John Durkan Memorial Chase at the same venue (7th December).

At a lesser level, it will be interesting to see what David Pipe can achieve with new arrival **EASTER METEOR**. A three times winner for Emma Lavelle, the eight year old was in the process of running a big race in last season's Paddy Power Gold Cup at Cheltenham when coming to grief at the second last. Despite being eight pounds higher than last season, the Midnight Legend gelding is shortlist material for the same event in November, even though his record at the track is 024PF6B. His first time out record is 3412P.

Owners Alan and Ann Potts invariably have runners at Cheltenham's Paddy Power meeting and, with that in mind, I wouldn't be surprised to see **SIZING GOLD** given an entry in the Paddy Power Gold Cup itself (15th November). A four lengths winner at Navan in December (2m 4f : Yielding/Soft), his trainer Henry De Bromhead said afterwards: **"He was deadly and that is his game. We have always liked him. We have some really good novices and he's up there with them."** A possible non stayer next time behind Foxrock in the Grade 2 Woodlands Park 100 Club Novice Chase at Naas over three miles, he may have found the ground too lively on his final two outings at Cheltenham (sixth in the Jewson Novice Chase) at Punchestown. The Flemensfirth gelding wants soft ground to bring out the best in him (form figures on soft or heavy 212212512) but there is little doubt he is potentially well handicapped off 135 over fences.

Staying Chasers:
The established top flight chasers are sure to have another big say in the outcome of the major races. These include the likes of **BOBS WORTH**, **CUE CARD** (missed Cheltenham due to a minor stress fracture of his pelvis – he will be ridden by Daryl Jacob this season), **DYNASTE**, **LORD WINDERMERE** (last season's Gold Cup winner) and **SILVINIACO CONTI** (Charlie Hall, *Betfair* Chase, King George & Gold Cup).

BOSTON BOB underwent a wind operation before running in the Ryanair Chase. A staying on sixth behind Dynaste at the Festival, he clearly benefited from the outing and was given a terrific ride by Paul Townend (11FF1) when winning the Grade 1 Melling Chase at Aintree. The nine year old then gained his fourth Grade 1 victory in the Punchestown Gold Cup later the same month. Stepping up to three miles one, he ran on strongly to beat First Lieutenant and Long Run by upwards of three and a quarter lengths. **"After that, we'll probably aim him at the Cheltenham Gold Cup. He could start off next season back here in the John Durkan Memorial Chase (7th December). The horse seems to have turned the corner and is becoming the horse I thought he would become,"** said Willie Mullins afterwards. The King George looks another option for the Andrea and Graham Wylie owned gelding.

The three mile Festive showpiece at Kempton may also come under consideration for stablemate **CHAMPAGNE FEVER**, who is set to step up in trip this season. The dual Cheltenham Festival winner came within a head of making it three successive wins at Prestbury Park in March when headed close home by Western Warhorse. Below par on his final run at Punchestown, the Stowaway gelding has only had four races over fences and is already being touted as a Gold Cup contender. The ability is undoubtedly there but it will be interesting to see how he settles over longer distances because he invariably races enthusiastically. Ruby Walsh certainly won't be in a rush on him. He is another who may be given an entry in the John Durkan Memorial Chase.

HOLYWELL is a dual Cheltenham Festival winner and, while he was smart over hurdles, he proved a revelation over fences last term. The seven year old was beaten on his first three races over the larger obstacles – Carlisle, Catterick and Wincanton – but he never looked back during the second half of the year. Victories came at Catterick, Doncaster, Cheltenham and Aintree in less than three months with his official rating escalating to 163. Having beaten Ma Filleule by a length and three quarters in the Baylis & Harding Affordable Luxury Handicap Chase at the Cheltenham Festival off 145, the seven year old then produced an even better performance to win the Grade 1 Mildmay Novices' Chase at Aintree by ten lengths. A.P.McCoy (12232111) said afterwards: **"I would never have said he was a Gold Cup contender before but he has beaten all of them today convincingly. In terms of form, this horse will be the best chaser we see all year. It is not impossible for him to win the Gold Cup."** His trainer added: **"He's definitely in the Gold Cup bracket."** The Gold Well gelding is unbeaten in two visits to Cheltenham.

Stablemate **SHUTTHEFRONTDOOR** provided 34 year old Barry Geraghty with his first win in the Irish National when scoring by three parts of a length at Fairyhouse in April. The seven year old's trainer Jonjo O'Neill believes: **"The National Hunt Chase was Plan A. He ran well at Cheltenham and today was Plan B. We can look forward to next season. He has a bit of class and could be a Gold Cup horse."** Raised eight pounds to a mark of 150, the Accordion gelding is only seven and remains open to plenty of improvement. He underwent a wind operation mid season and may not want the ground too soft (withdrawn from the Towton Novices' Chase at Wetherby in February due to heavy ground). There could be another big handicap to be won with him before turning his attentions to conditions chases.

O'FAOLAINS BOY, featured in the *Top 40 Prospects* last season, won the Reynoldstown Novices' Chase at Ascot and followed up in the RSA Chase at Cheltenham. Found to be wrong (scoped badly and stable out of form) when pulled up at Haydock in January, Rebecca Curtis' gelding bounced back at Ascot when beating Many Clouds by two and a half lengths. Despite pulling off a back shoe and twisting a front shoe, the seven year old won the RSA Chase by a neck from Smad Place. **"For whatever reason, he didn't sparkle but he still got the job done. I think there's better to come from him. He's a smart novice to win that when maybe he wasn't at his best. The Gold Cup is the big dream. Everyone wants a Gold Cup horse but there is no reason why he can't be,"** said Rebecca Curtis afterwards. Only fifth at Aintree, his trainer explained: **"He's absolutely fine but he has just run a little flat. It was in the back of our minds he would, but he seemed fine at home and Barry (Geraghty) has looked after him."** Lord Windermere won the RSA Chase en route to Gold Cup glory in consecutive seasons.

RSA Chase runner-up **SMAD PLACE** has the Hennessy Gold Cup (29th November) as his first target. Placed in the World Hurdle twice, Alan King's grey won over fences at Exeter and Newbury (unlucky not to win at Huntingdon on his chasing bow) before heading to the Festival. Only beaten a neck, the Barbury Castle based handler said afterwards: **"He did everything right bar win and you'd have to look on him as a Gold Cup type. He stays well and has run some marvellous races at Cheltenham."** The grey's first time out record is 6113U.

Granted decent ground, **LE BEC** looks capable of winning a good staying prize this season. Rated 149, the six year old has only raced ten times during his career, winning twice over fences last term. He beat Shutthefrontdoor by three parts of a length at Cheltenham's Paddy Power meeting in November before chasing home Sam Winner at the same track the following month. Absent until the RSA Chase, the Smadoun gelding was still going well when falling four out. His trainer was left frustrated saying: **"Le Bec was cantering, although it was too far out to say what would have happened. He took a horrible fall but thank god he was absolutely fine."** The underfoot conditions will determine his programme.

In terms of staying handicap chases, the following look capable of winning races this season. Robert Walford sent out 12 winners from only 65 runners last season, including French bred Umberto D'Olivate, who won four times over fences. The former rider will be hoping to repeat the trick with another new recruit from France, namely **CAMPING GROUND**. Only four, the gelded son of Goldneyev is a five times winner already. A winner over hurdles and fences (by ten lengths) at Auteuil, his other victories have been gained at Nantes, Chateaubriant (both May 2013) and Senonnes (March 2014). A nine lengths winner at Auteuil in March on his most recent start, he has yet to be given a rating but is a potentially exciting prospect for the Blandford based handler.

Evan Williams' runners at Haydock have proved profitable to follow in recent years (£60.50 to a £1 level stake during the last 5 seasons). It would be no surprise if the Welshman is eyeing races like the Tommy Whittle Chase (20th December) at the Merseyside track for **FIREBIRD FLYER**. Bought for 30,000gns in May 2012, the former Irish trained gelding was runner-up in the West Wales National at Ffos Las in February before winning at Ludlow next time. Placed twice at Haydock over hurdles and fences during the spring, he enjoys cut in the ground and can win races off 133.

Like Dr Newland, Brian Ellison has a superb record with other trainer's 'cast offs,' and it will be fascinating to see what he can achieve with **HERDSMAN**. Bought out of Sue Smith's yard for 18,000gns at the Doncaster May Sales, the nine year old has won two of his six races over fences and is a proven mudlark. Both his victories at Bangor (off 115) and Catterick (127) last season were gained on heavy ground. Placed at Carlisle in December, he is rated 132 and could be one for the Cumberland Handicap Chase (2nd November).

I was working at Ayr on Scottish National day and was taken by the performance of **SAMSTOWN** in the novices' handicap chase. Previously trained by Lucinda Russell, the seven year old was transferred to Alistair Whillans last season and he won twice over fences. A nineteen lengths winner at Ayr off a mark of 116, the handicapper has punished him, as a result, raising the Kingsalsa gelding by nineteen pounds. **"I thought he'd run very well. We didn't lay him out for this, but when he ran last time he'd had a few hiccups and the stable wasn't quite right,"** commented his trainer afterwards. The Ayr race has a terrific roll of honour – it includes Silver Birch (2nd in 2004), McKelvey (2nd in 2006), Always Waining (1st in 2006), Merigo (1st) & Ballabriggs (2nd in 2008), Auroras Encore (1st in 2009), On His Own (1st in 2011) and Johns Spirit (3rd in 2013). If he can defy the hefty rise in the weights, he remains unexposed over three miles plus (1714221).

The Emma Lavelle trained **SHOTGUN PADDY** overcame his lack of fencing experience to win the Grade 3 Betfred Classic Chase at Warwick (3m 5f : Soft) in January by six lengths off a rating of 145. A neck second in the National Hunt Chase at the Cheltenham Festival, he was surprisingly dropped two pounds afterwards and doesn't look badly treated off 149. **"Everything happened a bit quick for him on that ground and I think that is why his jumping wasn't as good as usual. We will gear up for the Welsh National next year,"** explained his trainer at the Festival. The Brian Boru is unbeaten in two runs at Chepstow.

THEATRE GUIDE was found to be lame on the same morning as stablemate Cue Card incurred a pelvic injury on the gallops in late February. The seven year old only raced three times last term but his third in the Hennessy Gold Cup implied he could have further improvement in him off 149. Still only seven, three miles plus is his trip and Colin Tizzard gave him a Cheltenham Gold Cup entry last season.

If Tim Easterby can sort **TRUSTAN TIMES**'s jumping out, the Heron Island gelding can win a big pot over fences. The former Irish pointer has only had half a dozen races over the larger obstacles and was arguably unlucky not to win the Scottish National in April. Only beaten a length and three quarters, the eight year old blundered at the first fence and was immediately shuffled to the back of the field. **"He hit the first fence very hard; he got right into the bottom of it and that did his race really. Wilson (Renwick) had to school him on the first circuit but, after that, he got into it and he's run a cracker,"** commented Easterby. Placed in the Long Walk, Rendlesham and Pertemps Final Hurdles during his career, he is also a former winner of the fixed brush handicap hurdle at Haydock in 2012 (beat Holywell conceding twelve pounds). He is handicapped to win a good staying chase off 142, if his jumping holds.

Moving across the Irish Sea, we almost certainly didn't see the best of **FOXROCK** in the four mile chase at Cheltenham. Ted Walsh's gelding didn't jump with any fluency and was well beaten in ninth behind Midnight Player. A dual Grade 2 winner at Naas and Navan, the six year old endured two hard races on those occasions in heavy ground and may have still been feeling the effects at Cheltenham. Third in Grade 1 company at Leopardstown over Christmas, he is fairly treated off 142 and strikes me as a future National horse. He could be one for the Welsh version this season (27th December) but he needs to jump much better than he did at Prestbury Park. It's possible he found the ground too lively in March. His record on soft/heavy ground is 1U23111.

When it comes to staying handicap chases, Tony Martin is invariably many people's first port of call. A winning pointer for Enda Bolger, **HEATHFIELD** is the sort of horse he could excel with this winter. Only rated 97 over fences, he remains a novice after six runs but caught the eye in no uncertain terms when third behind stablemate Wrong Turn at Leopardstown (2m 5f : Yielding/Soft) over Christmas. Absent until May, he was a staying on fifth at Killarney. I will be surprised if he can't make an impact off his current mark. Stablemate **SRAID PADRAIG** has a very good record on his seasonal reappearance (4111) and is one to watch out for first time out this season. The eight year old beat Cause of Causes over two miles at Fairyhouse in November with his trainer saying: **"He's a lovely horse and we've always liked him. He ran a lovely race when he won at Limerick last year but he's needed all the time he's got since. Things didn't go the right way for him after he won."** Eighth in the Byrne Group Plate at the Cheltenham Festival, he ran well for a long way in the Irish National before finishing thirteenth. Rated 135, his two Rules wins have been gained on right-handed tracks but he won his point-to-point going the other way round (Dromahane). The Paddy Power Chase at Leopardstown (27th December), which is 0-145, could be his race. Perhaps, he will go there first time out.

Two Mile Hurdlers:
JEZKI, who was third in the Supreme Novices' Hurdle in 2013, produced a terrific performance when going two better in the Champion Hurdle twelve months later. With A.P.McCoy electing to ride My Tent Or Yours, Barry Geraghty took over at Cheltenham and made it five out of five aboard Jessica Harrington's stable star. A neck winner, he followed it up with a three and a quarter lengths win in the *Racing Post* Champion Hurdle at the Punchestown Festival (one of six winners at the meeting for the stable) from Hurricane Fly. The six year old has won 9 of his 12 races over timber and, with time still very much on his side, he will continue to be a tough nut to crack. His record in Grade 1 company is 8113112411 and his form figures first time out are 111.

As discussed, compatriot **FAUGHEEN** could be heading down the Champion Hurdle route following a fantastic novice campaign, which culminated in victories at Cheltenham and Punchestown. A four and a half lengths winner at Prestbury Park, the Germany gelding had no trouble dropping back to the minimum trip in the Grade 1 Champion Novice Hurdle at Punchestown. Making all, he skipped a dozen lengths clear of stablemate Valseur Lido with Willie Mullins saying afterwards: **"That was very good. We might have to consider staying over hurdles next season. When we bought him, I thought he was a chaser but there'd be no harm in having another good hurdler."** His jumping has been an issue in the past and a lot depends on how he fares against battle hardened hurdlers over the minimum trip in Grade 1 company but he certainly deserves a crack at the best in the business. The six year old has a huge engine.

Stablemate **UN DE SCEAUX** is also unbeaten, having won 9 out of 9 during his relatively short career. A five times winner last season, the six year old has yet to race at Grade 1 level following his trainer's decision to skip Cheltenham and Punchestown. His final two wins came at Auteuil over two and a half miles but, on each occasion, he left the impression he will always be at his best over the minimum trip. It is well documented that he is highly strung and, hopefully, with another summer on his back, he will return a much more relaxed individual. Despite three Graded wins, the Denham Red gelding has been minded thus far but now is the time to find out whether he is genuine Grade 1 material.

Ireland's champion trainer was also responsible for one of the best juvenile hurdlers on either side of the Irish Sea during the first half of the season in **ANALIFET**. A winner over hurdles at Compiegne for Serge Foucher in May, she won twice for Mullins at Punchestown and Fairyhouse. A six and a half lengths winner of a Grade 3 contest at the latter venue, her trainer said: **"I wouldn't be afraid to go anywhere with her. She did what she has been doing at home and is a really strong type."** Ruby Walsh was equally impressed adding: **"She's very good. She's keen but she keeps going."** Sent off 30/100 favourite for the Grade 2 Knight Frank Juvenile Hurdle at Leopardstown on Boxing Day, she was pulled up and found to be suffering with a pelvic injury. The Califet filly hasn't been seen since but, all being well, she will be back in action and ready to resume her promising career. Rated 145, she is a talented filly.

Talking of enthusiastic racers, **MY TENT OR YOURS** continues to prove to be his own worst enemy, despite two Grade 1 victories at Newcastle and Kempton. Nicky Henderson's seven year old raced too keenly in the Champion Hurdle but was still only denied by a neck and then he didn't get home in the Scottish version at Ayr when fitted with a hood for the first time. In terms of natural ability, he is as good as there is but until he consents to relax, he will always be vulnerable. There is also the possibility he may go over fences this season.

There are plenty of people who feel **THE NEW ONE** was an unlucky loser at Cheltenham in March when hampered by the fatal fall of Our Conor at the third flight. Beaten less than three lengths by Jezki, there is no doubt Nigel Twiston-Davies' gelding was making up ground hand over fist after the last but he appeared tapped for speed coming down the hill. Stepped up to two and a half miles in the Aintree Hurdle, the King's Theatre gelding scrambled home by a head from Rock On Ruby. His record in Grade 1 company is 612231 and he is a four times winner at Cheltenham. I am still not convinced he is a Champion Hurdle winner. Did he miss his chance last season?

There is no disputing the fact **CALIPTO** was unfortunate not to win at the Festival after his stirrup leather broke after the second last flight in the Triumph Hurdle. Paul Nicholls' ex-French gelding finished fourth behind Tiger Roll and then may have found Aintree too sharp when third in the Grade 1 four year old hurdle. Described as **'a big baby'** last season by his trainer, the dual Newbury winner looks tailormade for the Greatwood Hurdle at Cheltenham (16th November) off his mark of 143. The champion trainer has won the race in the past with Rigmarole (2003) and Brampour (2012). The latter was also a four year old.

Stablemate **KATGARY** could also be aimed at the same two mile event. Formerly trained by Guillaume Macaire, he won twice over hurdles in France before failing by three parts of a length to win the Fred Winter Juvenile Hurdle at Cheltenham in March on his British debut. The Ballingarry gelding travelled strongly before being hampered by the fall of Clarcam at the penultimate flight. Reportedly over the top when only sixth at Aintree on Grand National day, he has a lot more to offer with his current rating of 137. He can win a good prize over timber before making his mark over the larger obstacles.

Arthur Moore's **SEA BEAT** was balloted out of the aforementioned Fred Winter Hurdle but it may prove a blessing in disguise as his trainer explained in the spring: **"My son J.D. (Moore) bought him well last year out of Juddmonte and he's a lovely horse. He didn't make the cut in the Fred Winter but that may have been for the better. He will go for a handicap hurdle at Punchestown and then we'll give him a break and bring him back in the Autumn."** Only tenth at Punchestown, the Beat Hollow gelding may have found the ground too quick, having previously won at Naas in February on heavy ground. Bought for 11,000gns last year, he was reportedly highly strung last season and hopefully he is another who will progress mentally this winter. If so, he can win a good handicap hurdle off his lenient looking mark of 124. The Boylesports Hurdle at Leopardstown in January could be a possible target.

Finally, the John Quinn trained **SWNYMOR** looks potentially very well handicapped off a mark of 129, compared to his Flat rating of 95. A high-class juvenile hurdler a couple of seasons ago, he looked all set to win the Grade 1 Finale Hurdle at Chepstow in January 2013 only to crash out at the final flight. Previously handled by Tim Vaughan and Rebecca Curtis, the five year old joined Quinn during the spring and he won impressively at Chester in May. The Dylan Thomas gelding then ran a terrific race from a poor draw in a valuable handicap at Galway in late July finishing fifth. Once rated 143 over timber, he could be 'thrown in' off his current mark.

Two and a half Mile Hurdlers +:

Unbeaten in five career starts, **MORE OF THAT** rapidly developed into the best staying hurdler in training last season. Jonjo O'Neill's six year old became the first horse to beat Annie Power when capturing the Ladbrokes World Hurdle at Cheltenham by a length and a half. The Beneficial gelding won a handicap hurdle at Wetherby in early November off a mark of 130 and is now rated 169. His trainer commented in January: **"He's a big fine sort and you have to think whatever he does this year is a bonus as he will make a nice chaser."** Even more worryingly for the opposition, the head of Jackdaw's Castle remarked at the Festival: **"He's still a big frame of a horse, coming to himself."** Whether he continues over hurdles or goes chasing, he is one of the most exciting horses in training – he is a class act.

Big Buck's, of course, provided Paul Nicholls and Andy Stewart with four consecutive victories in the World Hurdle (2009 – 2012) and the pair are hoping the progressive **SAPHIR DU RHEU** can develop into a top-class stayer. A three times winner last season, including the Lanzarote Hurdle at Kempton and Welsh Champion Hurdle (beat subsequent Grade 1 winner Whisper), the champion trainer remarked in January: **"I just told Andy (Stewart) we must look after him as he could be the best horse he has ever had with me over fences."** Despite that, connections are contemplating staying over hurdles for the time being. Either way, the five year old is an exciting prospect who could be 'awesome' over fences, according to his trainer.

LAC FONTANA is another who progressed from top-class handicaps to winning at the highest level during the spring. Paul Nicholls' five year old suffered with ulcers during the first half of the season but he looked a different horse when winning a handicap at Cheltenham's Trials meeting off a mark of 127. Victories in the County Hurdle (off 139) and the Grade 1 Mersey Novices' Hurdle at Aintree over two and a half miles soon followed. His trainer said: **"He'll jump a fence and has schooled over them already, but it would be nice to have another good staying hurdler."** The Ascot Hurdle (22nd November) has already been earmarked for his return with a race like the Relkeel Hurdle at Cheltenham (13th December) an option the following month.

COLE HARDEN was four lengths in arrears of Beat That at Aintree in the Grade 1 Sefton Hurdle. It was the first time Warren Greatrex's gelding had raced over three miles and he intends starting the five year old off in the West Yorkshire Hurdle at Wetherby (1st November). Twice a winner over hurdles at Fontwell and Newbury, he was seventh in the Neptune Investments Novices' Hurdle at Cheltenham.

LE ROCHER was ante-post favourite for the Triumph Hurdle for much of the winter following his two and a half lengths victory in the Grade 1 Finale Hurdle at Chepstow in late December. **"I would have been disappointed if he had got beaten. He has to be up there with Ptit Zig and Diakali as the top of his generation in France,"** said Nick Williams afterwards. A ten lengths winner of the Finesse Hurdle at Cheltenham's Trials meeting next time, he was forced to miss the Festival due to injury. The Saint Des Saints gelding has won 4 out of 6 and is rated 149. He could follow in the hoofprints of stablemate Reve De Sivola one day and develop into a World Hurdle contender. It remains to be seen whether soft/heavy ground is a necessity.

Ireland evidently holds a strong hand in the staying division. **ANNIE POWER** was runner-up in the World Hurdle last season and she will continue to be a major threat, if staying over the smaller obstacles. **SOLWHIT** won the race in 2013 but missed last season, due to a fetlock injury. Charles Byrnes' gelding is nearing his eleventh birthday and, while he has enjoyed a wonderful career with eight Grade 1 victories, there must be a doubt over whether he will return as good as ever. Compatriot and dual Champion Hurdle winner **HURRICANE FLY** is the same age and Willie Mullins is contemplating stepping the record breaking 19 times Grade 1 winner up in trip this winter. He said in early May: **"He's only ten and still a relatively young horse in National Hunt terms and he's injury free. I think he's still got one or two Grade 1s left in him and we might just go up in trip. I would have no problem going up in trip with him."**

Owner Graham Wylie won the World Hurdle three times with Inglis Drever and the plan is to target **BRIAR HILL** at the major staying events this winter. Sent off 2/1 favourite for the Albert Bartlett Hurdle at Cheltenham, the Shantou gelding fell at the seventh flight and suffered a broken cheekbone. A dual Grade 1 winner, he has only raced once over three miles under Rules but has always looked a strong stayer and is already a Cheltenham Festival winner. Rated 155, he doesn't have to improve too much to be competitive in the top prizes.

Only rated 143, **LIEUTENANT COLONEL** needs to improve appreciably if he is to be considered a World Hurdle but Dessie Hughes' Kayf Tara gelding has time on his side and he is a Grade 2 winner. Sixth in the Neptune Novices' Hurdle at Cheltenham, he beat subsequent winner Le Vent D'Antan by ten lengths at Fairyhouse's Easter Festival. Third of four behind Vautour at Punchestown last time, his trainer remarked in early April: **"He's a smashing horse who will make a lovely chaser in time. But he's only five, so we might stay over hurdles next season. He has plenty of pace and might be good enough to run in some good races like the Hattons Grace Hurdle at Fairyhouse (30th November)."** I think three miles will prove to be his trip, ultimately.

A potential improver when stepped up to two and a half miles plus this season is the Edward O'Grady trained **KITTEN ROCK**. A dual winner on the Flat in France, he won his first two races over hurdles at Navan and Limerick in March, with his trainer saying at the former: **"He's done lots of schooling but I've never actually galloped him. There must be plenty of improvement in him because we've never let him down. He's very promising."** Paddy Mangan rode him at Limerick and he said: **"He gave me a great feel and he's a very good horse."** Second and fourth in Graded company at Fairyhouse and Punchestown respectively during the spring, the Laverock gelding ought to progress when tackling longer distances this season. Runner-up over 1m 7f on the Flat, he has yet to race beyond two miles over timber. He looks well treated off 137, too.

Finally, at a considerably lesser level, I will be surprised if Anthony Honeyball can't win a race or two with the potentially well handicapped **ROUQUINE SAUVAGE**. A six year old mare by Loup Sauvage, she was heavily supported to make a winning debut in a bumper at Fontwell in October and duly did so by six lengths. Bought by J.P.McManus shortly afterwards, she has been well held in half a dozen subsequent outings, including four over hurdles. Yet to race beyond two mile three, she could be a different proposition over a longer trip and with another summer on her back. Her bumper win suggested she is far better than her current mark over hurdles of 93.

Talking of well handicapped horses, the same owner's **CUP FINAL** doesn't look overburdened off a rating of 125. Still a novice, the five year old is impeccably bred being a gelded son of Presenting out of the top-class mare Asian Maze. Well beaten in the Neptune Investments Novices' Hurdle at the Festival, Nicky Henderson's charge had previously chased home Irving at Taunton and Kempton (Grade 2 Dovecote Novices' Hurdle) over the minimum trip. Don't be surprised if his connections elect to make the most of his lenient rating.

INDEX

SELECTED HORSE = BOLD   *Talking Trainers = Italics*

173

EMAIL ONLY SERVICE

Similar to the last couple of years, I am running an **EMAIL ONLY SERVICE** from October to December exclusively. To give new clients an idea of what is on offer, I have included some examples from last year's service.

NOVEMBER & DECEMBER RESULTS

NOVEMBER – 5 WINNERS from 8 selections

URBAN HYMN		WON	11/4
CONDUCT	Advised @ 10/1	WON	8/1
THE LAST SAMURI	Advised @ 3/1	WON	5/2
	Advised @ 5/1	3rd	11/2
UMBERTO D'OLIVATE	Advised @ 4/1	WON	9/4
ZARZAL	Advised @ 4/1	WON	2/1
DANCING ART	Advised @ 100/30	6th	9/4
CLOUDINGSTAR	Advised @ 3/1	4th	13/8

DECEMBER – 4 WINNERS from 7 selections

ANTE-POST GRAND NATIONAL SELECTION		TBC	
MOORLANDS MIST	Advised @ 9/2	WON	7/2
HIT THE HEADLINES	Advised @ 9/1 (E/W)	2nd	9/2 (Nose)
BIG NEWS	Advised @ 8/1	PU	6/1
KAYFLEUR	Advised @ 7/4	WON	10/11
CHAMPAGNE WEST	Advised @ 7/2	WON	6/4
BYERLEY BABE	Available @ 6/5	WON	9/10

What The Clients Said:

"The email service bettered last year's, with Conduct at 10/1 undoubtedly being the highlight of a very successful November and December. A combination of genuine form insight and knowing racing insiders is making this service invaluable.......roll on October 2014." **P.G.**

"Just wanted to add my thanks for what has been some outstanding tipping. I gave up on tipping lines many years ago but chose to give your service a go due to the quality of your publications. I just love the fact that you are so genuine and really have your client's interests at heart." **A.C.**

"I have long been a fan of the OJA/AOTF books as these have served me well in terms of alerting me to superstars before they are well known. I have also enjoyed subscribing regularly to your 'updates' and have enjoyed success there. With such consistently good work with the books and the updates I felt it would be an interesting investment to give your e-mail service a try and this is, without doubt, the best horse racing service I have subscribed to. Insightful, well-judged and profitable, it is all a horse racing fan could ask for." **D.R.**

"As "first time" subscribers to your Email Service, we are very impressed with the service you offer and success achieved from the number of selections advised. This being supported with a good rationale for the selections made makes you stand out from similar providers. We use a similar service, this is an annual service providing daily advices, but we must say that you beat it hands down in relation to % of wins v horses advised." **I.G.**

NOVEMBER 2013 – 5 WINNERS from 8 selections

Winners: **URBAN HYMN** (11/4), **CONDUCT** (Advised @ 10/1), **THE LAST SAMURI** (Advised @ 3/1), **UMBERTO D'OLIVATE** (Advised @ 4/1), **ZARZAL** (Advised @ 4/1).

Quote: *"However, I have thought for sometime **CONDUCT** had the ideal profile for the twelve furlongs contest (please see page 9 of the Ahead On The Flat Autumn Update). William Haggas is currently on the 99 mark for the season (and he is likely to reach three figures on Thursday evening with Tweed, if not before) and he reports the six year old in good form. Indeed, I texted William on Monday evening and he said he has been very pleased with his preparation (unusually bullish for William). He did add though that the gelding has been plagued with problems throughout his career and it is a case of taking it day by day.*

A study of Conduct's career shows he has only raced five times (didn't run at all in 2011 and only once last year). Previously trained by Sir Michael Stoute, he joined Somerville Lodge at the start of this season. Four lengths fifth at Newmarket in August, he led two out only to weaken inside the closing stages, which was understandable having been off for 371 days. Returning to action a month later, he was only beaten a length by the Zetland Gold winner and Listed placed Clon Brulee (sold last week at the Newmarket Horses In Training Sales for 200,000gns) in a ten furlongs handicap at Doncaster. Despite that encouraging performance, the handicapper left him alone on a mark of 96.

Saved for this ever since, Conduct has yet to race beyond a mile and a quarter but, being out of a two mile winner (Coventina), he ought to improve over this longer distance. Cut in the ground shouldn't be an issue either because he is out of Selkirk and his dam was Listed placed on soft. In addition, having had leg problems, he wouldn't want the ground too quick in any case. The final piece of the jigsaw appears to be the booking of Seb Sanders. The former champion jockey is unbeaten on Conduct, having ridden him to victory on his racecourse bow in September 2010, and he boasts an impressive strike-rate for the stable. Sanders has won on 7 of his 16 rides for William Haggas during 2013 (strike-rate of 44% and a £1 level stake profit of £19.88). Given his health issues, Conduct is a risky betting proposition and there have only been two winning six year olds since 1987, namely Swingit Gunner and Yavana's Pace (1998). However, I feel it is a chance worth taking at 10/1." **Advised @ 10/ 1 WON at the November Handicap by 5 lengths at 8/1.**

Quote: *"The conditions at Chepstow are sure to be gruelling and that ought to play to the strengths of **UMBERTO D'OLIVATE**, who goes over fences for the first time in the UK in the two miles three handicap chase at 2.50. Robert Walford's gelding has chasing experience in France though and he is certainly bred and built for the larger obstacles. He runs off 110 and looks favourably treated. The five year old was runner-up on two occasions over hurdles at Exeter and Wincanton during the spring (both on soft ground) and he made an encouraging reappearance at the latter track last month. Beaten around ten lengths by Theatrelands, he would have been much closer but for slipping on the bend after the third last. The runner-up Maxi Chop finished a good fourth behind the well handicapped Quick Jack at Cheltenham on Friday to add substance to the form. Unexposed, he will appreciate the step up in trip provided he doesn't race keenly early on and his young trainer will be keen to send out a winner on his father-in-law Robert Alner's 70th birthday. One note of caution, all six of his UK races have been on right-handed tracks so it is taken on trust he will be as effective going left-handed. I will be disappointed if he can't reward each-way support at around 4/1."* **Advised @ 4/1 WON @ 9/4**

DECEMBER 2013 – 4 WINNERS from 7 selections (only 1 losing selection)

Winners: **BYERLEY BABE** (9/10), **CHAMPAGNE WEST** (Advised @ 7/2), **KAYFLEUR** (Advised @ 7/4), **MOORLANDS MIST** (Advised @ 9/2). Plus: **HIT THE HEADLINES** (Advised E/W @ 9/1 – beaten a nose @ 9/2).

Quote: *"There are three decent jumping cards in the UK tomorrow, including at Chepstow where the ground is likely to be good to soft. Stamina will be a premium in the three miles handicap hurdle at 2.35 and that ought to play to the strengths of **MOORLANDS MIST**. A course and distance winner when trained by Jeremy Scott in March, he was also runner-up at the Welsh venue over half a mile shorter on his previous outing, so we know he goes well there. Transferred to Philip Hobbs during the summer, the six year old made an encouraging start for his new trainer when finishing five and a half lengths fourth behind Ballyculla at Exeter last month. Challenging three out, he began to fade after the second last suggesting he was in need of his first run since April. The form of the race looks strong with the winner scoring again since and the third, Sir Frank, has also subsequently entered the winners' enclosure. Ten pounds claimer Thomas Cheesman rode him for the first time and he retains the mount here (he has ridden two winners this season, plus he partnered Pateese to finish second at Newbury's Hennessy meeting last week). His claim could prove crucial. Unexposed over three miles (134), the grey will handle the ground, has good course form and should be spot on fitness wise. Philip Hobbs intends sending Moorlands Mist chasing sooner rather than later but he clearly feels he is capable of winning another race over timber beforehand. I suggest backing him each-way at 9/2 with Betfred or Totesport."* **Advised @ 9/2 WON by 9 lengths at 7/2**

Quote: *"National Hunt enthusiasts will know that Shropshire based trainer Henry Daly is naturally pessimistic about his horses' chances, following years of learning his trade under the late Captain Tim Forster. I was therefore somewhat surprised when he said to my Racing UK colleague Niall Hannity and I at Carlisle on Sunday, "I will have a winner at Ludlow on Wednesday." The horse in question is **KAYFLEUR**, who lines up in the mares' novice hurdle at **3.00**. Daly won the event twelve months ago with Mickie, and Kayfleur has done very little wrong in four career outings. Beaten two and a half lengths by Carole's Spirit (now rated 130 over hurdles) in a bumper at Warwick on her racecourse debut, she then finished sixth in a Listed event at Aintree's Grand National meeting. Reappearing in another bumper at Warwick in November, she justified favouritism to get off the mark at the third attempt. From the family of Young Spartacus, Kayfleur then switched to hurdling and looked the most likely winner at Huntingdon until getting run out of it after the last. Five lengths behind Emma Lavelle's Woodland Walk (entered in a Listed hurdle at Haydock on Saturday), the pair finished fourteen lengths clear of the remainder. Henry said he was gutted when she got beaten that day but feels she may have bumped into a useful mare. The most noticeable aspect of her performance was her slick jumping. Henry Daly's horses are in terrific form at present with 23 winners already on the board (compared to 20 winners for the whole of last season). He sent out 10 winners last month and has added a further four during December. While I don't confess to knowing him well, I have spoken to him a few times and I have never known him so bullish about a horse."* **Advised @ 7/4 WON by 7 lengths at 10/11**

Quote: *"There have been few trainers in better form this month than Philip Hobbs, who has sent out 13 winners at a strike-rate of 25%. The Minehead based handler has done particularly well with his novices running in open handicaps. The Skyfarmer took advantage of a rating of 123 at Cheltenham's December fixture, while Sausalito Sunrise looked similarly well treated off 129 last weekend at Haydock. I am hoping the trend will continue in the Pertemps Qualifier at Wincanton (**2.15**) on Thursday (26th). The ground at the Somerset track is already described as heavy but that shouldn't be a problem for **CHAMPAGNE WEST**, who is set to tackle his first handicap off an official mark of 123. I will be amazed if he is not better than such a mark. The Westerner gelding won his only Irish point for Eoin Doyle on soft/heavy ground in November 2012, prior to being bought by Roger Brookhouse six days later for £120,000. Runner-up in a bumper at Ffos Las on bottomless ground (heavy), he was only denied by a head. His first start over hurdles is best forgotten because he made a bad mistake at the fifth flight at Exeter and never recovered. However, he was the only horse to give Beat That a race at Ascot next time. Beaten ten lengths, Nicky Henderson's winner was unlucky not to follow up in a Grade 2 at Sandown next time and is rated 142. The third home Knock House won comfortably at Plumpton on his only subsequent start. The form is rock solid. Champagne*

West then went one better when getting the better of the highly regarded and dual bumper winner Deputy Dan at Warwick. The pair had a protracted duel from the second last with the Hobbs runner prevailing by a length. It was 22 lengths back to bumper winners Ulzana's Raid and Tullyesker Hill. There is a possibility Champagne West is better going left handed (form figures 121 compared to 92 going right-handed) and he did show a minor tendency to jump to his left at Ascot on his penultimate start. It is not a major concern though, especially as they are likely to only jump ten flights (the hurdle after the stands is expected to be omitted). Tom O'Brien is reunited with the five year old, having partnered him in the Ffos Las bumper."
Advised @ 7/2 WON by 10 lengths at 6/4

Quote: *"Robert Tyner won the mares' beginners chase at Limerick (**2.50**) twelve months ago with Oscars Business and the County Cork based handler may have the answer to the 2013 renewal, too. **BYERLEY BABE** is out of the stable's 2001 Paddy Power Chase winner I Can Imagine, and she has won 4 of her 11 career starts. Successful in a point-to-point, bumper and over hurdles twice, she is having only her second start over fences. Beaten around twenty lengths on her chasing bow at Naas (Yielding/Soft) in November, she finished sixth behind the likes of Road To Riches (third in the Grade 1 Drinmore Novice Chase since), Foxrock (won next time and contests the Grade 1 Topaz NC at Leopardstown today), Golanbrook (won next start by 79 lengths) and You Must Know Me (third in the Grand Sefton over the National fences at Aintree next time). The race is worth watching on the ATR website (still in contention jumping the second last). It was a very good run, especially as it was her first run since April and Philip Enright was by no means hard on her. His record on the Beneficial mare is 32116. A course and distance winner over hurdles in March, Byerley Babe's record on heavy ground is 11211 and the fact she ran in two points means she doesn't lack jumping experience. Back amongst her own sex, I would like to think she will outclass her rivals. The Racing Post Betting Forecast of 5/2 looks generous to say the least. To add further substance to her cause, Irish point expert Declan Phelan emailed me last night to say he had spoken to Robert Tyner earlier in the day and he expects Byerley Babe to win."* **WON easily @ 9/10**

The service will run for 3 months (ie. October, November & December) with the option of buying each month at £25 or £60 for all 3 (save £15).

OCTOBER 2014	£25.00
NOVEMBER 2014	£25.00
DECEMBER 2014	£25.00
OR ALL 3 MONTHS	£60.00

Total Cheque / Postal Order value £.............. made payable to **MARK HOWARD PUBLICATIONS Ltd.**
Post your order to: **MARK HOWARD PUBLICATIONS. 69 FAIRGARTH DRIVE, KIRKBY LONSDALE, CARNFORTH, LANCASHIRE. LA6 2FB.**

NAME: ....

ADDRESS: ....

....

.... POST CODE: ....

Email Address: ....

Alternatively, order via www.mhpublications.co.uk

EMAIL ONLY
ONE JUMP AHEAD UPDATES

I shall be producing **5 One Jump Ahead *Updates*** throughout the 2014/15 National Hunt season. Each *Update* comprises information about the horses in ***One Jump Ahead*, an update from top Bloodstock Agent Anthony Bromley, Bumper News, Ante-Post Advice** (recommendations for the major races), **Big-Race Previews** and **News from Ireland** from one of the most informed Irish experts Declan Phelan. **Please note, the *Updates* are ONLY AVAILABLE VIA EMAIL (Not Post).**

It is £6 per *Update* (except £8 for the Cheltenham Festival version) or £32 for ALL 5 via **EMAIL**.

Summary of the 2013/2014 *Updates*:

What The Clients Said:
"Thank you for your exceptional publications. Without any doubt, the books and Updates are the best of their kind on the market, giving incredible value for money." **R.S.**

"I just want to pass on my thanks for the Cheltenham Update 2014. I thought it was a superb read and was excellently put together." **C.O'R.**

"Thanks to Declan Phelan and Tammys Hill, I cleared £1300 profit last week. I have subscribed to your OJA publication for the last 5 years and your interim Updates for the last 3 years. I took a real gamble in the run up to the Festival because your Xmas & Feb Updates were so positive about Vautour & Faugheen, especially, I backed ante post and in a double. I will remain a firm admirer of the quality of the information you provide and will continue to happily subscribe to your excellent service for many years to come." **J.S.**

"I have been a client for about two years now – I would like to commend you for the excellent work with the regular Updates and information you pass on. I think its immense value for money. I find it difficult to bet without such information." **P.E.**

"Well done with the Cheltenham Update – it was a fantastic read. The info this year has been spot on, and not just at Cheltenham, but also the ante-post info re O'Faolains Boy. Keep up the good work." **J.J.**

"A big thanks for the fantastic information you have provided in your publications this season. I took your advice re Faugheen and Vautour in the February Update and backed them individually and in a double ante-post. I was born and bred in Cheltenham and have had close to the best 2 days of my life. I also have to say the quality of Declan Phelan's advice in the Updates is brilliant." **J.S.**

"The Cheltenham Update was absolutely marvellous – Declan Phelan needs Knighting for his services to punting." **J.B.**

The PADDY POWER MEETING 2013

6 WINNERS: QUICK JACK (15/8), THE LIQUIDATOR (6/4), KID CASSIDY (4/1), DELL'ARCA (Advised @ 14/1), RED SHERLOCK (7/2). Plus: COLOUR SQUADRON (2nd in the Paddy Power Gold Cup – Advised @ 14/1)

Quote: "***DELL'ARCA** is one of the most intriguing runners of the whole three day fixture. Only a four year old, he was purchased for €280,000 at the Arqana Sale in July, having won over hurdles at Compiegne. Runner-up next time at Auteuil, it is his first run over hurdles, which warrants plenty of scrutiny. Beaten a nose by Un Temps Pour Tout (receiving eight pounds) at Bordeaux in May, the winner has won twice more since and finished seven lengths third in the Grade 1 Prix Renaud Du Vivier at Auteuil this month (behind the 145 rated Ptit Zig). If that form is taken literally, he could be thrown in off 128 for his British debut. In some respects, he reminds me a lot of Rodock, who won the race for Martin Pipe in 1999 on only his third start over hurdles off a mark of 131. Could history repeat itself fourteen years later?"* **Advised @ 14/1 WINS the Greatwood Hurdle on his British debut.**

Quote: *"The one I like is **QUICK JACK**, who will be partnered by Ruby Walsh for the first time. Trained by Tony Martin, the Footstepsinthesand gelding has only run four times over obstacles, winning at Listowel in September. A dual winner on the Flat in 2013, he was a good second in the Movember Handicap at Leopardstown this month. Tony Martin has his team in good fettle and he looks sure to go well."* **WON @ 15/8**

Quote: **COLOUR SQUADRON**: *"Fifth in the novice handicap at the Festival, he is rated 139 (compared to 143 over hurdles) and is well treated. I also think he will jump much better on a sounder surface – all four of his chases last season were on soft or heavy. He goes well fresh (first time out 12) and is a leading contender, if he gets his jumping together. Tom O'Brien rides him for the first time."* **Advised @ 14/1 – 2nd – beaten three parts of a length in the Paddy Power Gold Cup**

Plus: **ARDKILLY WITNESS (3/1 & 8/11), COOZAN GEORGE (11/4), FORCED FAMILY FUN (11/10 & 5/1), GOODWOOD MIRAGE (6/4), IVAN GROZNY (8/13 & 5/1), KELVINGROVE (5/1), PEARL CASTLE (17/2 & 4/6), RUTHERGLEN (8/11, 5/4, 4/5), SURE REEF (5/2 & 9/4), TAGLIETELLE (3/1), TIDAL DANCE (5/6)**

Quote: **COOZAN GEORGE**: *"I was working at the Scottish track for Racing UK and Brian Hughes was very complimentary about the four year old afterwards. He feels he is more than capable of winning a bumper and one for the future."* **WON a bumper next time at Musselburgh (3/1/14) @ 11/4**

Quote: **HAWK HIGH**: *"He could develop into a Fred Winter Hurdle type."* **WON the Fred Winter Juvenile Hurdle at the Cheltenham Festival @ 33/1**

Quote: **IVAN GROZNY**: *"I was speaking to Graham Wylie at Wetherby on Charlie Hall day and he said he had purchased **IVAN GROZNY**. A three year old by Turtle Bowl, he was successful in two of eight races on the Flat for Daniel Rabhi. Without a win last term, he won at Lyon in early March (1m 1f : Standard) before following up by three lengths from Eurato (won twice since) at St-Cloud (1m 2f : Heavy) eleven days later. A length and three quarters third behind Triple Treat (won Group 2 since) in a Group 3 at Longchamp, he rounded off his Flat campaign by finishing fifth in the Group 2 Prix Greffulhe at St-Cloud. By all accounts, he has done everything asked since arriving at Closutton."* **WON a Grade 3 Hurdle at the Fairyhouse Easter Festival (21/4/14) @ 5/1**

BROMLEY'S BEST BUYS – Part II: WINNERS: ACTIVIAL (9/4), BROTHER DU BERLAIS (5/1), CALIPTO (5/2 & 4/6), VICENZO MIO (Evens)

Quote: **CALIPTO**: *"Ran a lovely debut race at Auteuil for Guy Cherel to finish a good second in the prestigious Prix Finot Hurdle in mid September. He is due to start at Newbury's Hennessy meeting (29th November) and is potentially smart."* **WON on his British debut at Newbury @ 5/2**

TALKING TRAINERS: **MALCOLM JEFFERSON: WINNERS: CAPE YORK (3/1), ENCHANTED GARDEN (8/1), FIRTH OF THE CLYDE (9/5 & 11/4), HI GEORGE (12/1), KING OF THE WOLDS (5/4), PAIR OF JACKS (3/1), RETRIEVE THE STICK (9/4 & 11/8), SECRETE STREAM (9/4), SUN CLOUD (5/1 & 4/1), URBAN HYMN (8/11 & 9/4)**

Quote: **ENCHANTED GARDEN**: *"He handles cut in the ground and is a nice prospect for novice hurdles. He looks very well at moment."* **WON on his hurdles debut at Market Rasen (16/1/14) @ 8/1**

Quote: **HI GEORGE**: *"Half-brother to Attaglance, he has also had a few problems with his wind so we have operated on his soft palate. He will be going over fences and I think he will make a nice chaser. His schooling has gone very well and he isn't short of speed. We will keep him to two and a half miles for the time being but I don't see why he won't stay a bit further."* **WON @ 12/1 on his chasing debut at Catterick (4/12/13)**

Quote: **SUN CLOUD**: *"There are definitely races to be won with him over fences."* **WON his next two starts @ 5/1 & 4/1, including the North Yorkshire Grand National at Catterick.**

CHRISTMAS SPECIAL

CHRISTMAS HURDLE: **MY TENT OR YOURS (WON @ 11/8)**
WELSH NATIONAL: **HAWKES POINT (2nd – beaten a head - @ 14/1)**

Anthony BROMLEY's Festive Nap – **SILVINIACO CONTI (7/2)** in the King George at Kempton on Boxing Day.

OWNERS' ENCLOSURE: **RICH RICCI: WINNERS: ARVIKA LIGEONNIERE (2/7 & 1/2), BALLYCASEY (2/1), CLONDAW COURT (2/9), VAUTOUR (1/4, 7/4 & 7/2), ZAIDPOUR (5/4)**

TALKING TRAINERS: **WARREN GREATREX: WINNERS: CHALK IT DOWN (11/10), COLE HARDEN (4/1), DOLATULO (9/1), ELLNANDO QUEEN (8/1, 9/2, 4/7), MADNESS LIGHT (4/1)**

Quote: **ELLNANDO QUEEN**: *"Third on her reappearance over hurdles at Ludlow, she needed the run that day and has had a wind operation since. She jumps well and is a lovely mare who I like a lot."* **WON next time at Kempton @ 8/1, plus 2 more victories @ 9/2 & 4/7.**

Quote: **MADNESS LIGHT**: *"The handicapper has raised him nine pounds to a mark of 124. We could run him in another novice hurdle but I think he could be a tasty proposition in a handicap off such a rating."* **WON @ 4/1 on his handicap debut at Uttoxeter (31/12/13)**

The IRISH ANGLE: **DECLAN PHELAN**
Quote: **NO MORE HEROES**: *"He was a non runner on Saturday, apparently due to a stone bruise, the simple fact that Gigginstown had the favourite in the same race might have been the real reason for non participation. A son of Presenting, he was one of the highly successful batch of four year old pointers that Michael O'Leary sent pointing last spring. He won a good quality point at Dromahane: the third and fourth from that race, Powerstown Dream and Fort Worth have since won bumpers in the UK. Now in training with Gordon Elliott, No More Heroes debuted over hurdles at Down Royal in early November: racing over an inadequate two miles, he was noted staying on takingly towards the finish in placing fourth. I rate this horse a moral to win a hurdle race at 2m 4f or above and the winter soft ground will aid his quest to win. He has multiple entries over the Christmas period and I think he will offer each way value in whatever engagement he fulfils."* **WON a bumper at Leopardstown (27/12/13) by 39 lengths @ 15/8**

Quote: **MAYFAIR MUSIC**: *"Given her preference for decent ground, don't be surprised if she makes a trip to Doncaster en route."* **WON at Doncaster (15/8) in March.**

Quote: **VAUTOUR**: *"Rather like Pont Alexandre twelve months ago, the former Guillaume Macire trained gelding made a sparkling start to his new career with Willie Mullins at Navan this month. It may not have been a strong maiden hurdle, even though there were thirty runners, but the manner in which the Robin Des Champs gelding moved through the race and readily saw off his rivals was hugely impressive. He looks to have everything needed to be a top-class jump horse – size, scope, pace and quality and in the right hands. He has been given two entries over the Festive period at Leopardstown (Grade 1 Champion Novice Hurdle (1.50 on Friday) and Limerick (1.35 on Thursday). Either way, I can't wait to see him in action again. He is a tremendous prospect."* **WON his next three starts, including the Supreme Novices' Hurdle (7/2) at the Cheltenham Festival in March.**

FEBRUARY 2014

BETFAIR HURDLE: **DELL'ARCA (Advised e/w @ 14/1 – 2nd at 15/2)**

Quote: **FAUGHEEN**: *"He is a very good novice who, provided his jumping improves, will be hard to beat at the Festival in March."* **WON the Neptune Novices' Hurdle @ 6/4**

Quote: **O'FAOLAINS BOY**: *"In many respects, the ex-pointer has something to prove now but I wouldn't write him off. Ascot showed what he is capable of and Haydock was too bad to be true. Obviously, he needs to produce a good performance next time and get his chasing career back on track. However, he still could emerge as a leading contender for something like the National Hunt Chase at the Festival. Currently available at 33/1 with William Hill (as short as 12/1 with Boylesports & Paddy Power), that could look a huge price if he wins on his next start."* **WON the Reynoldstown at Ascot @ 8/1 & RSA Chase @ 12/1**

Quote: **VAUTOUR**: *"Unbeaten in two starts since joining Willie Mullins during the summer from France, he is one of the most exciting novice hurdlers on either side of the Irish Sea and looks set to play a major part at the upcoming Cheltenham Festival. ...... Already favourite for the Festival opener, he will take some stopping. He is a class act."* **WON the Supreme Novices' Hurdle at Cheltenham @ 7/2**

TALKING TRAINERS: **OLIVER SHERWOOD: WINNERS: BEFOREALL (4/1), CARRY ON SYDNEY (8/15), FINANCIAL CLIMATE (5/2), STIFF UPPER LIP (15/8 & 9/2)**

Quote: **BEFOREALL**: *"He has been winning over shorter trips but I think a step up to three miles will bring about further improvement."* **WON over 3m 1f at Ffos Las (6/4/14) @ 4/1**

Quote: **STIFF UPPER LIP**: *"I think he will improve when encountering better ground."* **WON on good ground at Towcester (20/4/14) @ 9/2**

The CHELTENHAM FESTIVAL 2014

WINNERS: VAUTOUR (7/2), FAUGHEEN (6/4), TIGER ROLL (Advised @ 12/1)

Quote: **VAUTOUR**: *"Another ex-French trained gelding who looks a budding star for Willie Mullins. He, too, is unbeaten since joining his current yard having run twice over timber for Guillaume Macaire. Workmanlike when beating Western Boy in a Grade 3 novice at Punchestown, he may not have been suited by the inner track there and looked much more at home at Leopardstown last time. Given a fine ride by Ruby Walsh, he proved too good for dual Grade 1 winner The Tullow Tank in the Deloitte NH (Champagne Fever won the same race en route to Supreme NH glory). A three lengths winner, the five year old will almost certainly be ridden handily as he attempts to draw the sting out of the smooth travelling Irving. He has looked a class act this season."* **WON the Supreme Novices' Hurdle @ 7/2**

Quote: **TIGER ROLL**: *"**TIGER ROLL** is a half-brother to the Lonsdale Cup winner and Irish St Leger runner-up Ahzeemah. Ex-Godolphin, the son of Authorized didn't race on the Flat and was bought by Nigel Hawke for 10,000gns in August last year. Having won on his debut at Market Rasen in November, he was sold the following month to Gigginstown House Stud for 80,000gns. Transferred to Gordon Elliott, he stayed on well to finish second behind Guitar Pete in a Grade 1 at Leopardstown. Beaten two and a quarter lengths, he would have been even closer had he not made a mistake at the last. Both his races have been on soft or heavy ground. Gordon Elliott believes he has improved a lot since his last run and is a major contender."* **WON the Triumph Hurdle @ 10/1**

The IRISH ANGLE by DECLAN PHELAN: 3 WINNERS from only 6 selections: PRESENT VIEW (8/1), SIRE DE GRUGY (11/4), TAMMYS HILL (15/2). Plus: BALLYALTON (2nd @ 20/1)

Quote: *"Ex-Irish pointer **PRESENT VIEW** is now beginning to fulfil the potential he displayed within the flags in Ireland: He struggles to see out the three mile trip, and a fast run 2m 4f-2m 6f race are perfect for this son of Presenting: he bolted up last time at Kempton: raised 11lbs to 137, he is capable of being competitive off that elevated rating as this race will be run to suit him: a drying sod will not inconvenience as he has plenty of speed. **ATTAGLANCE** enjoyed a terrific 2012, landing a spring Festival double over hurdles at Cheltenham and Aintree: unsuccessful from eight previous outings over fences, he may not be comfortable jumping fences: taken in isolation a repeat of his promising fourth in the Paddy Power in the autumn off the same rating as now, would give him an excellent each way chance."* **PRESENT VIEW (1st) @ 8/1 & ATTAGLANCE (2nd) @ 10/1**

Quote: **BALLYALTON**: *"Ballyalton another ex-pointer has enjoyed a decent campaign: a second season novice, a course winner and dangerous on a sound surface, a definite place candidate at least."* **2nd in the Neptune Novices' Hurdle @ 20/1**

Quote: **SIRE DE GRUGY**: *"I will be concise: I think that Sire De Grugy is the best bet of the four day fixture. On my figures, I rate this improving chestnut at least 7 to 8 lengths superior to these rivals and he should be an odds on shot: the fact that you can back him at odds close to 5/2 should be accepted with thanks."* **WON the Queen Mother Champion Chase @ 11/4**

Quote: **TAMMYS HILL:** *"My preference is for Tammys Hill: he failed to sparkle on his sole UK trip last term at Stratford: but that run came at the end of a long winter when he was over the top. A wind operation in the close season has definitely improved him: he won a point hard held in December: then lost out narrowly to On The Fringe at Down Royal (jockey carried overweight). He avenged that defeat with Robbie McNamara nipping up the rail late and fast at Leopardstown. I thought he ran another cracker when third over an inadequate 2m 5f at Fairyhouse last time: he was beaten less than four lengths conceding eight pounds to Warne (a specialist hunter at that trip) and Seabass (receiving 3lbs): he finished best of all. I like that he is thundering home and, with as good as a professional on his back, he may provide the north of Ireland with a second winner in this race in the space of three years. With three point to point wins on good/fast ground over the past eighteen months, he operates on any ground."* **WON the Foxhunters' Chase @ 15/2**

TALKING TRAINERS: **PAUL NICHOLLS: WINNERS: BROTHER DU BERLAIS (5/1), LAC FONTANA (11/1)**

Quote: **BROTHER DU BERLAIS:** *"He won over hurdles at Auteuil for Robert Collet and was being prepared for the EBF Final at Sandown yesterday. However, he incurred a nasty cut following his UK debut at Wincanton last month and wasn't ready in time. He is considered favourably treated though off 132."* **WON on his handicap debut at Ayr (12/4/14) @ 5/1**

Quote: **LAC FONTANA:** *"Eighth in last season's Triumph Hurdle, we purposely put him away after that. Having won well at Cheltenham in October, he ran a dire race next time at the Paddy Power meeting. We found that he was suffering with ulcers and therefore after some treatment returned at Cheltenham in January and bolted up. The handicapper raised him twelve pounds which ensures he will get a run in the County Hurdle. He worked well at Wincanton last week and, provided the ground is on the slow side, I think he will have a massive chance."* **WON the County Hurdle @ 11/1**

TALKING TRAINERS: **DAVID PIPE: WINNERS: BALLYNAGOUR (12/1), DYNASTE (3/1), GOULANES (13/2)**

Quote: **BALLYNAGOUR:** *"He holds a couple of entries but will run in the Byrne Group Plate rather than my father's race (Martin Pipe Conditional Jockeys HH). Eighth in the former last season, it is well documented that he has bleeding problems and he is best fresh. On his day, he is a very good horse but he isn't the easiest to predict. Pulled up in the Paddy Power Gold Cup in November, he blew up that day because he hadn't been back in yard that long. Hopefully, he will be at his best this week and run well."* **WON the Byrne Group Plate @ 12/1**

Quote: **DYNASTE:** *"He is in good nick and the Ryanair Chase on Thursday is his most likely target. Having run well in the Betfair Chase at Haydock, we thought he would go close in the King George but he ran below par. Found to have pulled some muscles afterwards, he was sore for a long time afterwards. We have purposely given him plenty of time to recover and I have been pleased with him during the last couple of weeks."* **WON the Ryanair Chase @ 3/1**

Quote: **GOULANES:** *"Entered in the three mile handicap chase on Tuesday and the Kim Muir, it is possible he will skip Cheltenham and wait for the Midlands National on Saturday (15th). He likes cut in the ground and, if back to his best, he would have a chance in whichever race he contests next."* **WON the Midlands National @ 13/2**

The AINTREE GRAND MEETING 2014

WINNERS: THE NEW ONE (4/9), BEAT THAT (6/1). Plus: CHELTENIAN (E/W 4th @ 8/1), LADY BUTTONS (E/W 2nd @ 8/1)

Quote: *"**PARSNIP PETE** was second behind Filbert at Newbury's Hennessy meeting and is only two pounds higher. A disappointing sixth at Ludlow last time, he is better than he showed that day. The key to him is flat left handed tracks (731112) and he gets on well with Paddy Brennan (4 from 15). A career best by some way is needed but he is a good traveller and these are his optimum conditions."* **WON the Red Rum Chase @ 16/1**

Quote: *"**MA FILLEULE** has won half of her eight races over fences and is rated 150. Nicky Henderson's mare produced a career best effort when narrowly denied by Holywell at the Cheltenham Festival last month. Beaten less than two lengths by Jonjo O'Neill's gelding, she did well to finish so close after her rider lost his iron after the third last. The drop in trip shouldn't be a problem for the six year old and her stable won the race last year with another French recruit Triolo D'Alene."* **WON the Topham Chase @ 9/1**

Quote: *"**BEAT THAT** hasn't been seen since finishing second behind Killala Quay (fourth in the Neptune NH since) in a Grade 2 novice hurdle at Sandown in December. Nicky Henderson's gelding was unlucky not to win, having made a bad mistake at the last. Prior to that, he beat subsequent three times winner and Albert Bartlett NH fourth Champagne West by ten lengths. Rated 142, his form is very solid and he is bred to appreciate the step up to three miles (from the family of Foxhunters' winner Drombeag). The six year old is fresh but may not want it too soft. His trainer won this in 1988 with Rustle."* **WON the Grade 1 Sefton Novices' Hurdle @ 6/1**

CONNECTIONS' VIEW: **WINNERS: PINEAU DE RE (25/1), RHYTHM STAR (7/1).**

Quote: **PINEAU DE RE**: *"Pineau De Re is Dr Newland's first ever Grand National runner. The horse comes into the race on the back of a near miss in the Pertemps Network at the Cheltenham Festival. Only beaten a neck, he can be considered an unlucky loser as he met the last hurdle wrong. A 23 length winner of the Ulster Grand National over three and a half miles last year, the eleven year old has the ability to run a big race. Filmed by the Racing UK cameras, Pineau De Re also went to Lambourn last week to school over National style fences. Leighton Aspell put him through his paces and will ride him on Saturday. Pineau De Re has previous Aintree experience having fallen at the eight in Becher Chase. However, he was a little unlucky, jumping the fence fine but slipping on landing. He will be given a waiting ride, creeping into contention late on. Arguably one of the form horses going into the race, he has solid claims granted a clear round."* **WON the Grand National @ 25/1**

Plus: **EDUARD (7/4)**

Quote: *"Despite winning twice and earning an official rating of 144 over fences, it has been a frustrating season for **EDUARD**. Nicky Richards' gelding was in the process of giving Pendra a race when sprawling on landing at the second last on his chasing bow at Carlisle in October. Returning to the Cumbrian venue in early December, he was only workmanlike in victory, having mastered the tough Mwaleshi after the last. The Morozov gelding didn't return until early March and, having overcome a mistake at the fourth last, he went on to record a comfortable eleven lengths victory over Imjoeking (beaten again since) conceding seven pounds. The fact he didn't race between December and March suggests Nicky Richards was keen for him to avoid heavy ground and leave him fresh for a spring campaign. With that in mind, the **Future Champions Novices' Chase** at Ayr (2.05) on Scottish National day (12th April) looks tailormade for him. Eduard has only raced once over two and a half miles when a well held fourth at Aintree's Grand National meeting last year but he had endured a hard race at Kelso on his previous start, which may have left its mark. The Ayr event has been kind to Greystoke over the years, with the late Gordon Richards winning it five times (Cromwell Road (1976), Little Bay (1981), Noddy's Ryde (1984), Jim Thorpe (1988) and Addington Boy (1996)), and Nicky won the prize in 2006 with Monet's Garden. It is time for Eduard to deliver."* **WON the Future Champions Novices' Chase by 20 lengths @ 7/4**

ONE JUMP AHEAD UPDATES 2014/2015
ORDER FORM (EMAIL ONLY)

AVAILABLE AT £6.00 EACH (£8 Cheltenham) OR £32 FOR ALL 5

- **CHELTENHAM PADDY POWER MEETING 2014**
  (Will be emailed on Thursday 13th November 2014)

- **CHRISTMAS SPECIAL 2014**
  (Will be emailed on Friday 19th December 2014)

- **FEBRUARY 2015**

- **MARCH 2015 - CHELTENHAM FESTIVAL PREVIEW**
  (Will be emailed on the Sunday before the Festival)

- **APRIL 2015 – AINTREE PREVIEW**
  (Will be emailed on the Tuesday before the Meeting)

Total Cheque / Postal Order value £.............. made payable to MARK HOWARD PUBLICATIONS Ltd. Post your order to: MARK HOWARD PUBLICATIONS. 69 FAIRGARTH DRIVE, KIRKBY LONSDALE, CARNFORTH, LANCASHIRE. LA6 2FB.

NAME: ....

ADDRESS: ....

....

.... POST CODE: ....

Email Address: ....

If you have not received your *UPDATE* via email 24 hours before the meeting starts, please contact us immediately.

Available to order via www.mhpublications.co.uk

AHEAD ON THE FLAT 2015

The 15th edition of *Ahead On The Flat* will be published in early April for the 2015 Flat season. It will be formulated along the same lines as previous years with a ***Top 40 Prospects*** (included Night of Thunder (40/1) in the 2000 Guineas in 2014)**, *Maidens, Handicappers, Gallic Gems*** (included Gallante (33/1 & 62/1 on PMU in 2014)**, and *What's The Craic In Ireland?*** In addition, there will be the usual stable interviews with some of the top trainers in Great Britain (last year's included **Andrew Balding, David Barron, Marco Botti, Roger Charlton, Luca Cumani, James Fanshawe, William Haggas, Mark Johnston, David O'Meara** and **Roger Varian**). *Ahead On The Flat* will contain 152 pages and the price is £8.99.

I shall also be producing **three *Ahead On The Flat Updates*** (EMAIL ONLY). There will be a **Royal Ascot Preview** (8 winners in 2014 including Born In Bombay (14/1)), a **York Ebor Preview** (Mutual Regard Advised @ 25/1 in the Betfred Ebor in 2014), and an **Autumn *Update***. Once again, the price remains the same at £6.00 each or £15 for ALL THREE.

ORDER FORM

•	**AHEAD ON THE FLAT 2015 (Book ONLY)**	**£8.99**

AHEAD ON THE FLAT UPDATES 2015 (can be ordered individually at £6.00 EACH or ALL 3 updates for £15.00):

•	**ROYAL ASCOT PREVIEW 2015**	**£6.00**
•	**YORK EBOR MEETING PREVIEW 2015**	**£6.00**
•	**AUTUMN PREVIEW 2015**	**£6.00**
•	**ALL 3 UPDATES (EMAIL ONLY)**	**£15.00**
•	**AHEAD ON THE FLAT + 3 UPDATES**	**£23.99**

Total Cheque / Postal Order value £............. Made payable to **MARK HOWARD PUBLICATIONS Ltd. Please send to: MARK HOWARD PUBLICATIONS Ltd. 69 FAIRGARTH DRIVE, KIRKBY LONSDALE, CARNFORTH, LANCASHIRE. LA6 2FB.**

NAME: ....

ADDRESS: ....

....

.... POST CODE: ....

Email Address: ....

Now you can watch Racing UK... anywhere

Sky / Freeview

Online

iPad

Mobile Web / Android / iPhone

100% PROFITS BACK INTO RACING

Racing UK just got better. With Racing UK Anywhere you can now watch live coverage of the best UK racing on up to 3 devices of your choice from our 7 available platforms*. There's NO EXTRA COST on top of the usual Sky subscription so enjoy every race live from 34 of the UK's best courses... anywhere.

1 channel – 3 devices – 1 price

RACING UK

racinguk.com/anywhere

More than 3 devices can be chosen for an additional fee.
*Racing UK Anywhere is not available for subscribers on Virgin Media or UPC.

racinguk @racing_uk